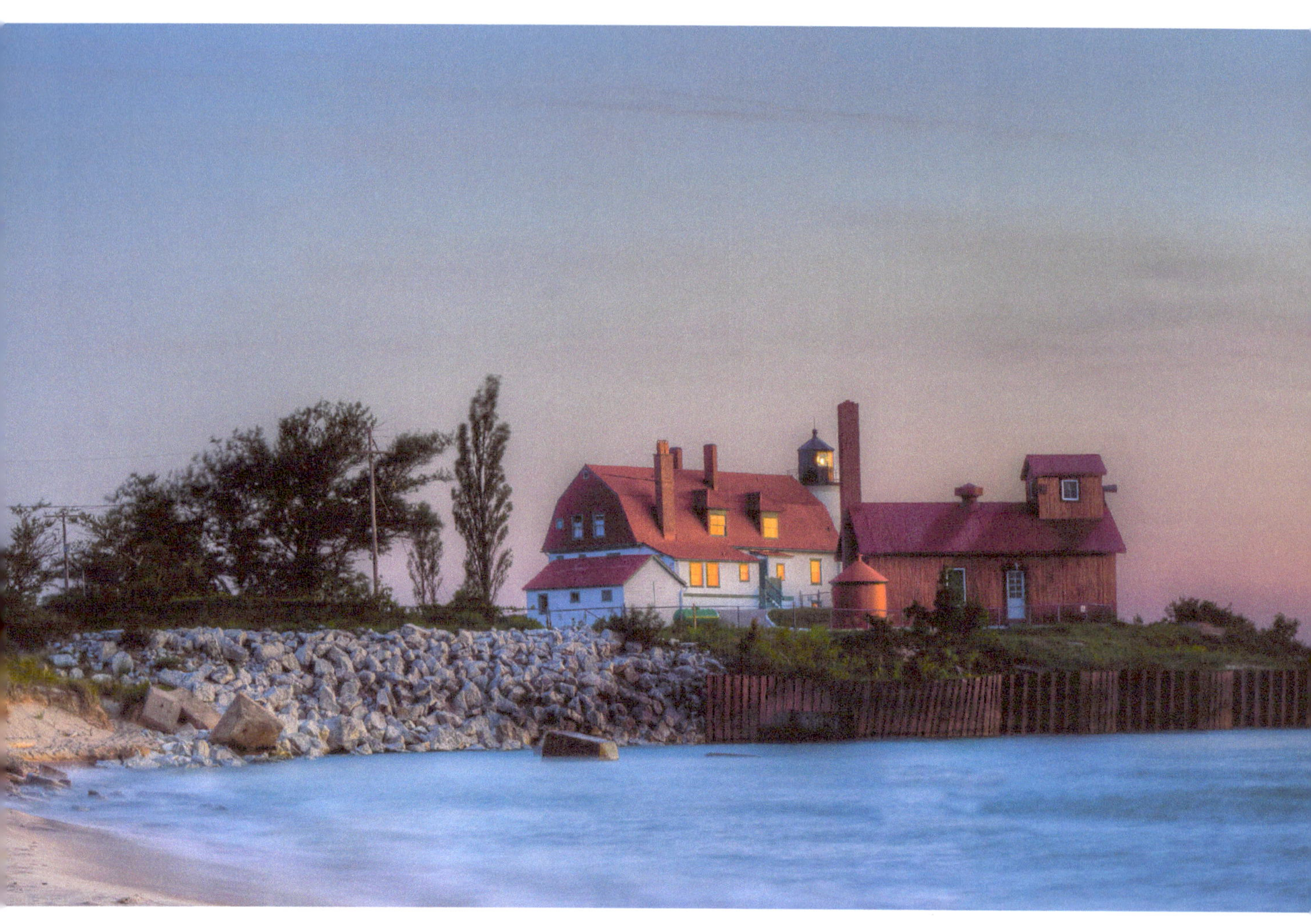

Point Betsie Lighthouse

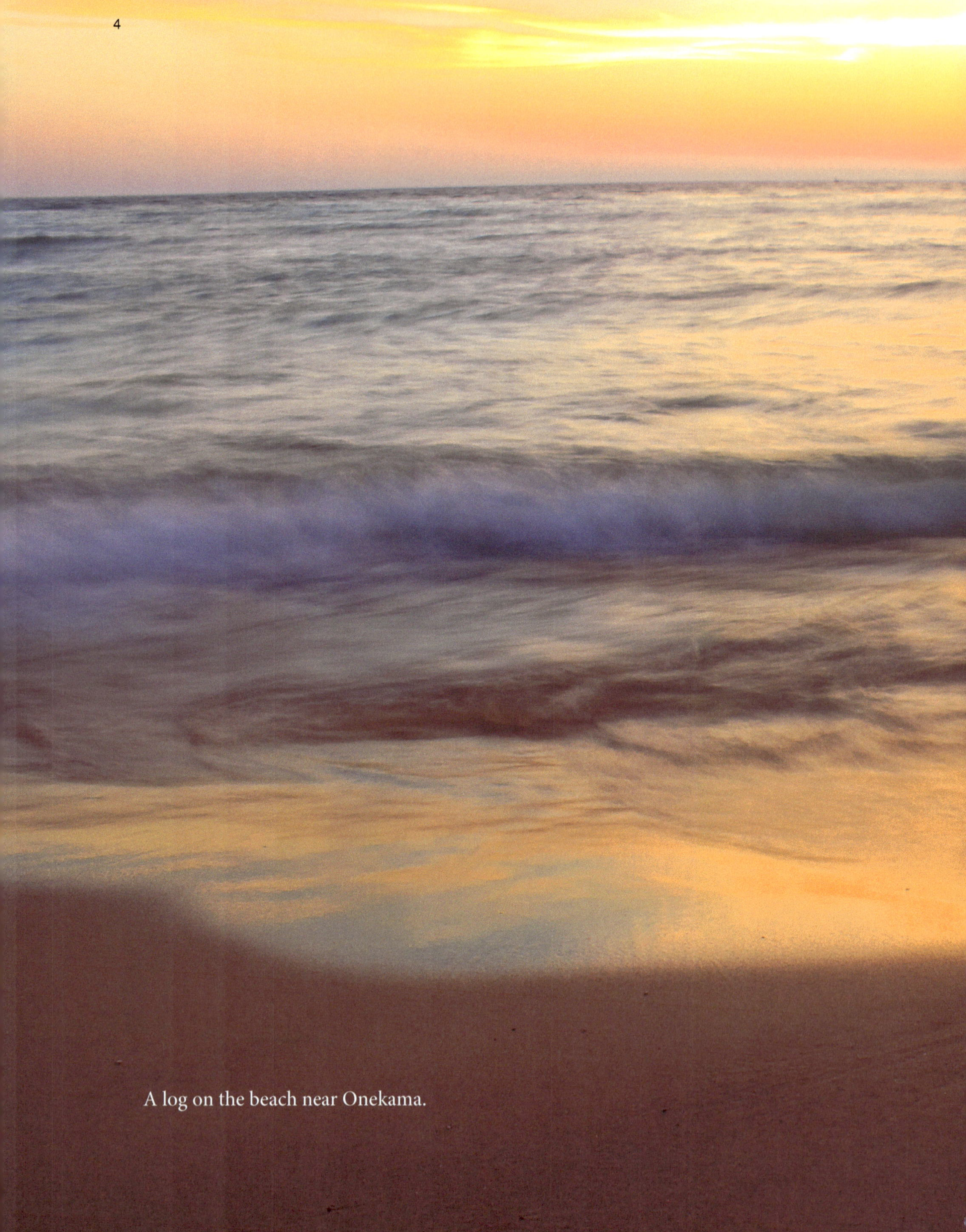

A log on the beach near Onekama.

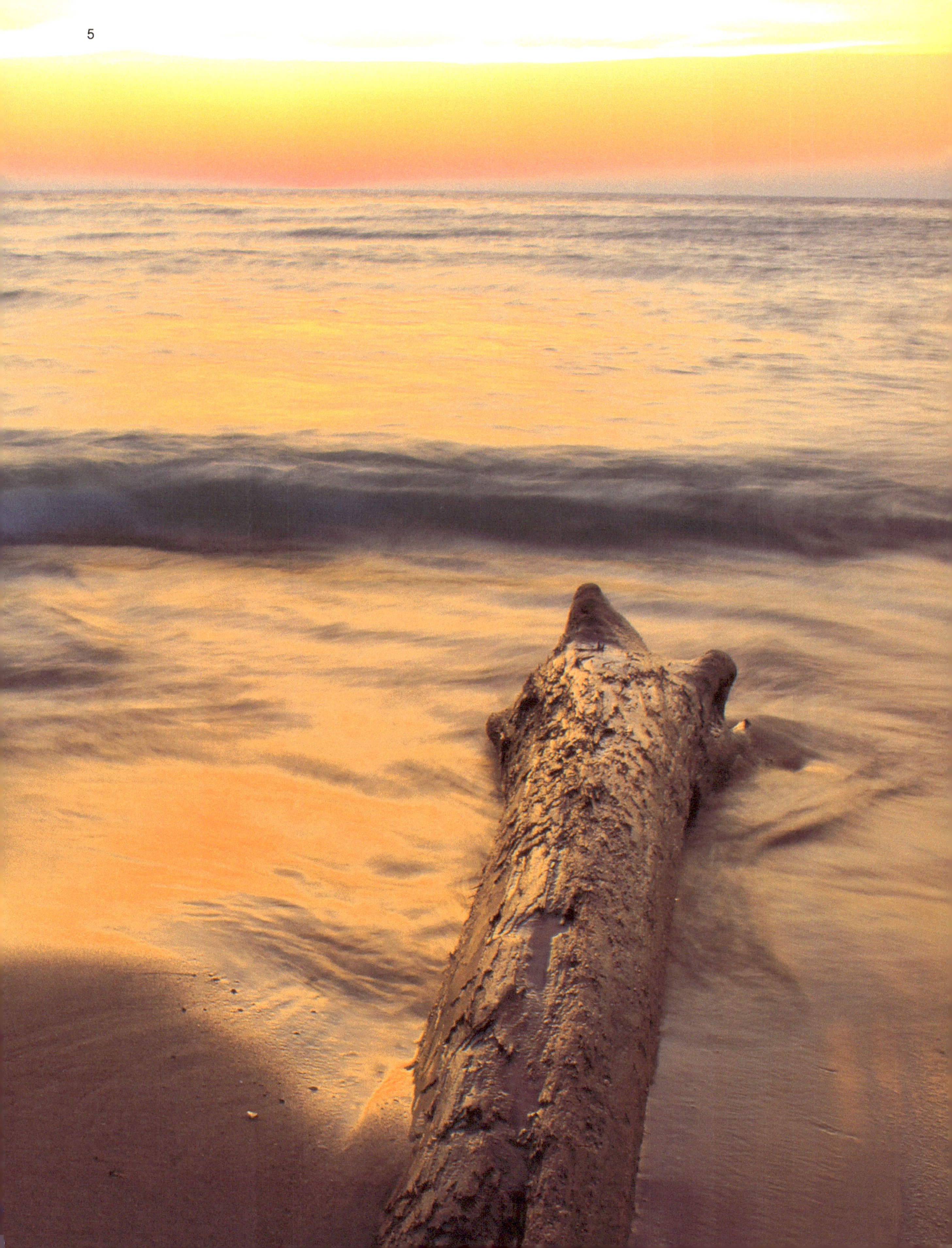

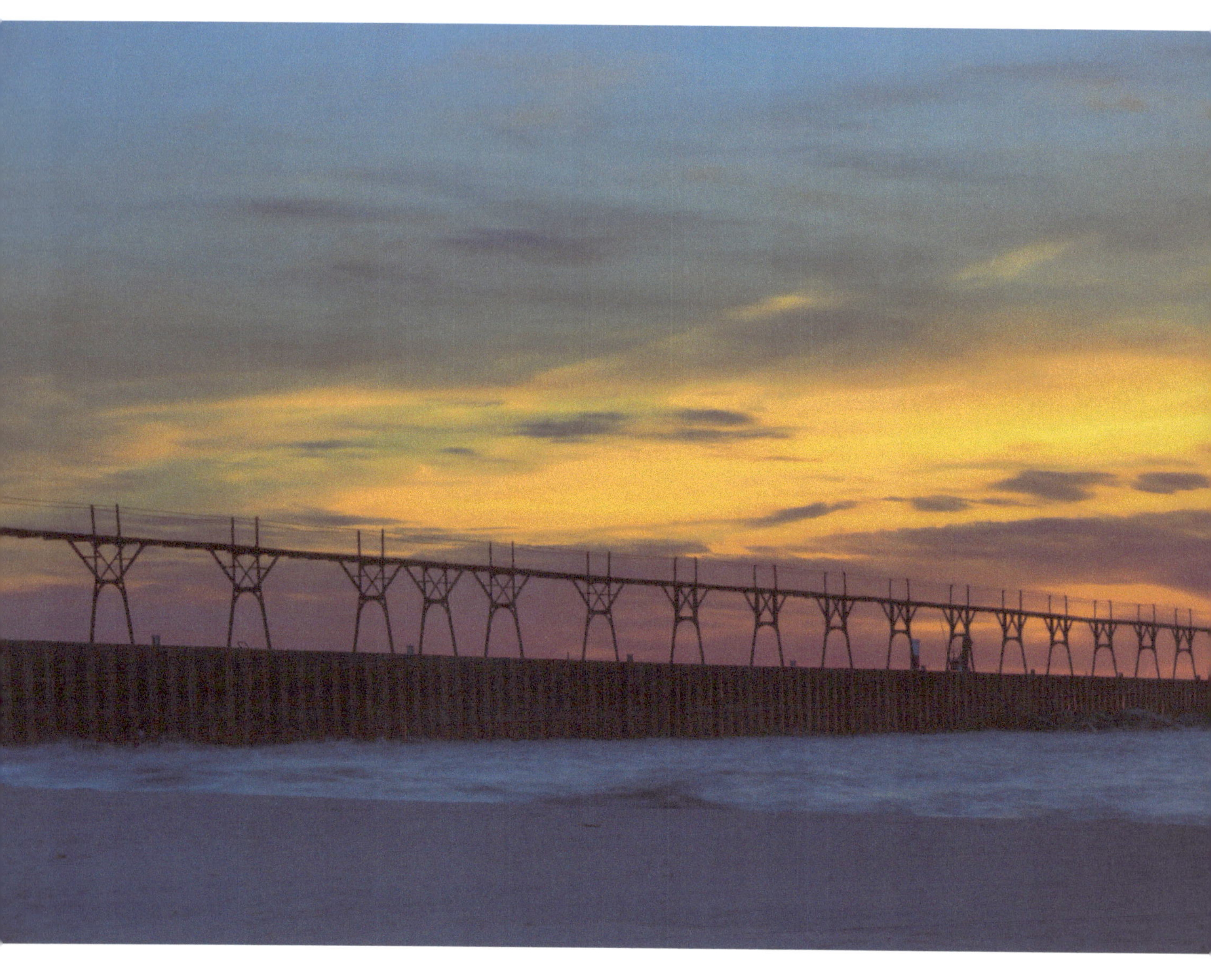

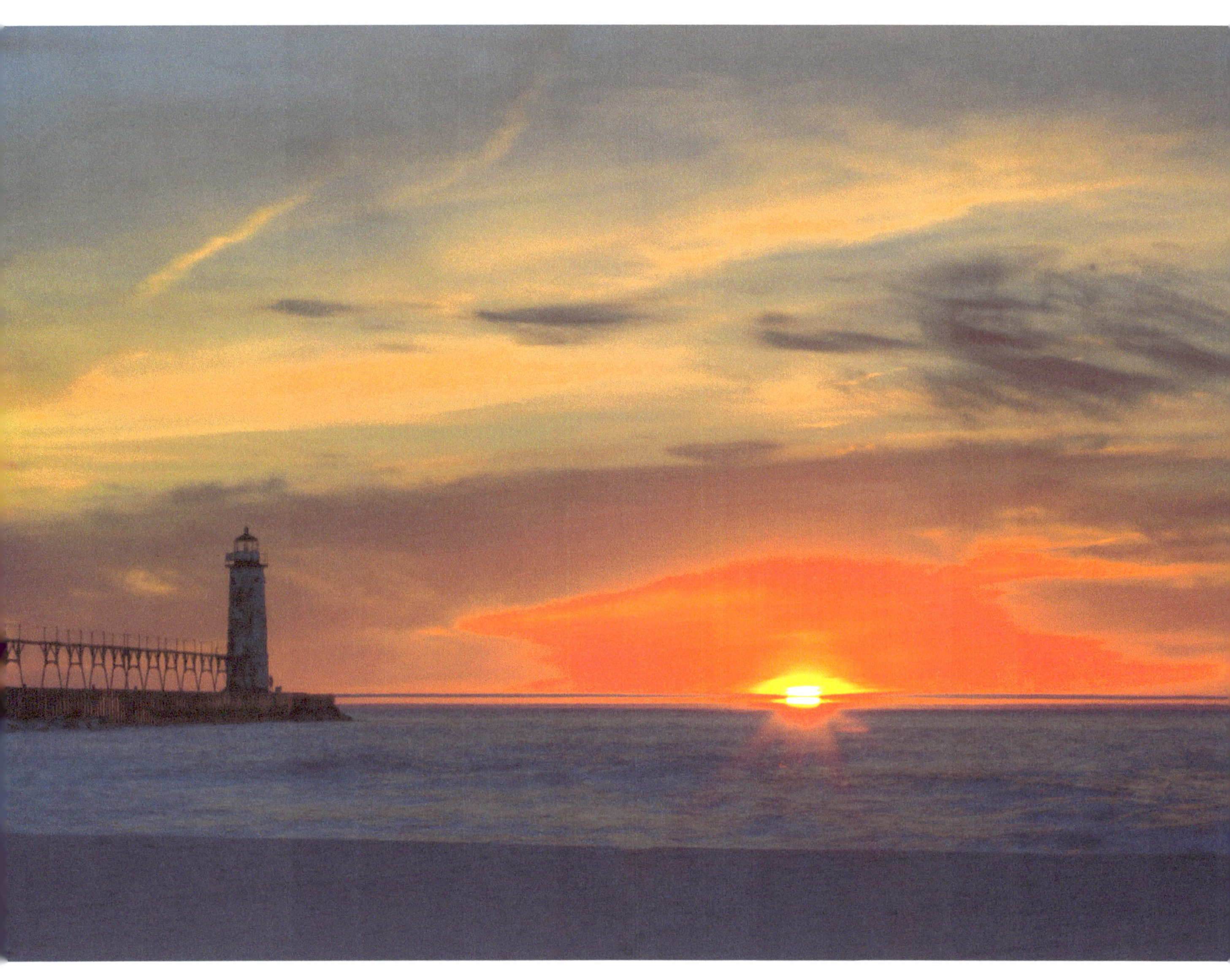

Manistee North Pierhead Lighthouse and Lake Michigan at sunset.

The Northwest Shore

Photography along Michigan's Northwest Lower Peninsula Shoreline

by Twenty-Two North Photography

www.22northphotography.com

Contents

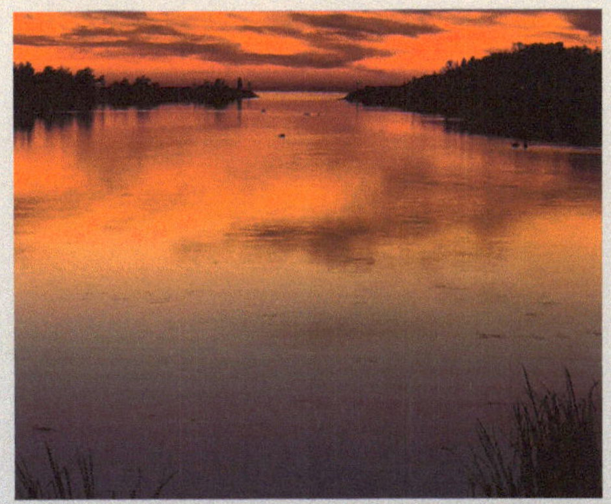

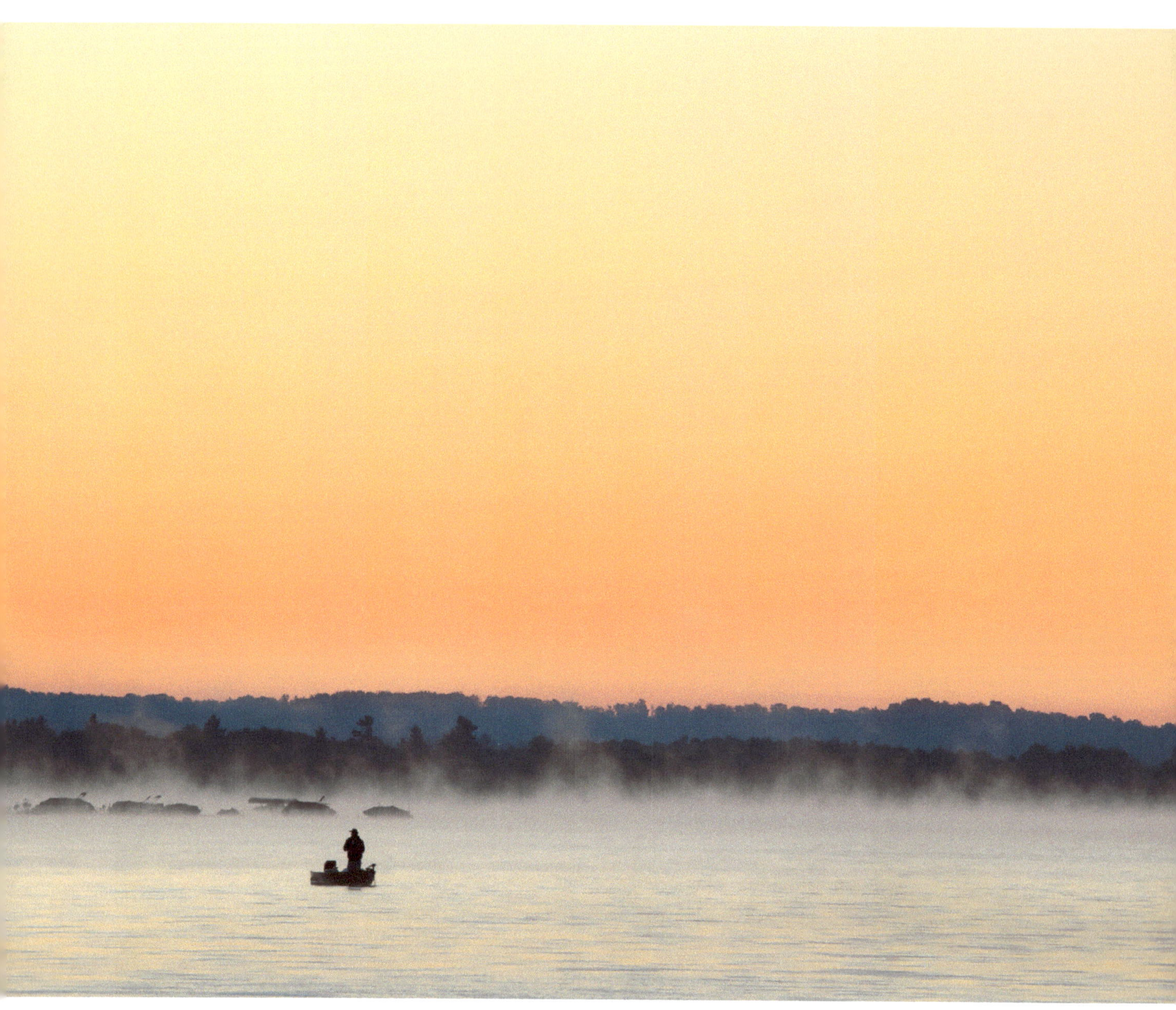

A fisherman at sunrise on Bear Lake.

Introduction

Michigan's landscape was formed by the gradual advance and retreat of glaciers over many thousands of years. The glaciers deposited fine sand and soil and dug the basins that form Lakes Michigan, Superior, Huron, Erie, and Ontario. These forces, along with thousands of years of erosion, created what is today one of the most beautiful stretches of shoreline in the world -- Michigan's Northwest Lower Peninsula shoreline. Stretching from Ludington in the south some 100 miles north to the tip of the Leelanau Peninsula, The Northwest Shore features miles of sugar sand beaches, towering dunes, inland lakes, and numerous unique lakeside towns.

Any discussion of The Northwest Shore must begin with the Sleeping Bear Dunes National Lakeshore, recently named the Most Beautiful Place in America by Good Morning America. It is one of two federally protected lake shores in Michigan under the management of the National Park Service. The dunes are the symbol of Michigan's natural beauty. Stretching approximately forty miles along Lake Michigan, the Sleeping Bear Dunes

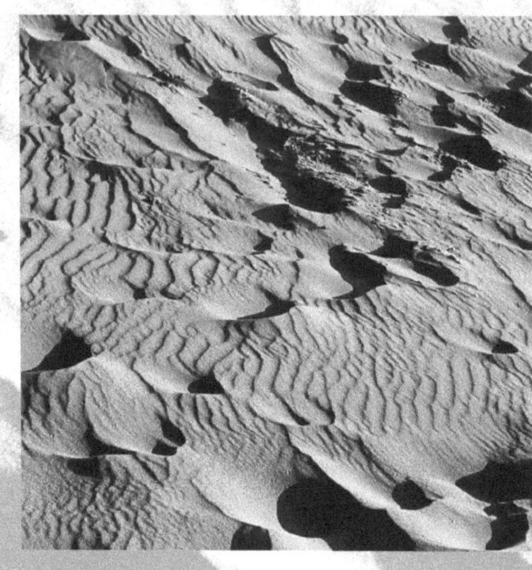

feature towering dunes along the lakeshore, grand views over Lake Michigan, thousands of acres of native forest, and numerous rivers and inland lakes, all easily accessible by car or short hike.

To the north and south of the dunes, beach and port towns line Lake Michigan, each offering unique natural, historical, and recreational attractions. Starting to the south, the journey begins in Ludington, a popular beach and port town in Mason County. Ludington features a thriving downtown, busy marinas, and miles of beaches. Ludington′s two lighthouses, Ludington Light and the Big Sable Lighthouse, are beautiful landmarks along Lake Michigan.

Proceeding north along US-31, the City of Manistee sits at the mouth of the Manistee River, which winds its way for 180 miles through Michigan's northern Lower Peninsula before emptying into Lake Michigan. The Manistee River is one of the most scenic rivers in the world, and is a mecca for kayaking, canoeing, hiking, and camping. Downtown Manistee features a scenic river walk leading to Lake Michigan, the Manistee Pier, and the Manistee North Pierhead Lighthouse.

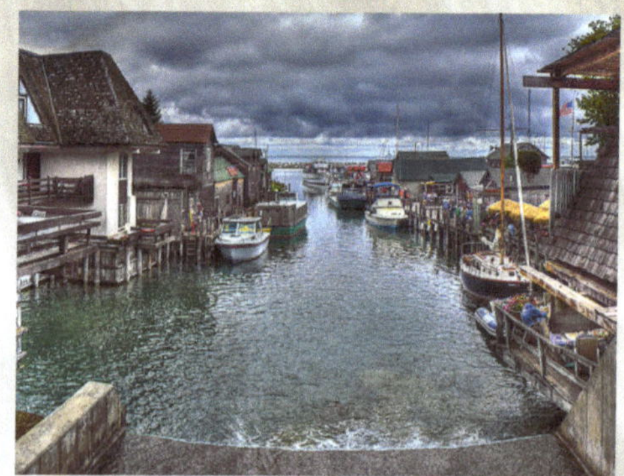

About ten miles north along M-22, Portage Lake and the town of Onekama sit along Lake Michigan's shoreline. Sometimes identified by the symbol "1," after years of tourists mispronouncing the town's name as "One Comma," Onekama offers recreational and scenic opportunities along both lakes, and is home to shops, marinas, and upscale resorts.

A few miles north on M-22 sits secluded Pierport Beach. There are no businesses and is no town at Pierport, just miles of unspoiled sandy beaches and the best opportunity in the area to escape from other more frequented destinations.

Next, one comes to the town of Arcadia, with popular destinations including the Arcadia Ice House, serving visitors sandwiches and ice cream for decades, and the Arcadia Overlook roadside park, which sits hundreds of feet over Lake Michigan and provides some of the best views in Northern Michigan. Arcadia is also home to Arcadia Bluffs Golf Club, one of the most scenic courses in the world and the youngest course in Golf Digest's top-50. On summer days, Arcadia's marina thrives with fishermen launching into Lake Michigan.

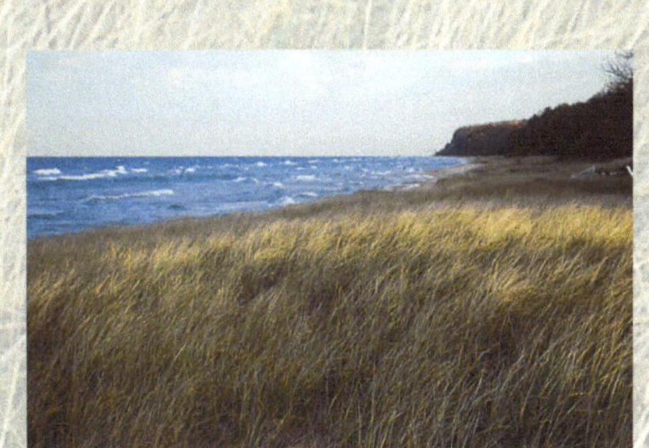

About ten miles north of Arcadia are

Frankfort and Elberta, which sit on opposite sides of Betsie Lake at the mouth of the Betsie River. Former logging towns in the 1800s, these towns thrive as tourist destinations today. Frankfort's downtown offers numerous gift shops, restaurants, cafes, and bars, and is an easy walk to the town's beach, pier, and lighthouse.

Just off of M-22 a few miles north of Frankfort sits Point Betsie Lighthouse. The lighthouse has been in service continuously since the mid-1800s, is easily accessible, and is surrounded by miles of pristine beaches. Due to its beauty and accessibility, Point Betsie Lighthouse is one of the most photographed in the United States.

After entering the Sleeping Bear Dunes National Lakeshore, the next towns are Empire and Glen Arbor, both of which are surrounded by the Sleeping Bear Dunes. Empire has numerous shops and restaurants and a small beach and lighthouse. Glen Arbor is the home not only to miles of Lake Michigan shoreline, but also to Glen Lake, a beautiful inland lake surrounded by hills and dunes to all sides. Glen Arbor has an upscale downtown with wine tasting rooms, galleries, and local shops.

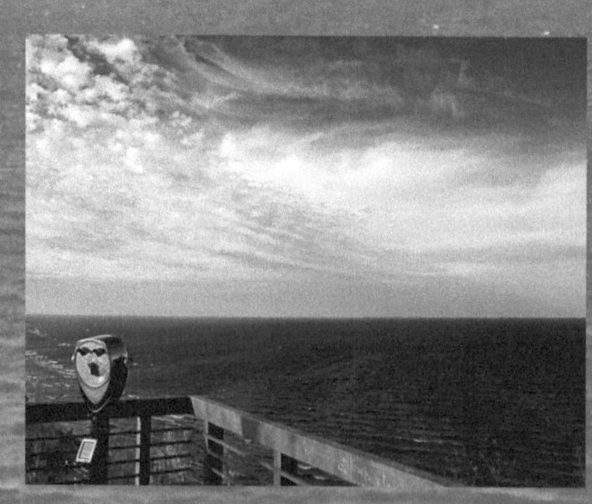

The last town along the Northwest Shore is the popular fishing town of Leland. Leland's primary attraction is Fishtown, an assortment of weathered shanties sitting along the Leland River between Lake Leelanau and Lake Michigan. One can enjoy fresh Lake Michigan smoked salmon from the smokehouses or have drinks at the popular Cove Restaurant along the channel.

In between these towns and attractions lie miles of forests, trails, country roads, and roadside shops. Each season transforms the area's landscape and feel. In Summer, the area is a busy hub for visitors from around the world, all taking advantage of warm temperatures and long summer days to enjoy the lakes. In Fall, the forests are in full color, with trees turning to brilliant shades of red, orange, and yellow. In Winter, the lake brings snow and the area transforms into a prime destination for skiing and snowmobiling. Together it all forms one of the most beautiful areas in the world. Even the finest photographs cannot do it justice, but we hope that the pages of this book can give you a flavor of what Michigan's Northwest Lower Peninsula has to offer.

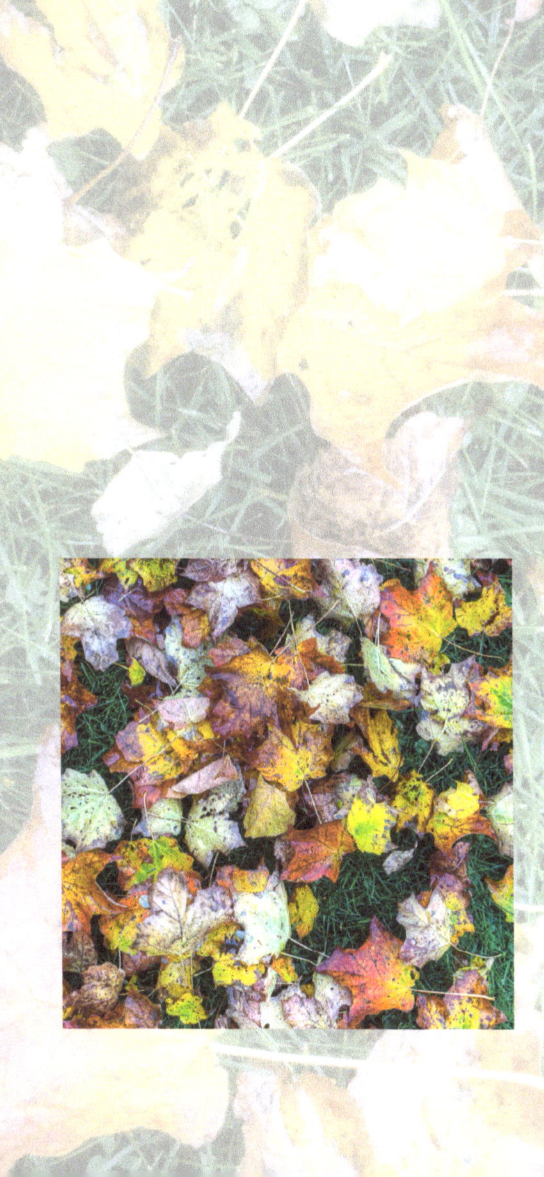

Ludington

Ludington sits at the intersection of M-10 and US-31 along the Lake Michigan shoreline. M-10 divides the northern from southern half of the Lower Peninsula, so Ludington is a great place to start any journey along the Northwest Shore.

Originally named Pere Marquette after the Pere Marquette River that empties into Lake Michigan, the town of Ludington is home to miles of beaches, a thriving downtown, Hamlin Lake, Ludington State Park, and two historic lighthouses.

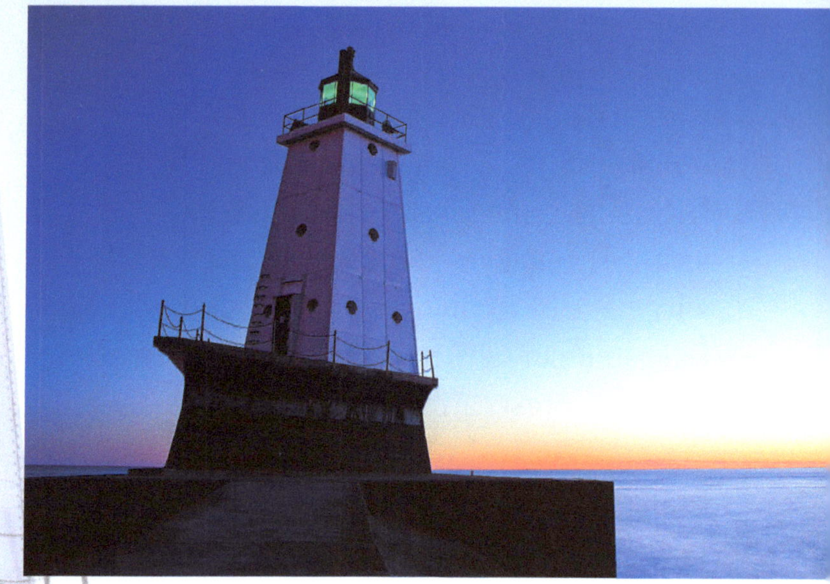

Ludington Light at dusk.

Entering from the east, one is greeted by a downtown featuring local shops, restaurants, and bed and breakfasts. Just steps away sits Lake Michigan, Ludington's pier, and one of Ludington's two historic lighthouses, known simply as Ludington Light. The historic SS Badger docks in the harbor by downtown, and provides daily ferry service to Wisconsin. Ludington State Park, home to lakeside dunes, the Big Sable Lighthouse, and the Sable River, starts just a few miles north of downtown.

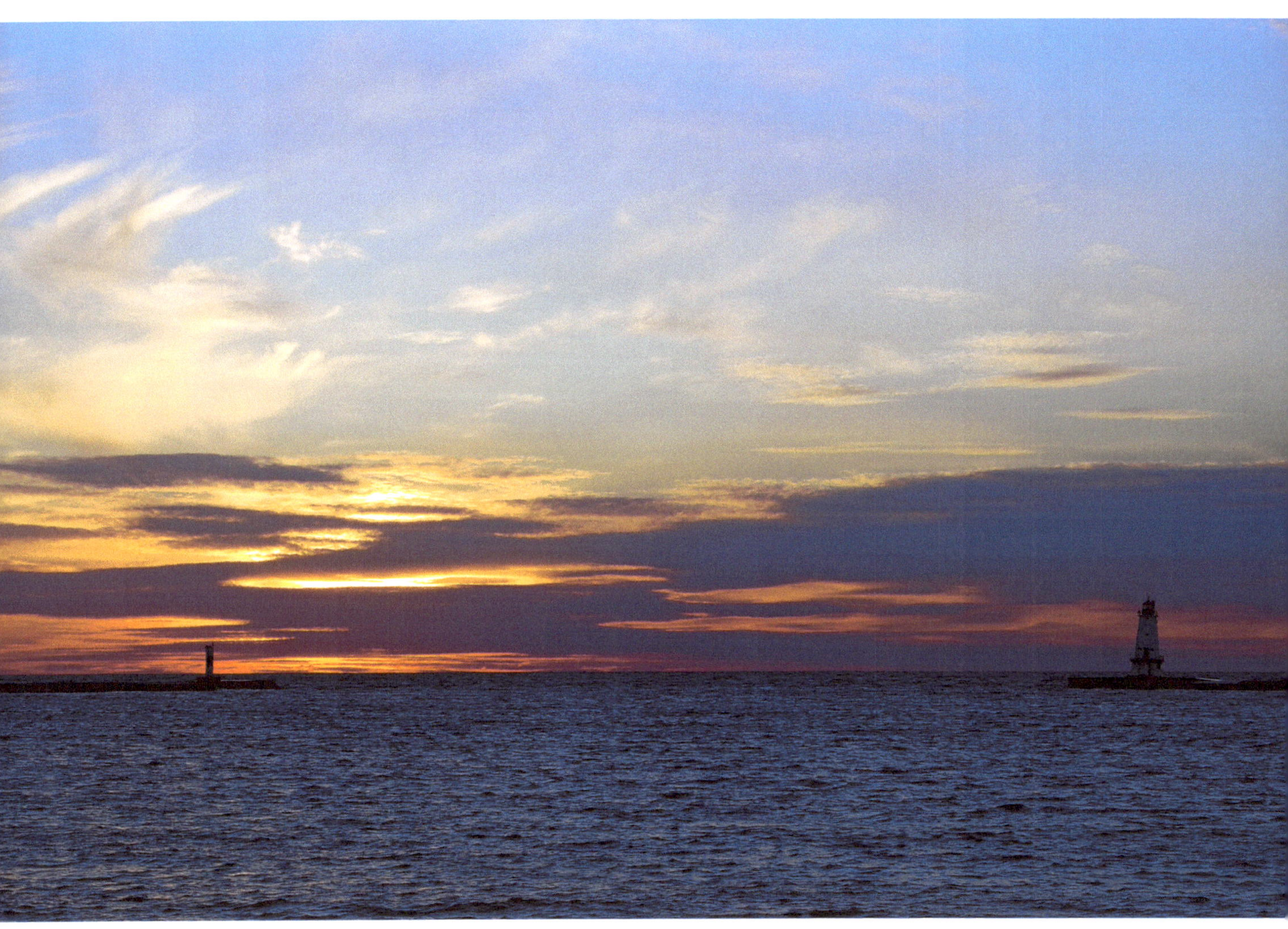

The Ludington Light and fog horn at sunset. These landmarks sit at the end of long piers in Lake Michigan and shelter Ludington Harbor at the mouth of the Pere Marquette River.

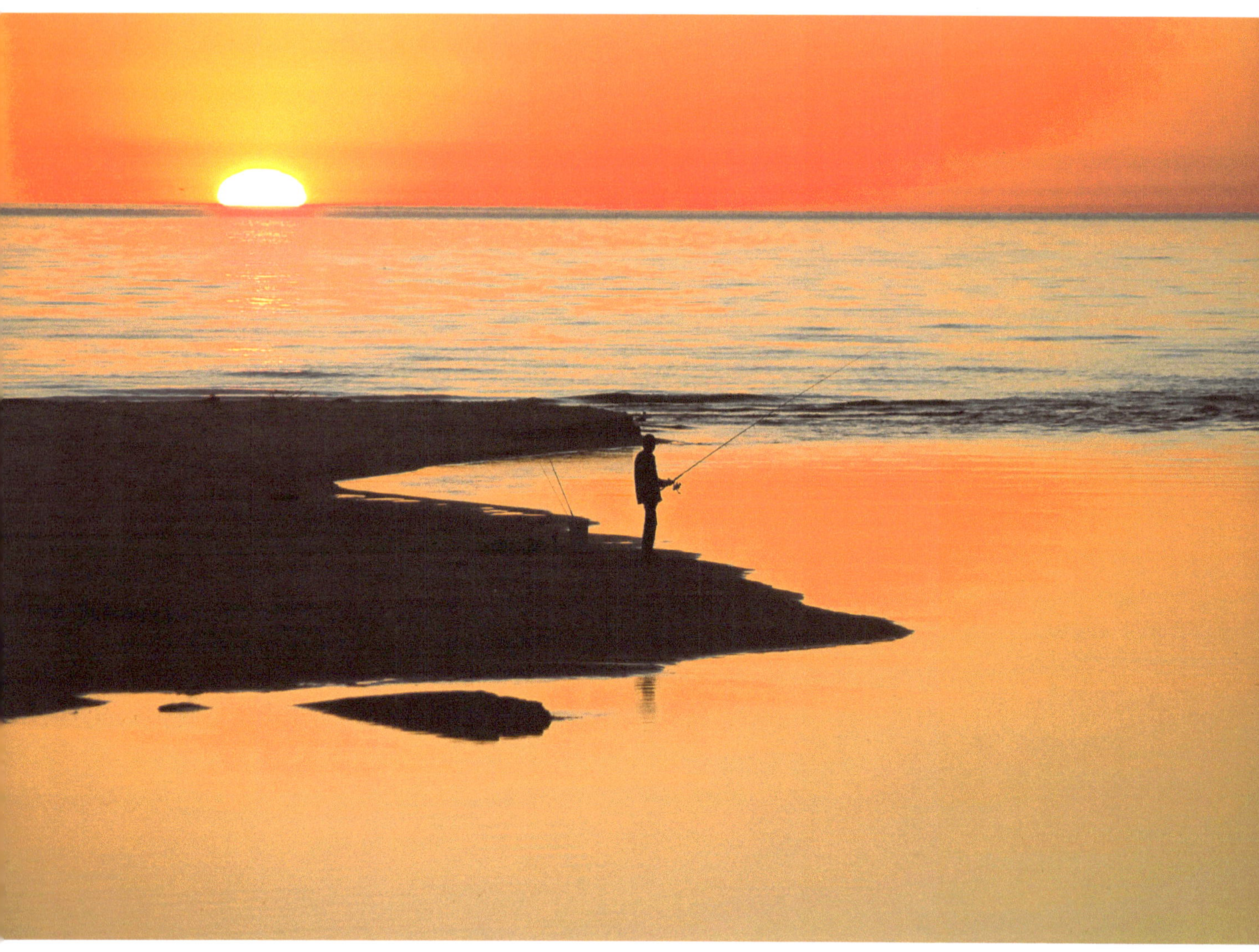

A fisherman stands along the Lake Michigan shoreline at sunset at the mouth of the Sable River. The mouth of the Sable River is accessible from nearby parking within Ludington State Park. The Sable River connects Lake Michigan to Hamlin Lake, which runs for ten miles northeast of Ludington.

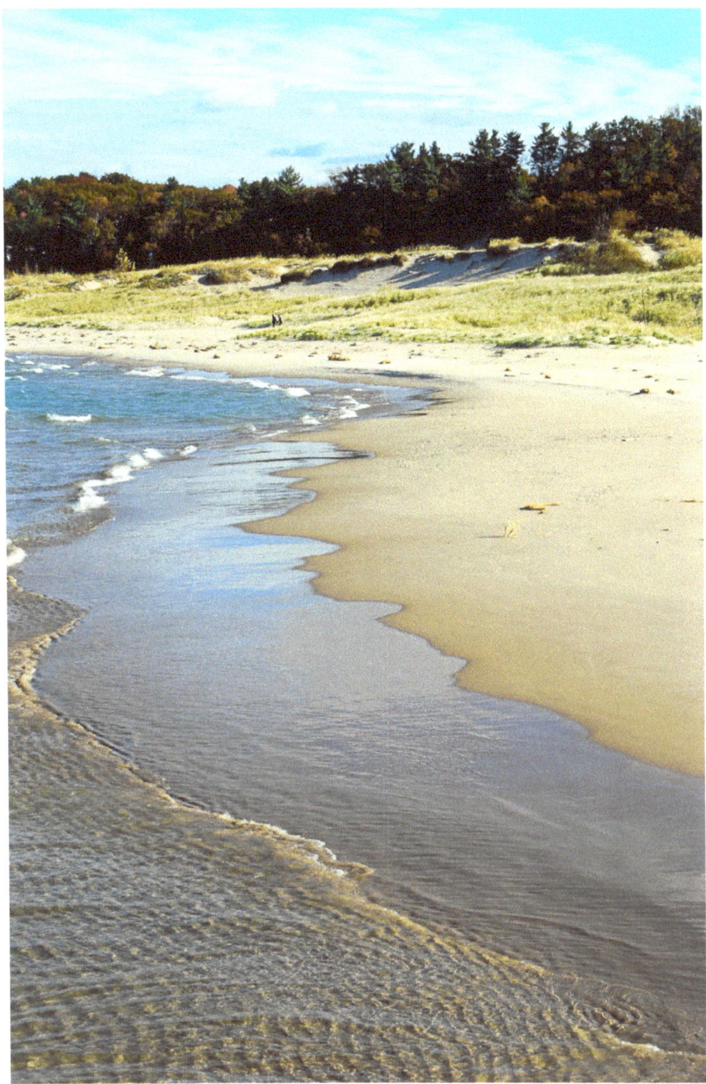

The beach at Ludington.

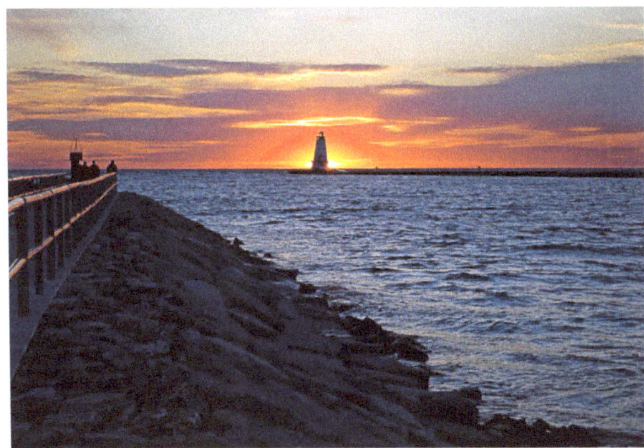

Sunset over Ludington Light.

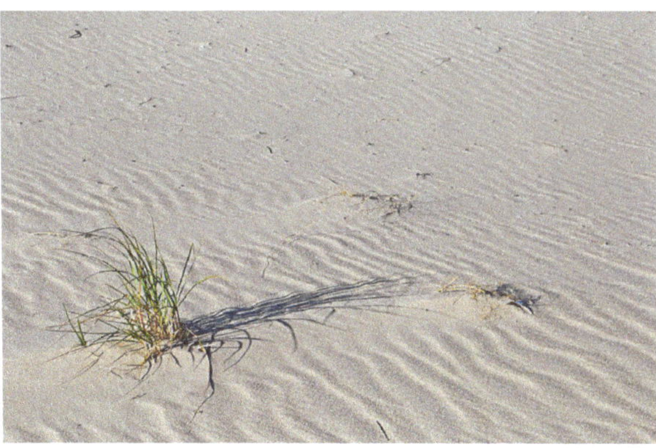

Dune grass grows on the beach.

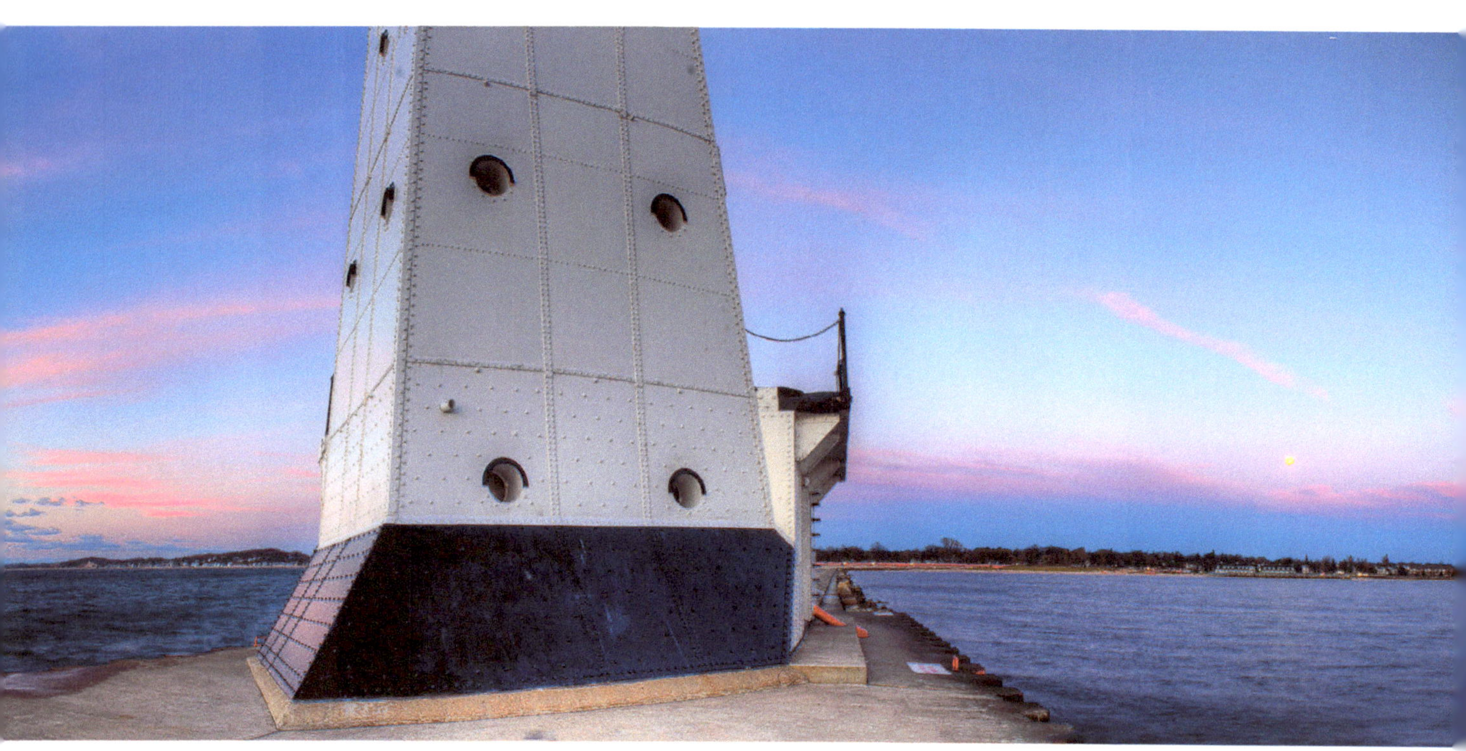

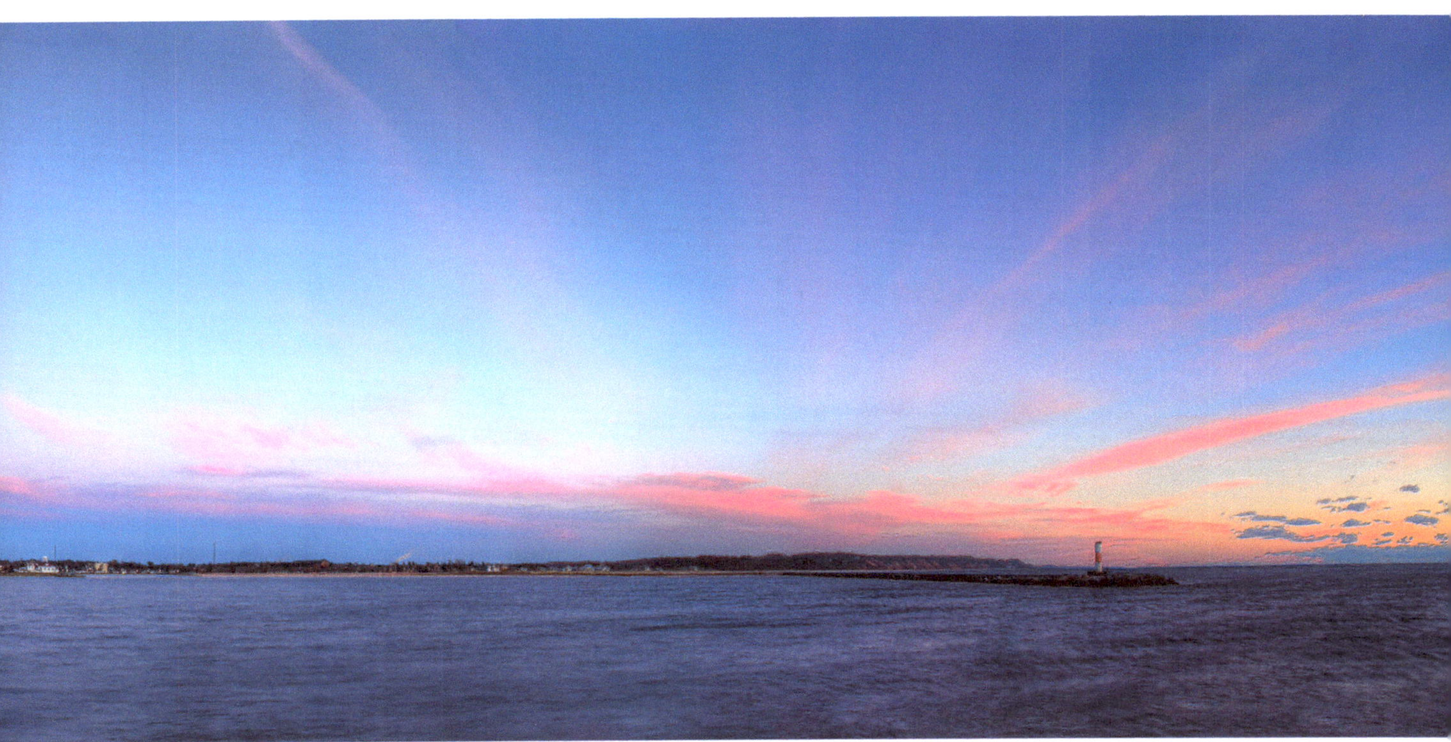

Ludington Light and Ludington shoreline at dusk. Ludington Light is one of Ludington's two landmark lighthouses. It sits at the end of a pier and is a popular place for visitors to take in the sunset, fish, or watch the passing boats. Ludington Light was completed in 1924. It still illuminates every night at sunset.

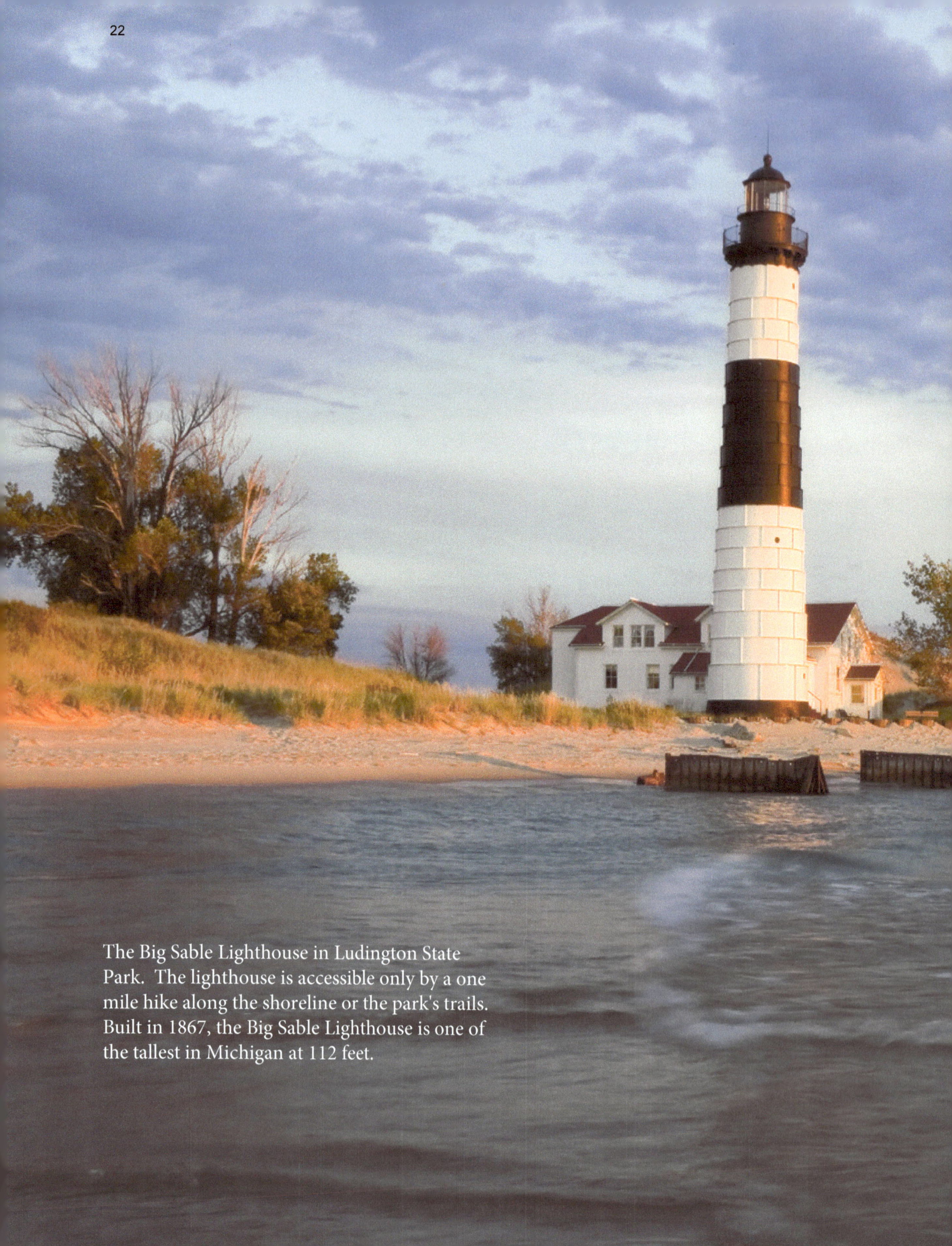

The Big Sable Lighthouse in Ludington State Park. The lighthouse is accessible only by a one mile hike along the shoreline or the park's trails. Built in 1867, the Big Sable Lighthouse is one of the tallest in Michigan at 112 feet.

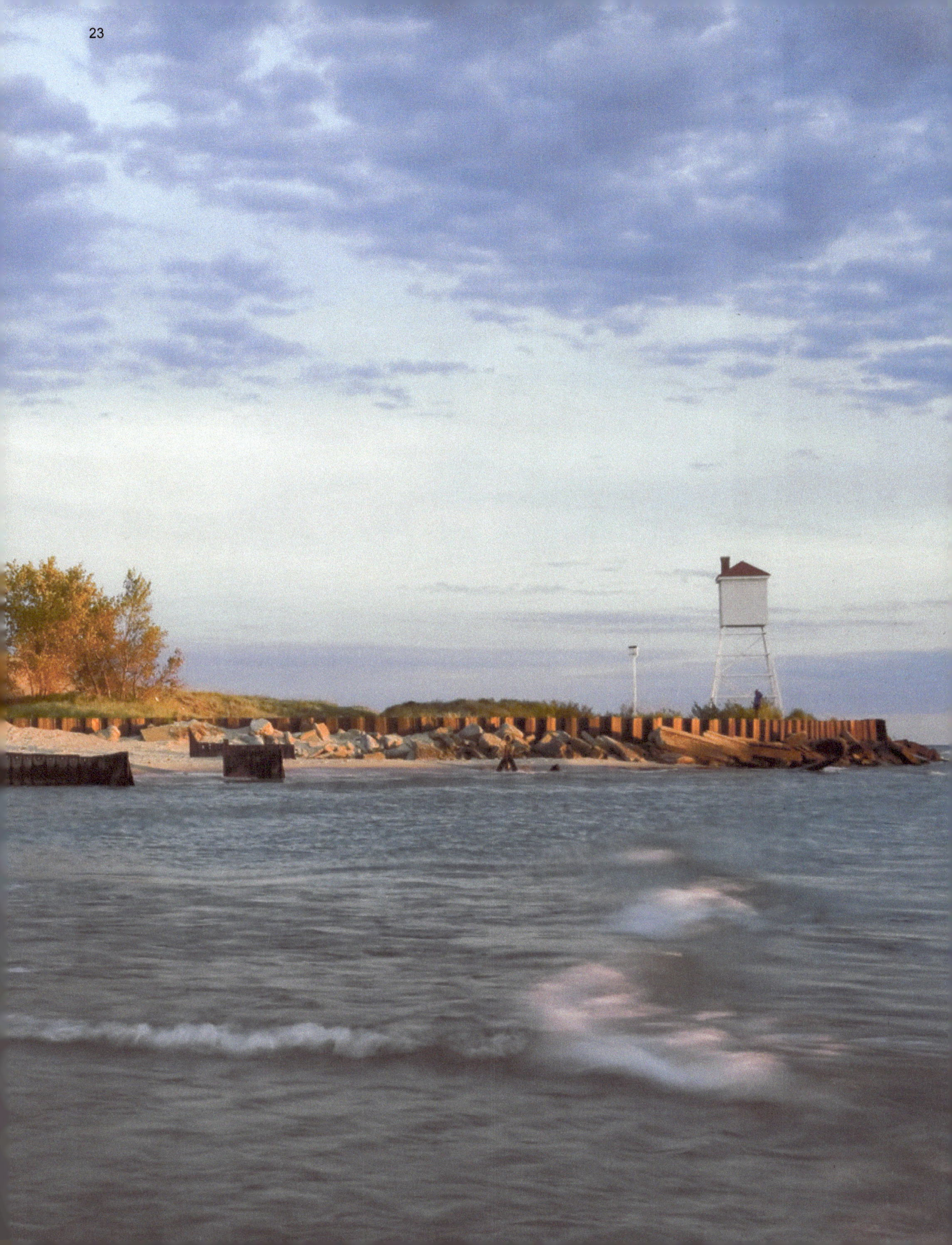

Manistee

Getting its name from an Ojibwe Indian term meaning "spirit of the woods," Manistee sits twenty miles north of Ludington at the mouth of the Manistee River. The town grew rapidly in the logging era. In the 1880s, Manistee was home to more millionaires per capita than anywhere in the United States.

Today, the river serves a few commercial enterprises along Manistee Lake, but is better known as a mecca for fishing, hiking, kayaking, and canoeing. The river winds its way 180 miles through Northern Michigan and is easily accessible from River Rd. and M-55 a few miles north of downtown.

Manistee's downtown features numerous shops and eateries and some of the oldest buildings in Northern Michigan, such as the Ramsdell Theatre. Streets line both sides of the river and lead to Lake Michigan, where the Manistee North Pierhead Lighthouse towers over the shoreline and pier.

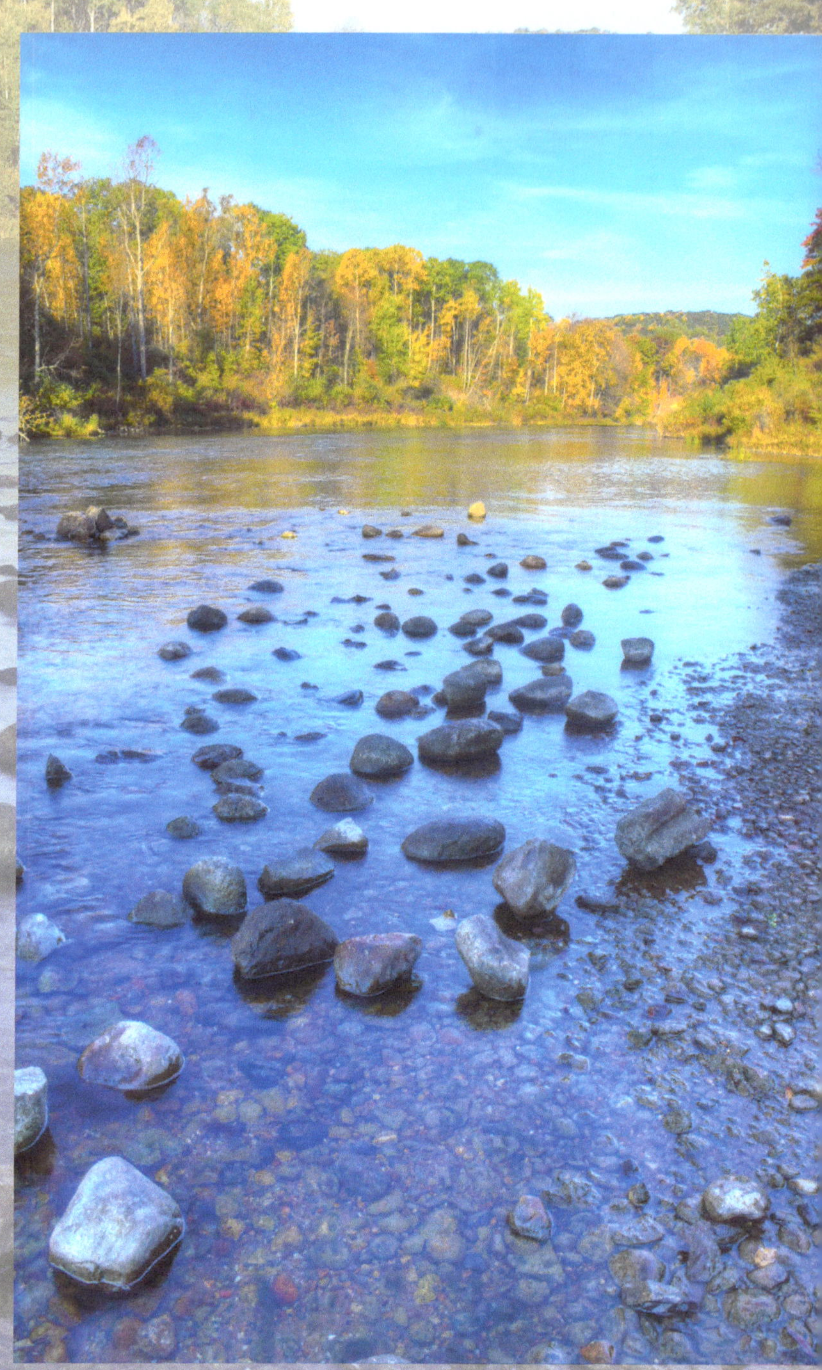

The Manistee River in the Fall.

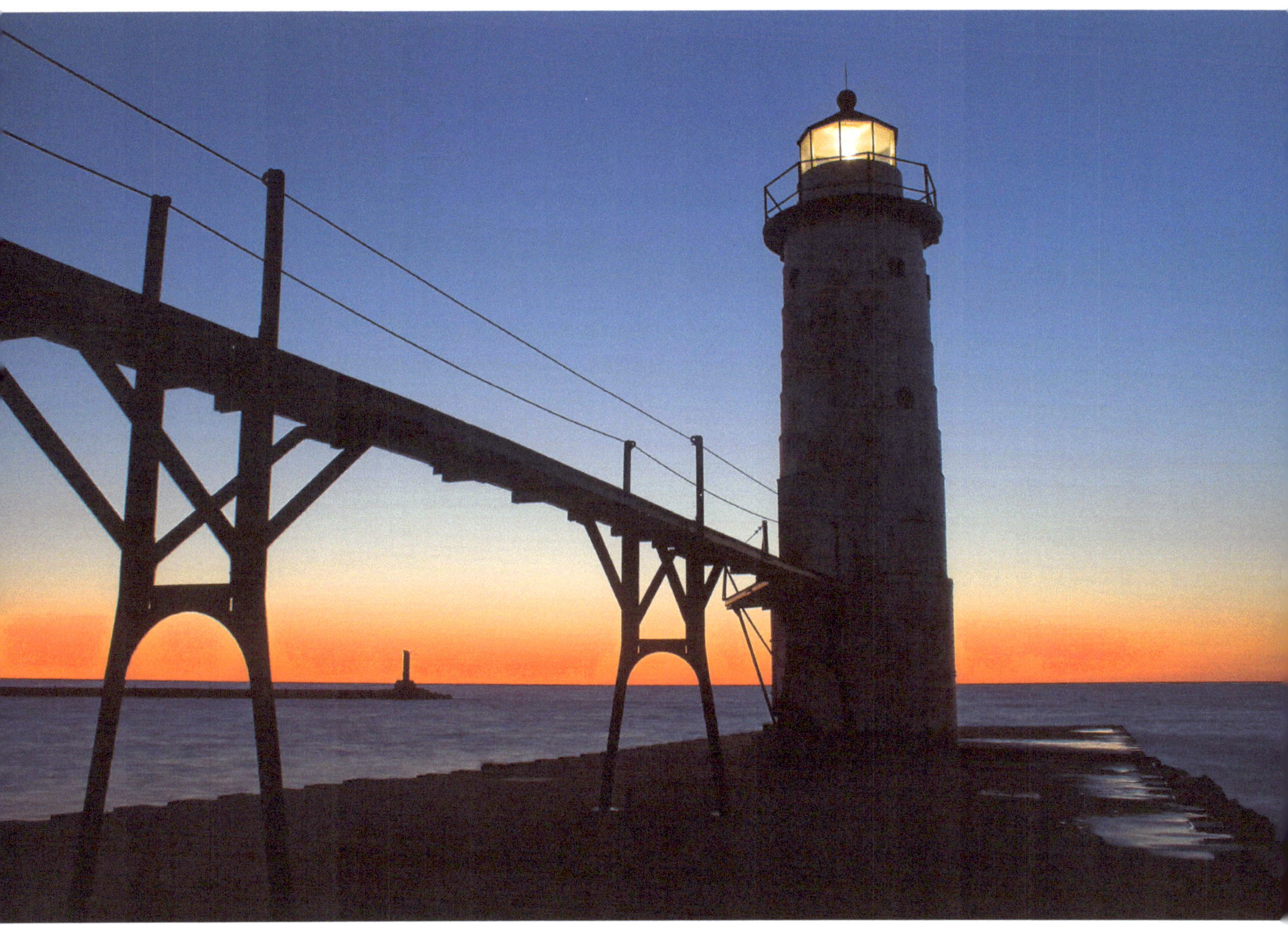

The Manistee North Pierhead Lighthouse at dusk. The Lighthouse was originally built in 1870, but was lost the next year in the Great Fire of 1871. The fire destroyed the town of Manistee. The lighthouse burned on the same day as the Great Chicago Fire of 1871. It was replaced the following year, and remains an active aid to navigation.

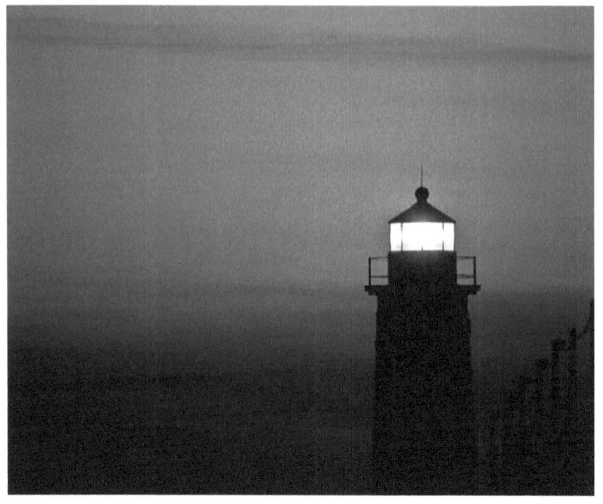

The Manistee North Pierhead Lighthouse.

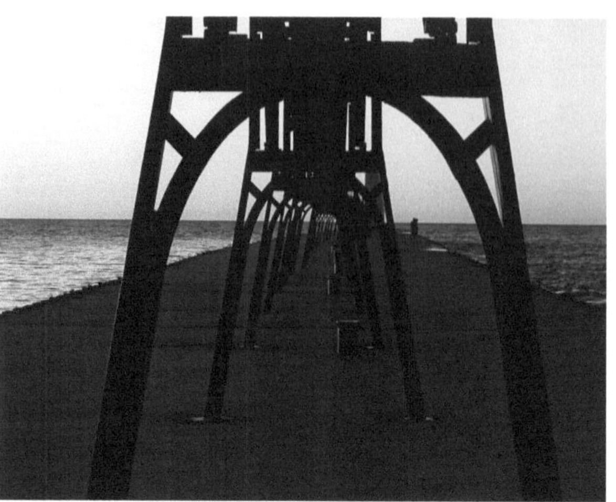

Support beams on the pier.

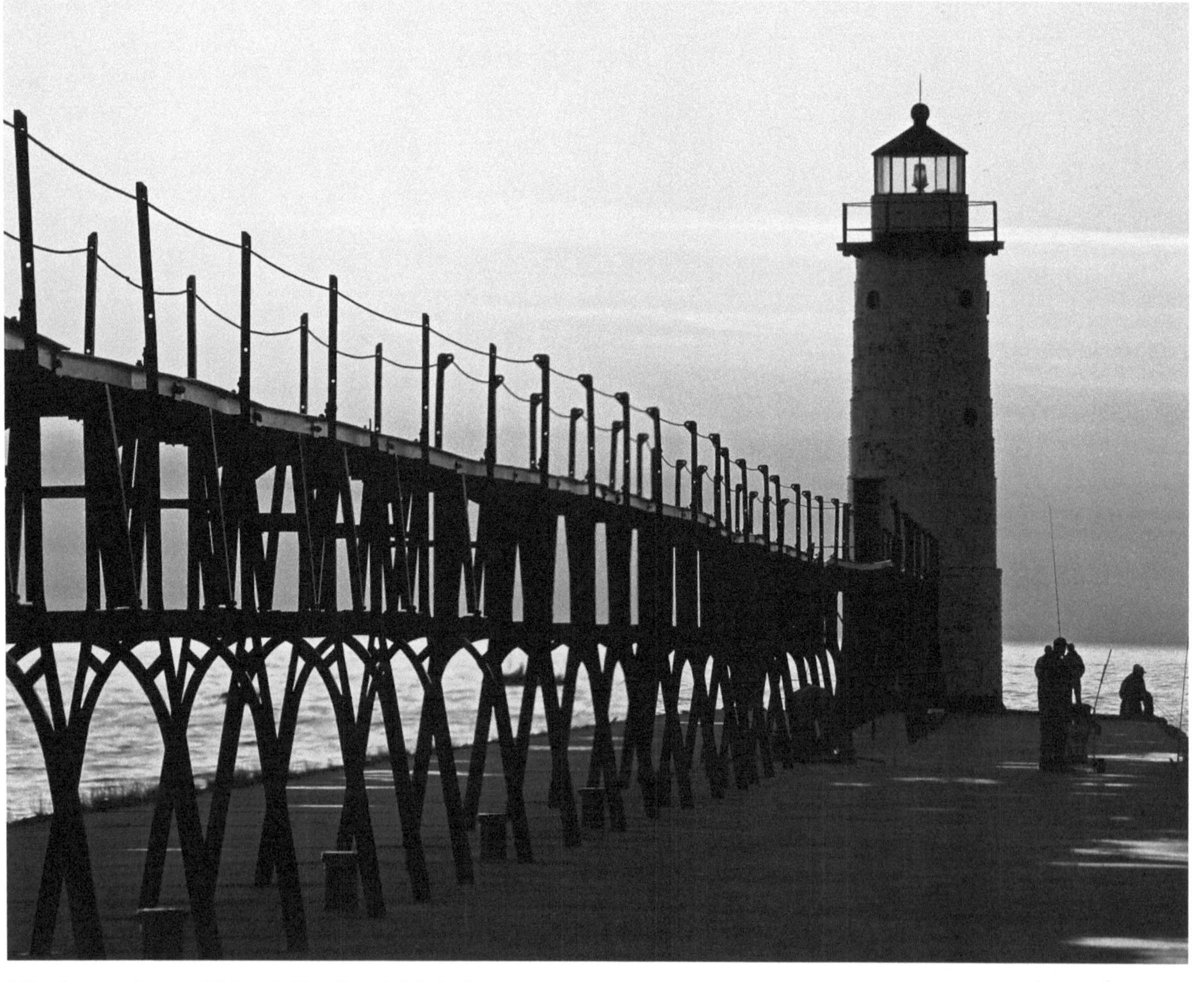

Manistee pier and North Pierhead Lighthouse.

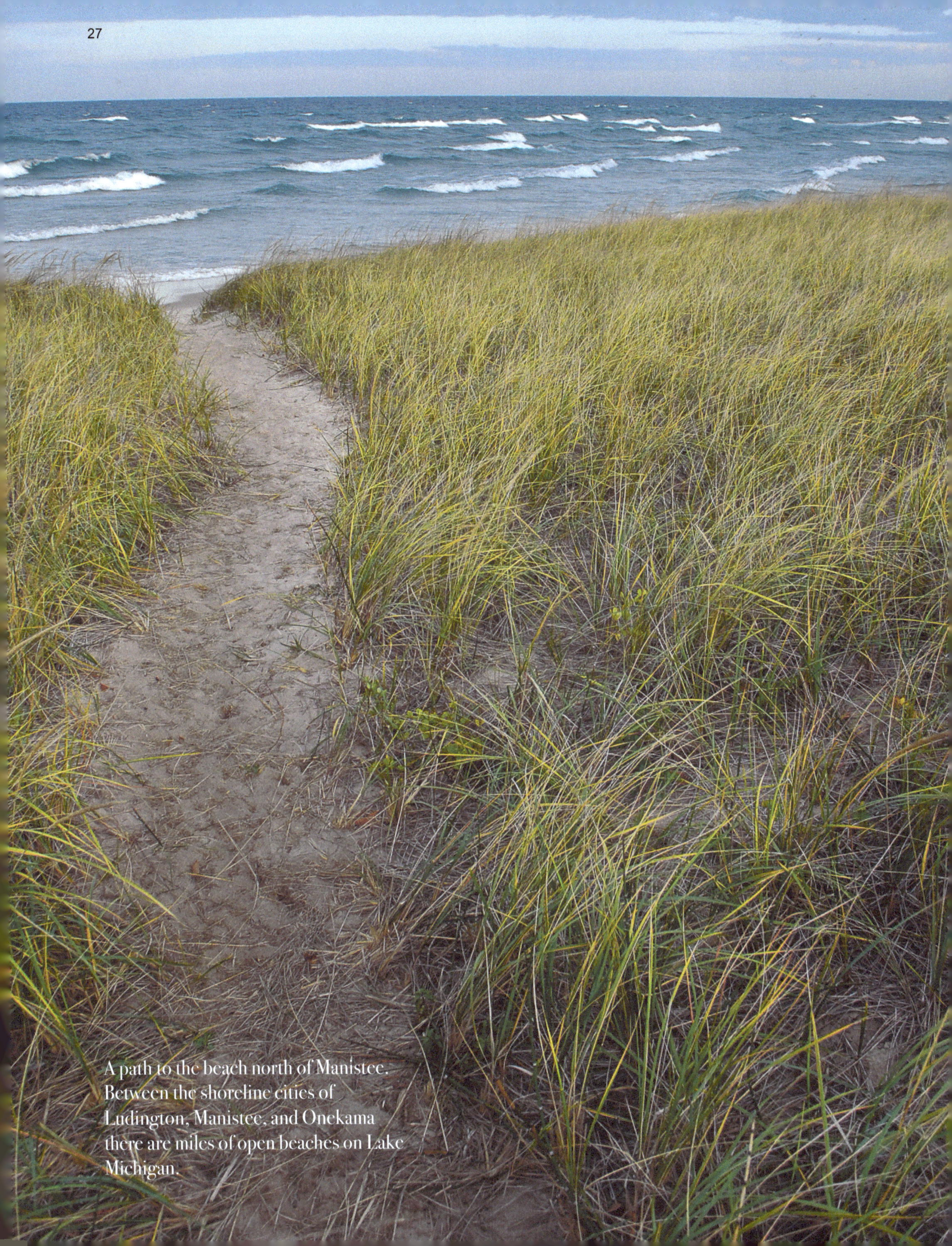

A path to the beach north of Manistee. Between the shoreline cities of Ludington, Manistee, and Onekama there are miles of open beaches on Lake Michigan.

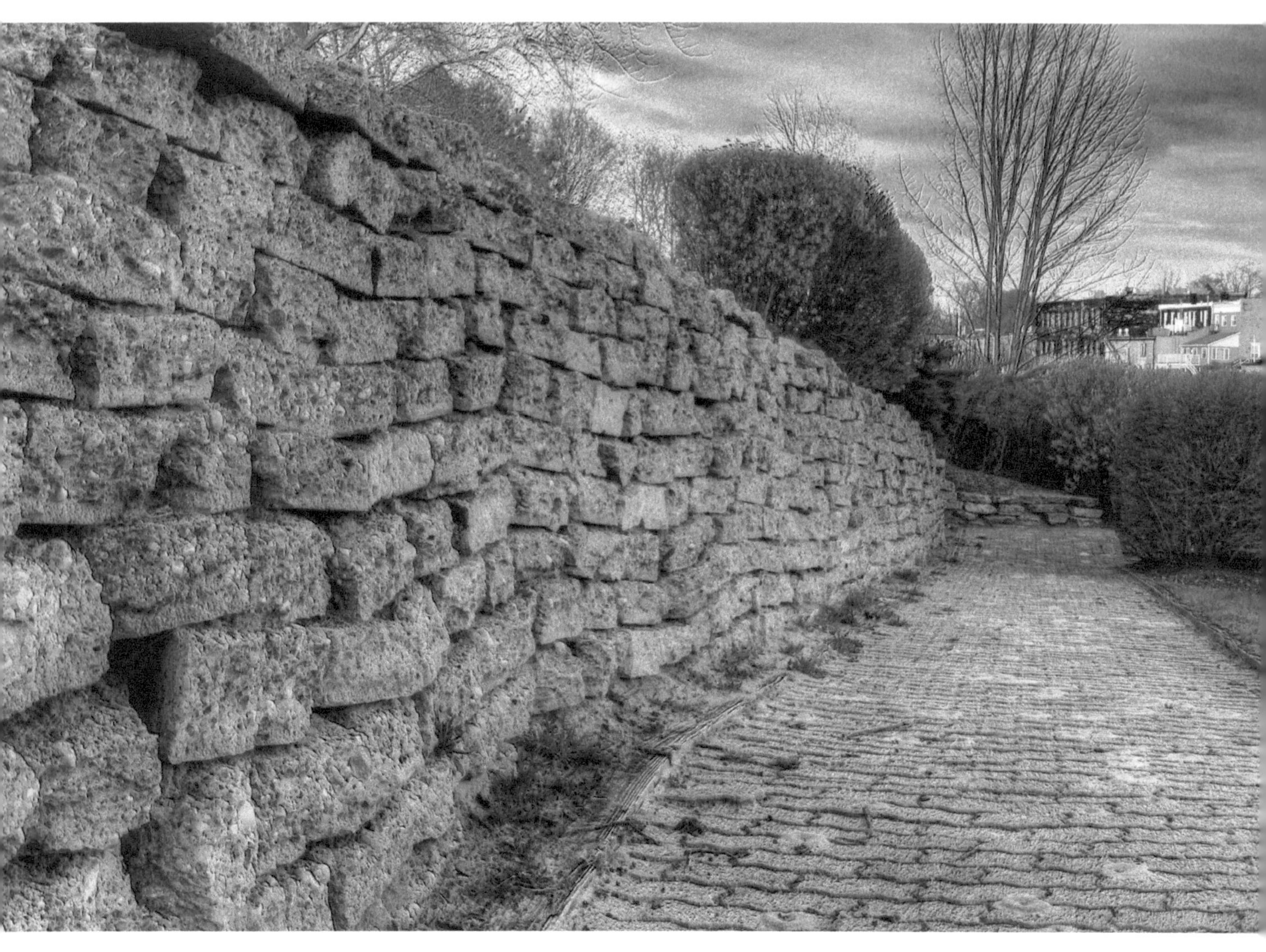

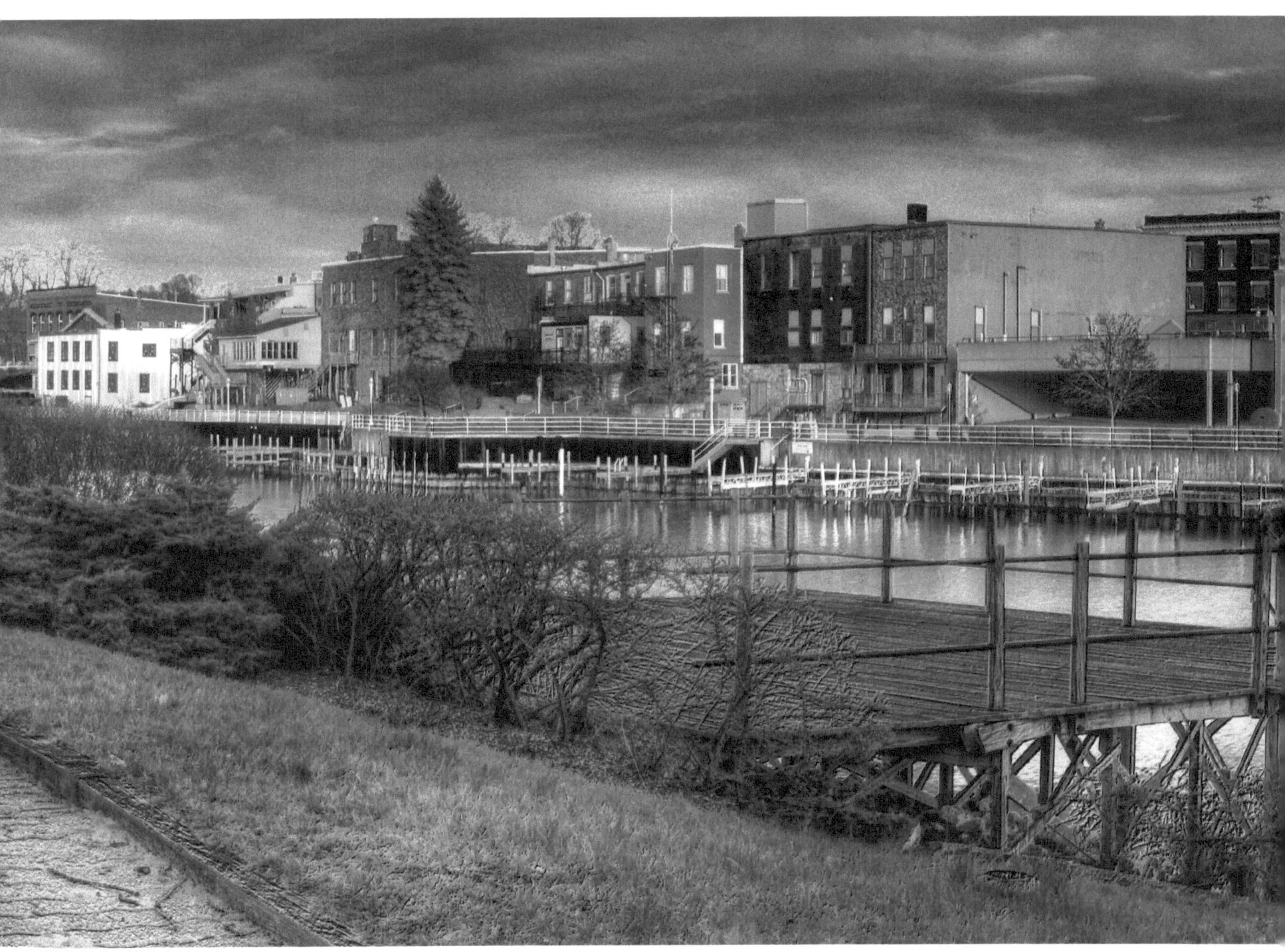

A path runs along the north bank of the Manistee River. The backs of numerous turn-of-the-century downtown buldings line the south bank.

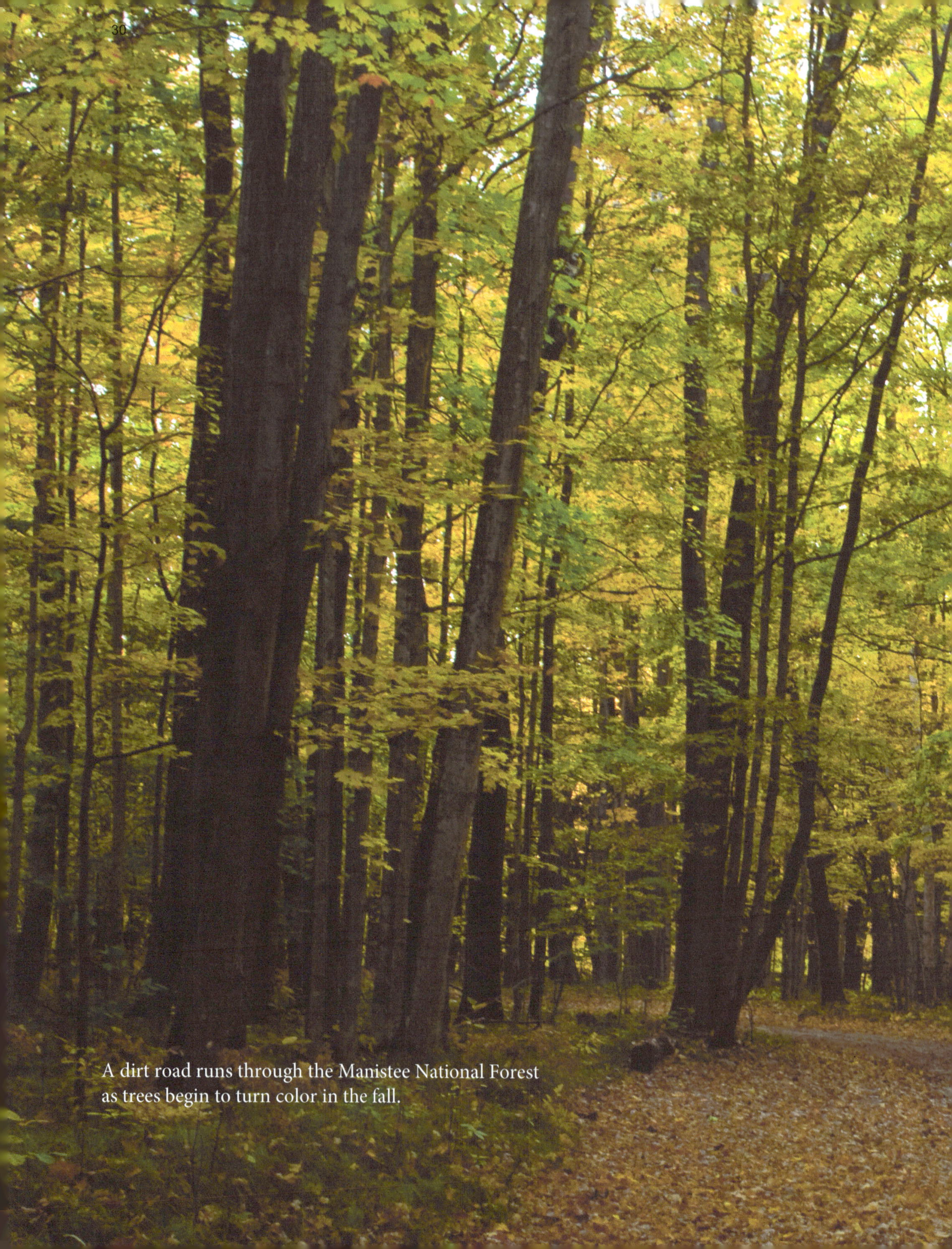

A dirt road runs through the Manistee National Forest as trees begin to turn color in the fall.

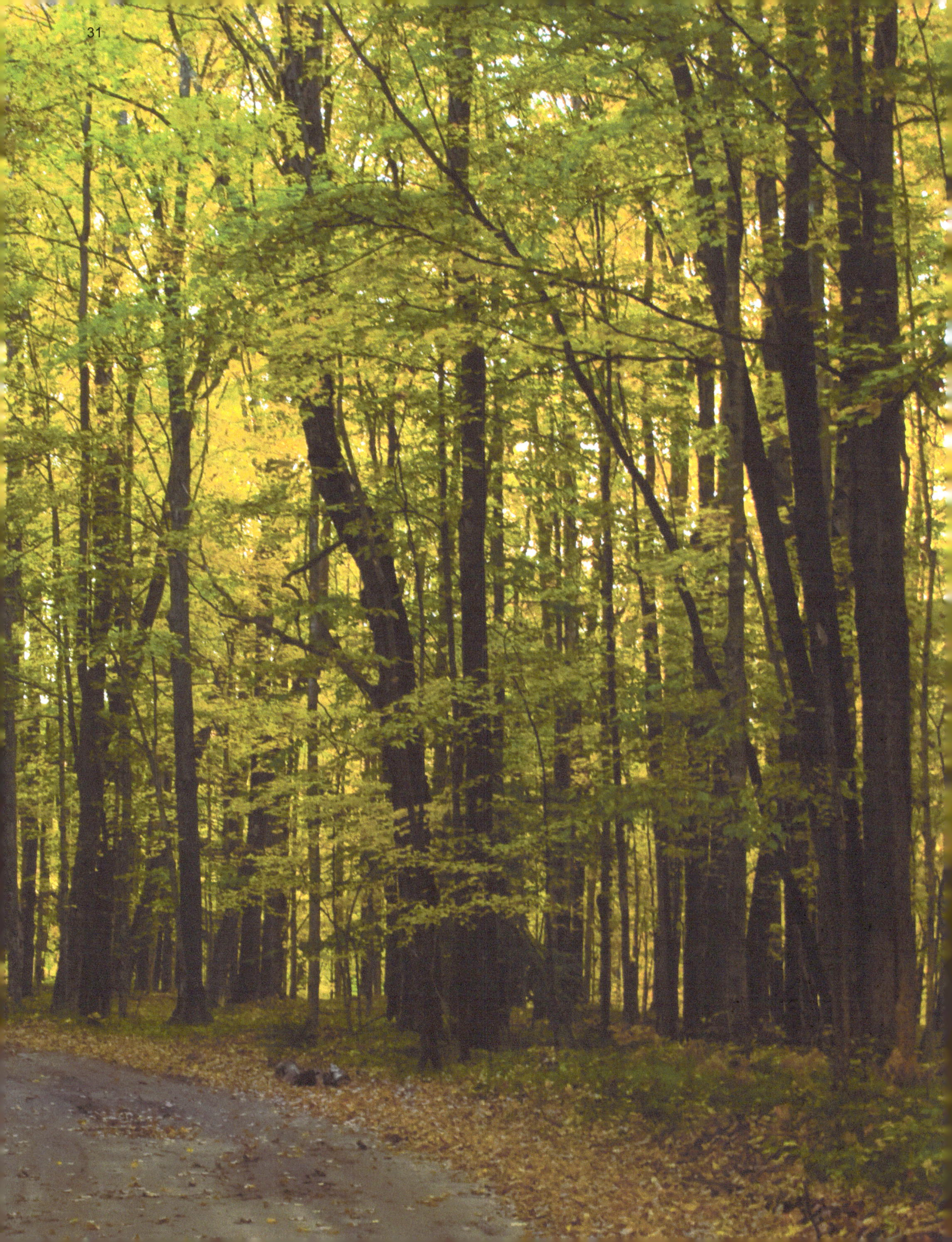

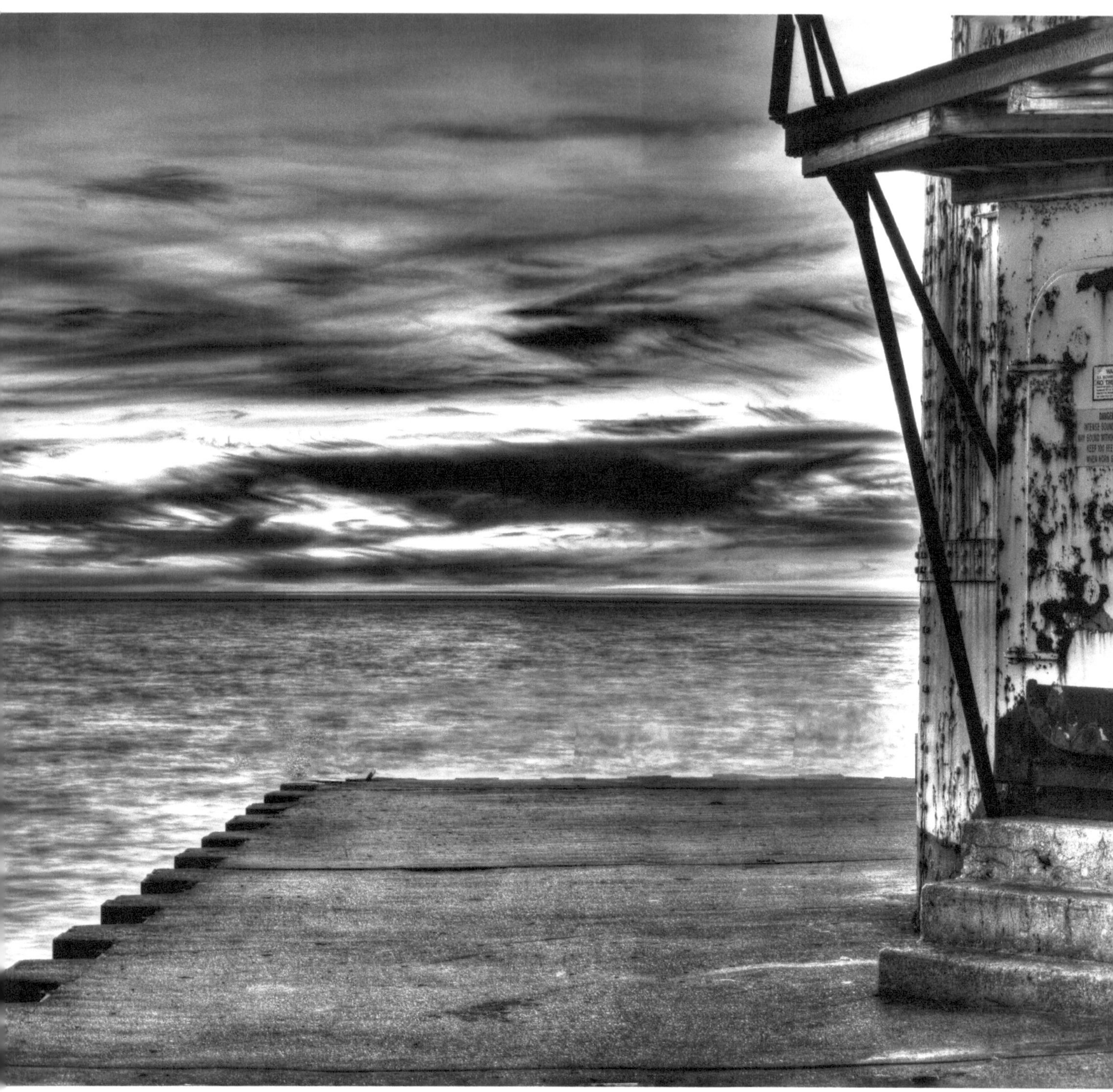

The weathered base of the Manistee North Pierhead Lighthouse at the end of the Manistee Pier.

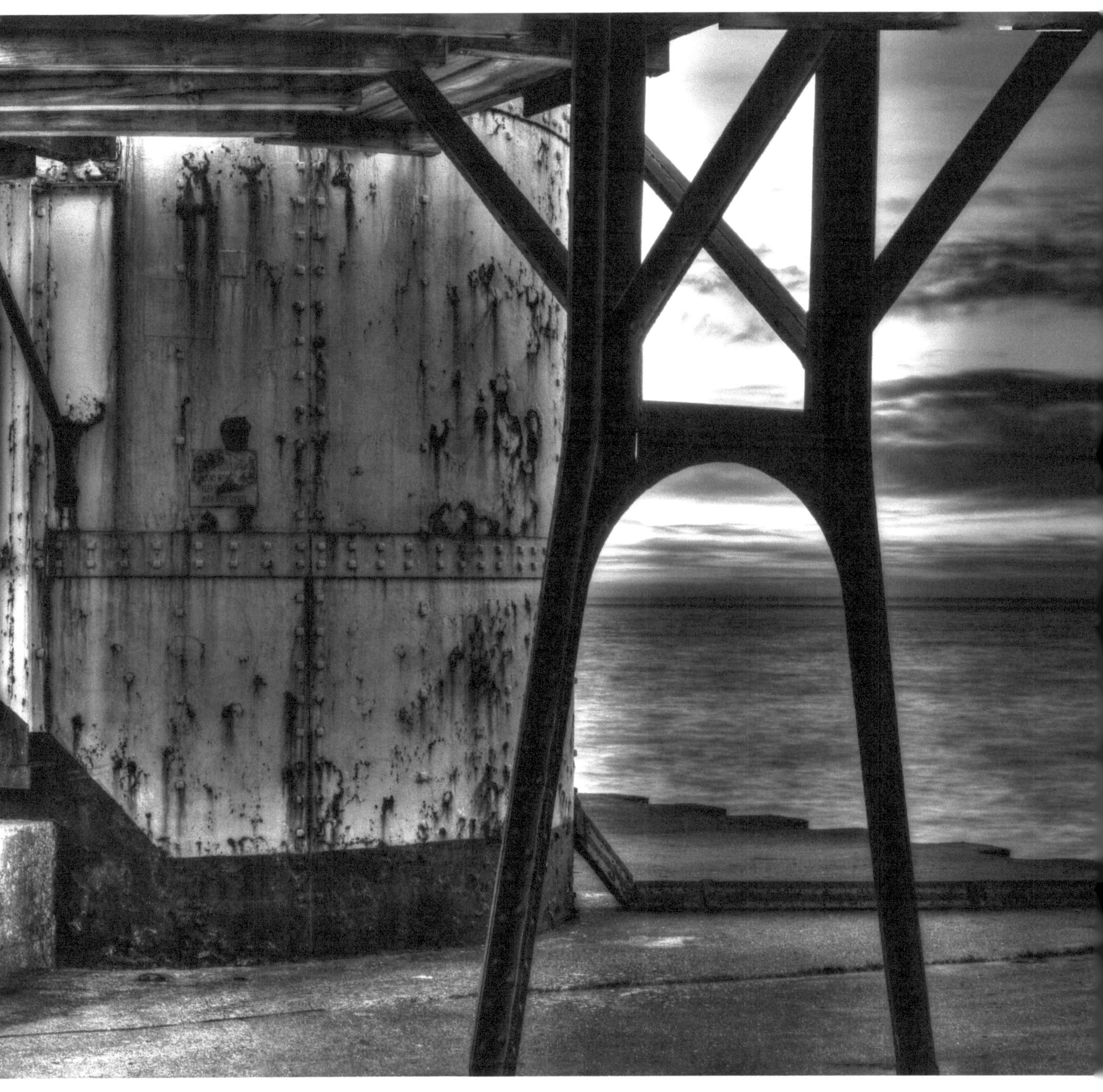

Onekama

North of Manistee one must veer left on to M-22 to continue along the Northwest Shore. M-22 continues for another 100 miles and is widely considered one of the most scenic roads in the United States. Onekama is the first town north along M-22.

The town's name is derived from "Ona-ga-maa," an Anishinaabe Indian word meaning "singing water." Onekama is centered around Lake Michigan and Portage Lake, which sit only a few hundred feet apart and are connected by a channel. There are miles of beaches along the Lake Michigan shoreline and a large pier which provides great opportunities for fishing and taking in the sunset.

Portage Lake is surrounded by seasonal houses, a small downtown area with a few local shops and restaurants, and a number of resorts, including the turn-of-the-century Portage Point Inn.

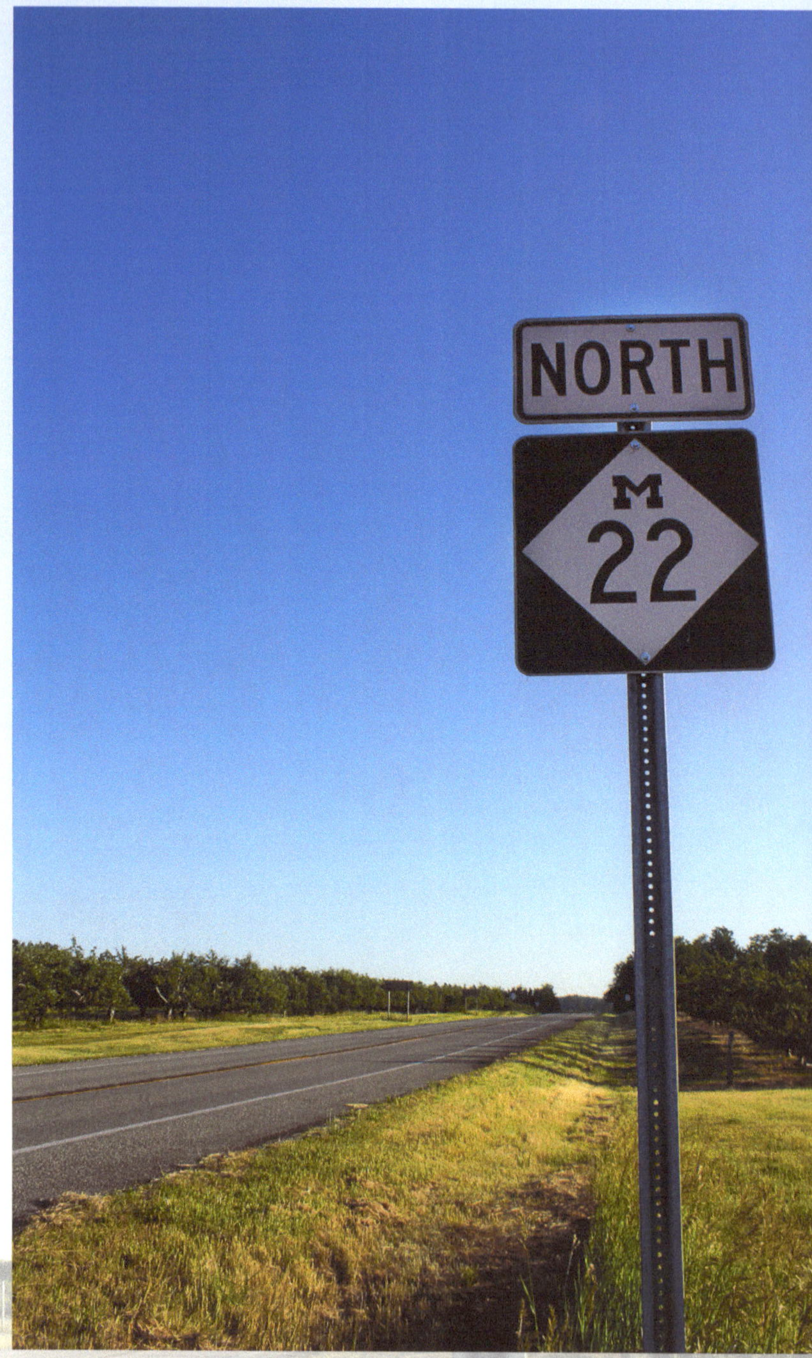

M-22 Scenic Highway near Onekama.

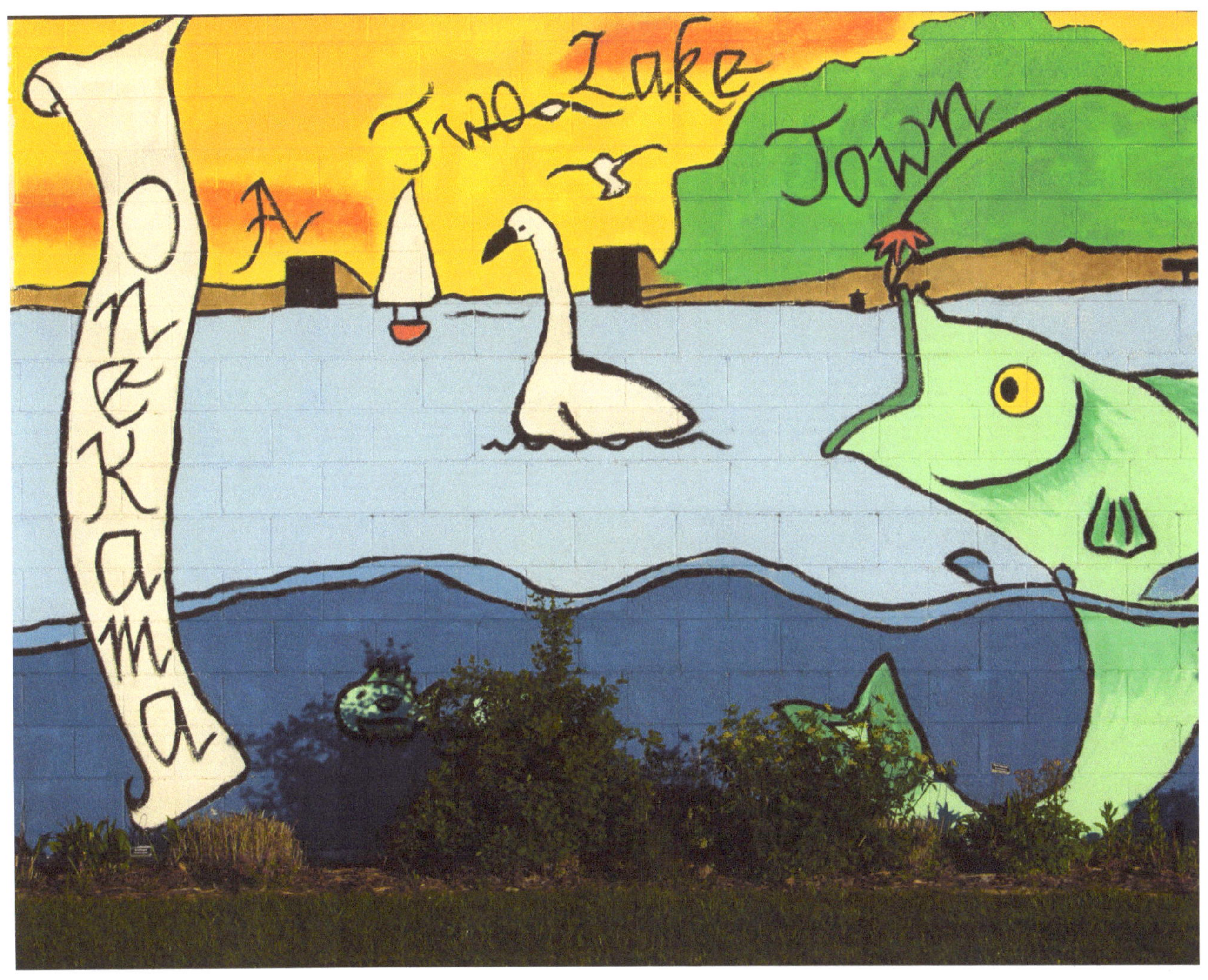

A mural on the side of Onekam Township Hall

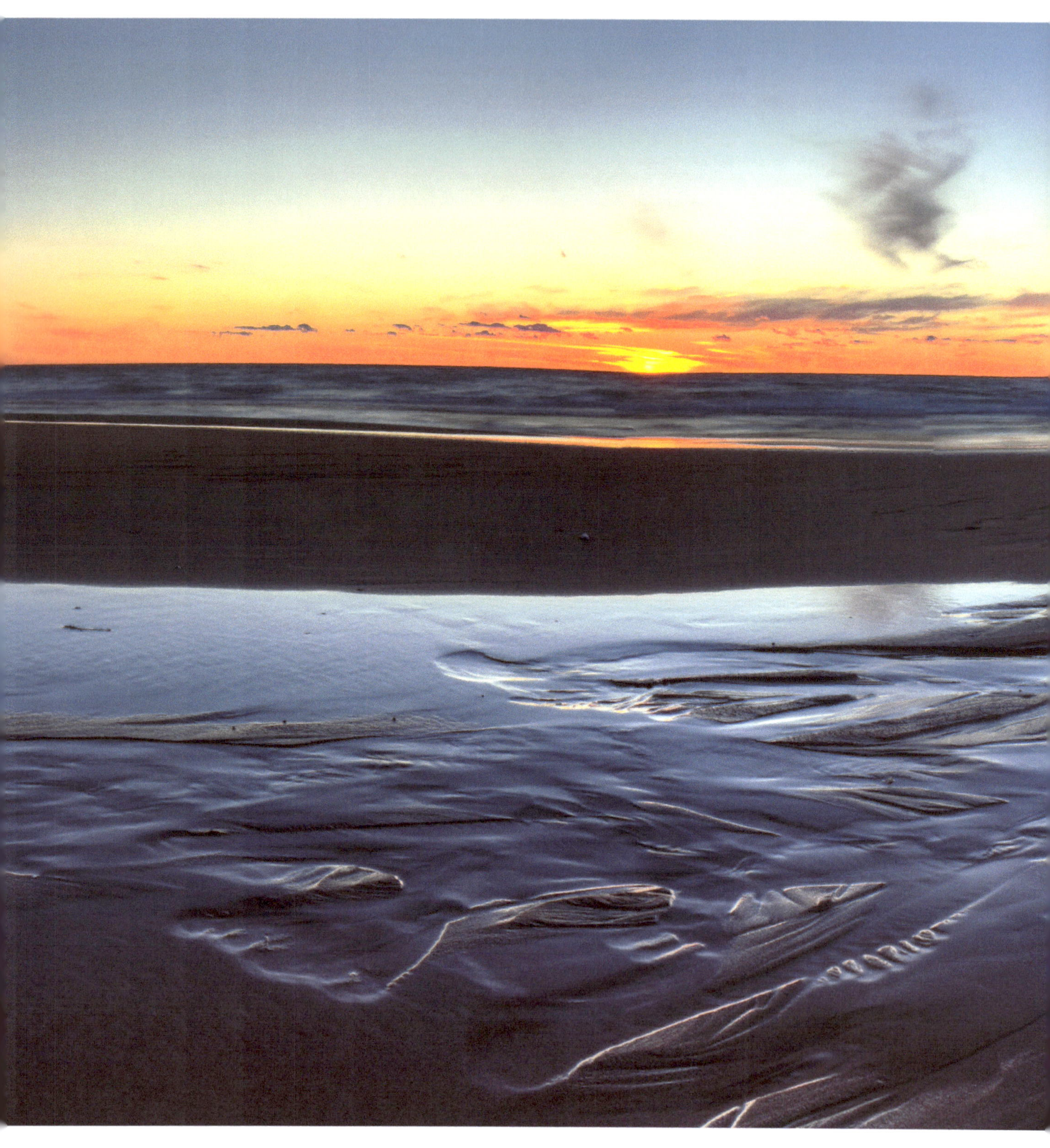

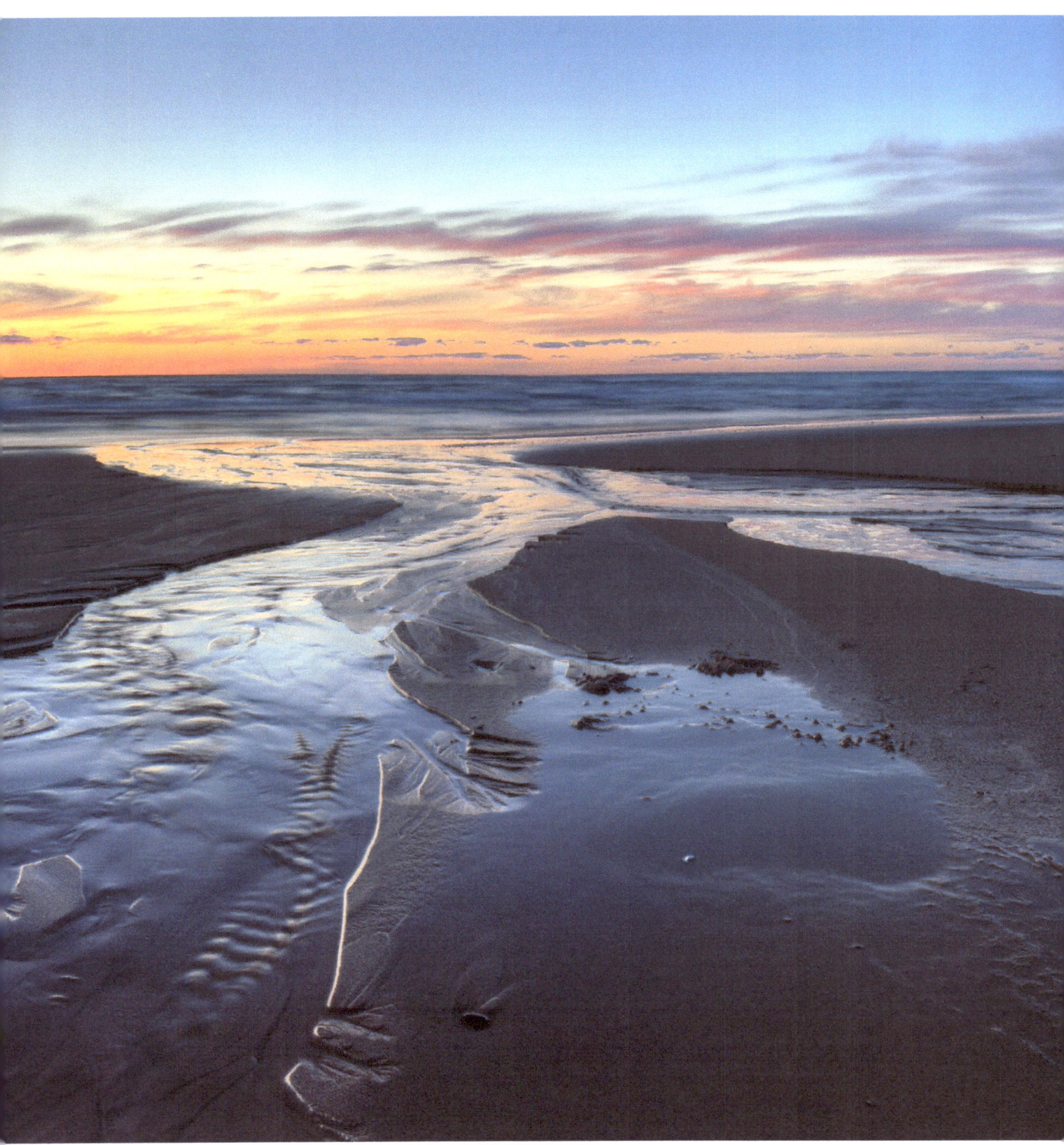

A small stream enters Lake Michigan on the beach in Onekama

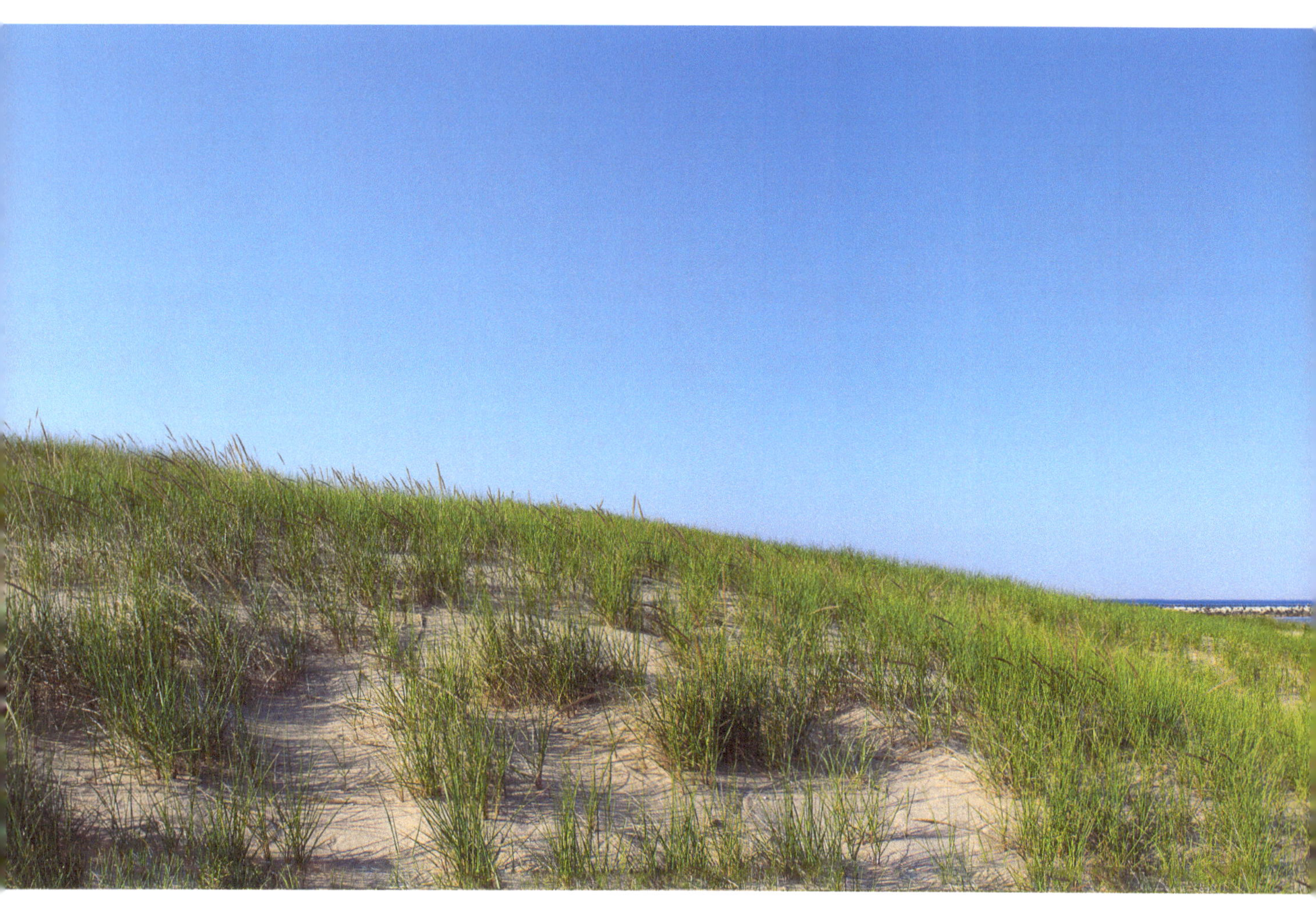

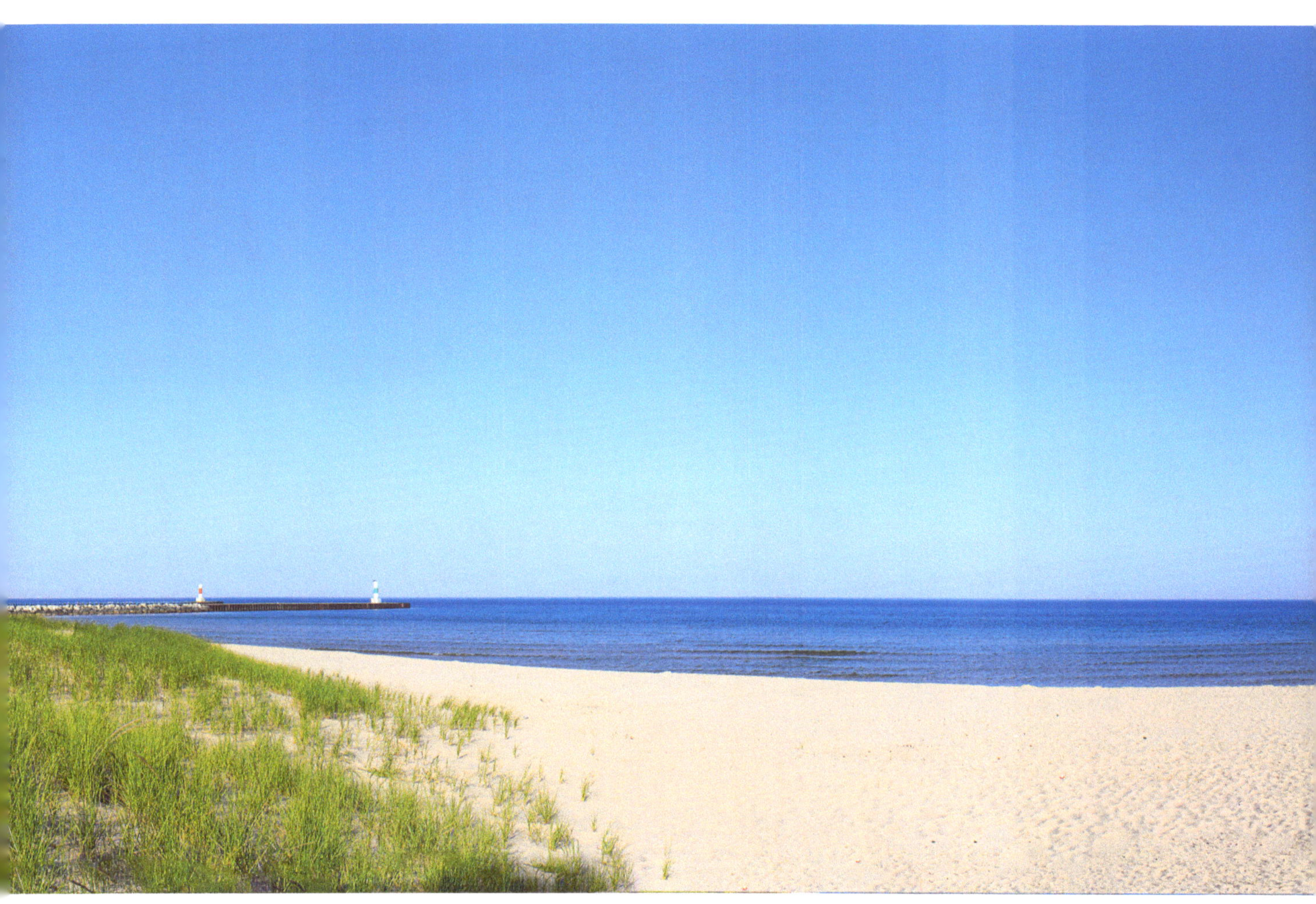

The Onekama shoreline with the pier in the distance. Onekama's public beach features wide expanses of sand and rolling hills of dune grasses. Since it is located about two miles from M-22 and Onekama's downtown, the beach is less crowded than neighboring beaches in Manistee and Frankfort.

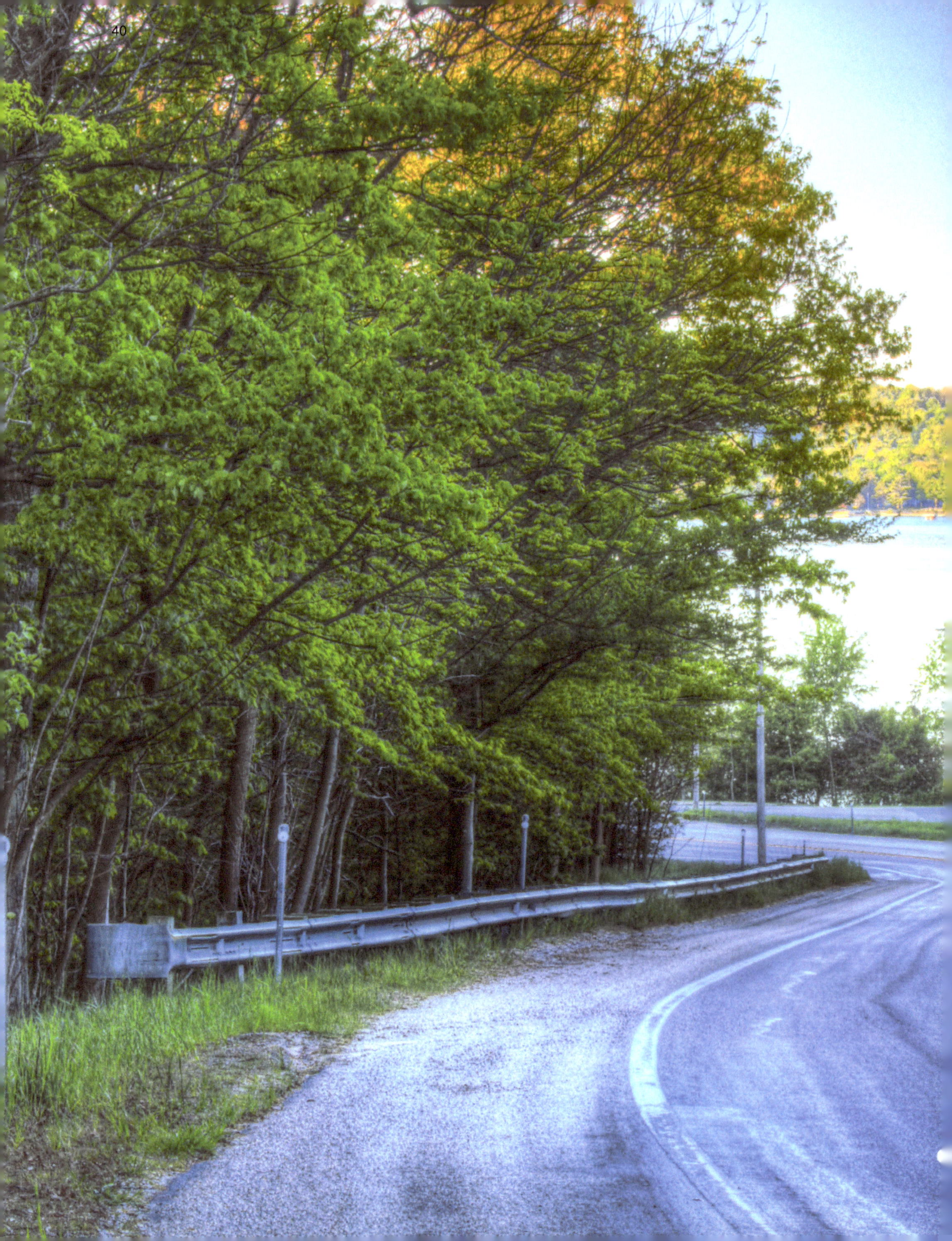

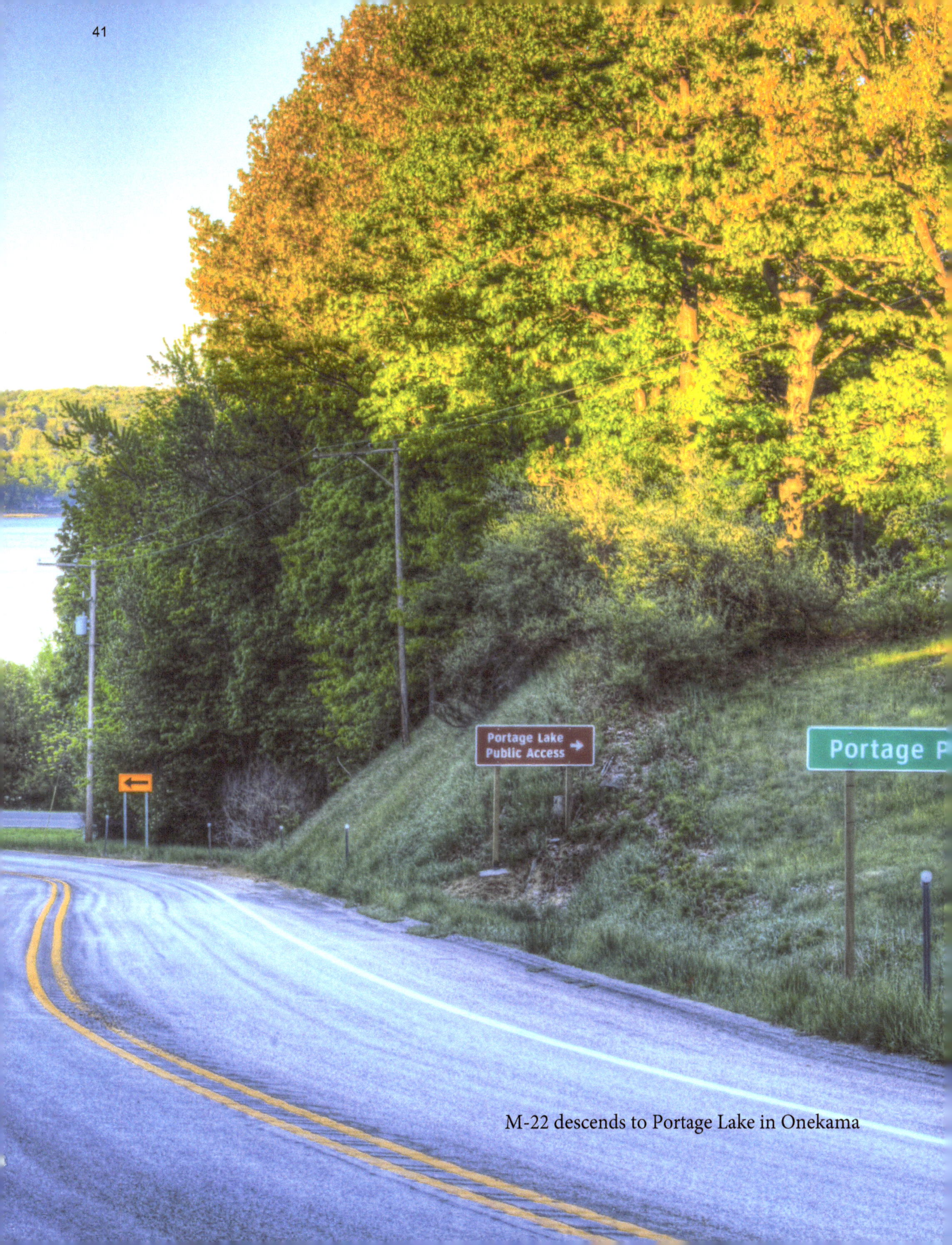

M-22 descends to Portage Lake in Onekama

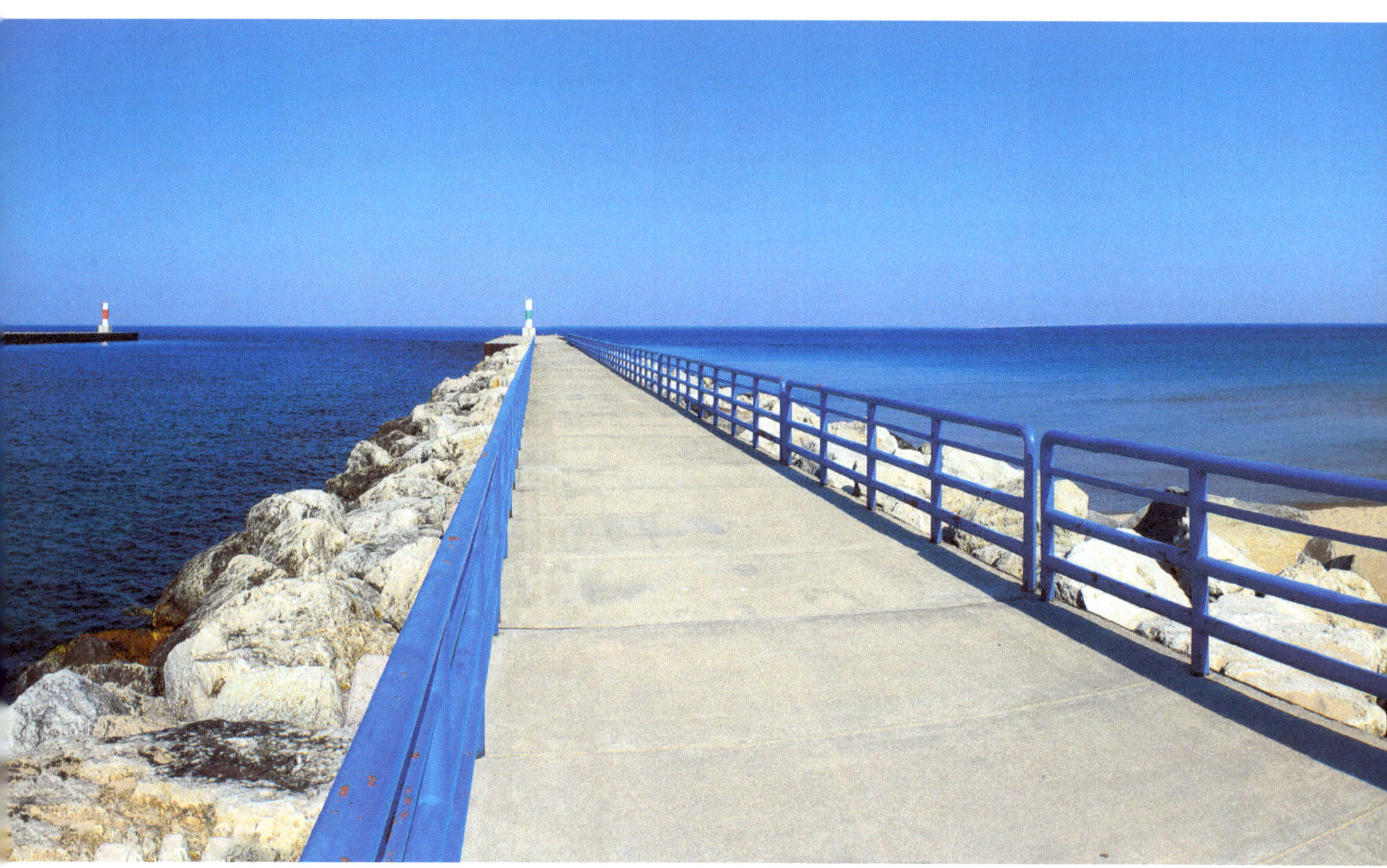

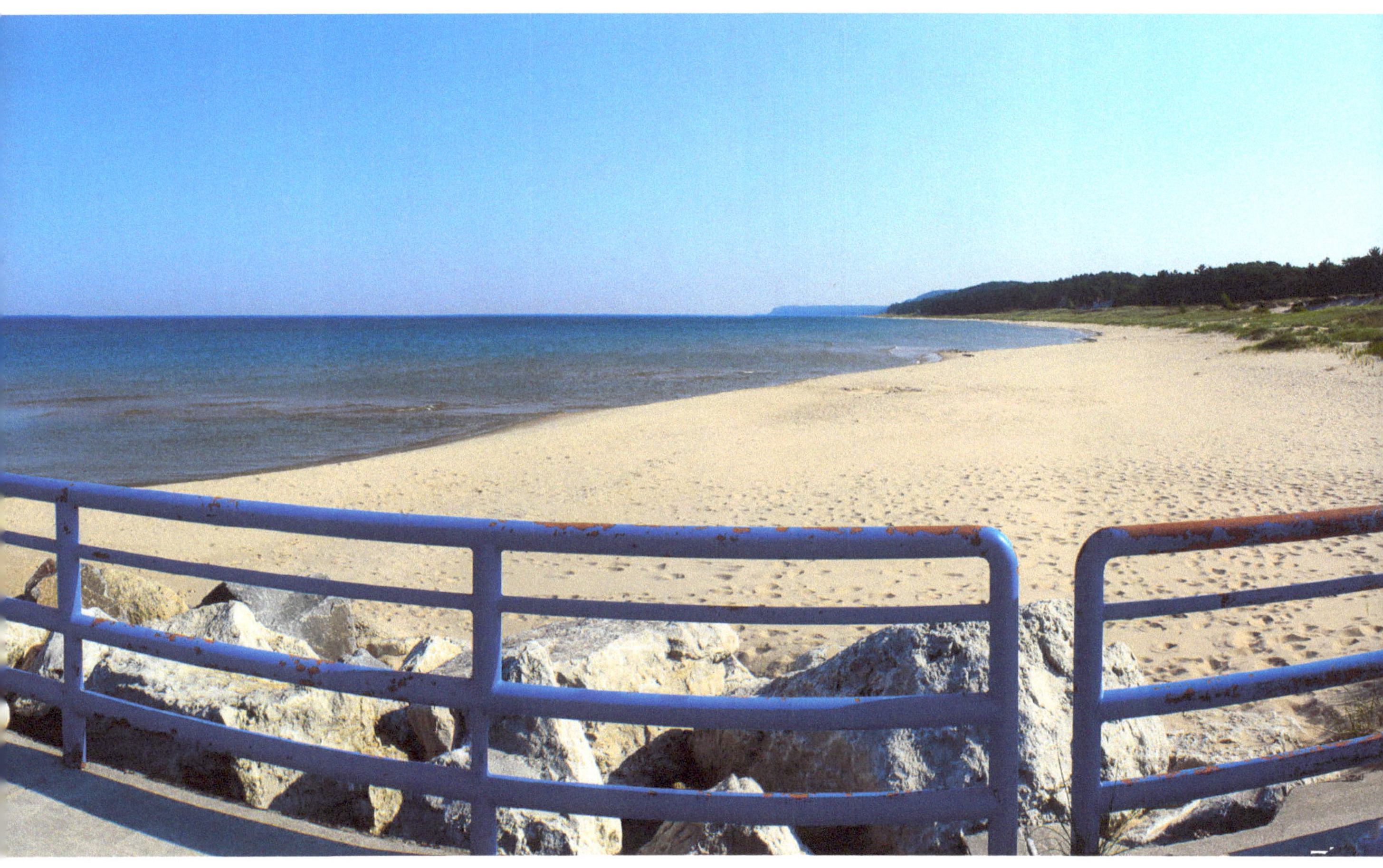

Entrance to the Onekama Pier. Onekama's twin piers extend into Lake Michigan and shelter the channel connecting to Portage Lake. The pier is a popular place for fishing and viewing the sunset. Unlike the piers in nearby Manistee and Frankfort, Onekama's pier does not have a lighthouse. Instead, each pier has a fog horn station.

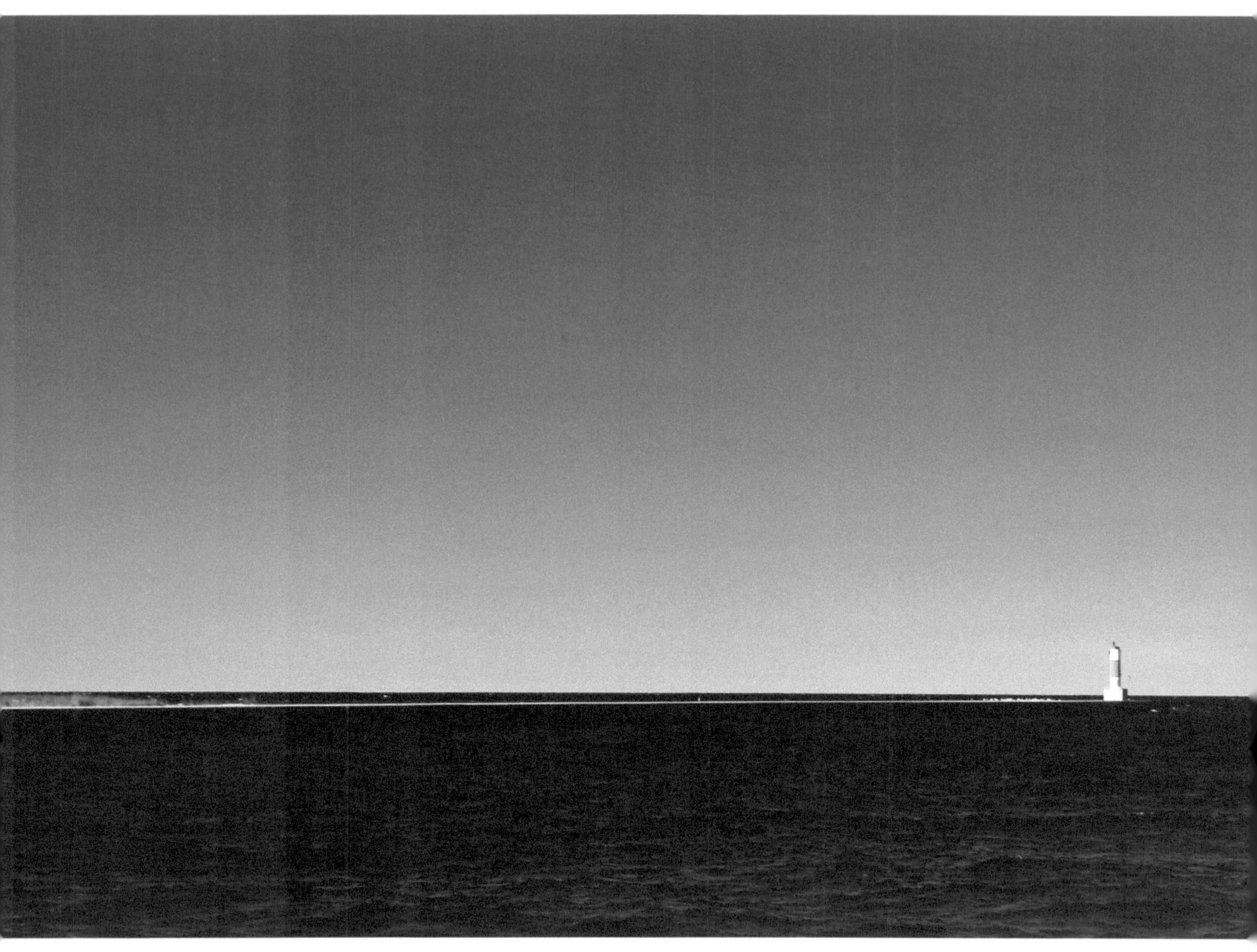

The Onekama south pier and fog horn station.

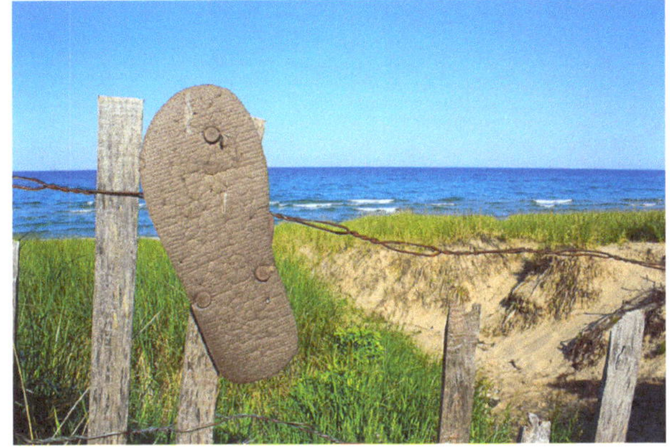
A sandal on a fence at the beach.

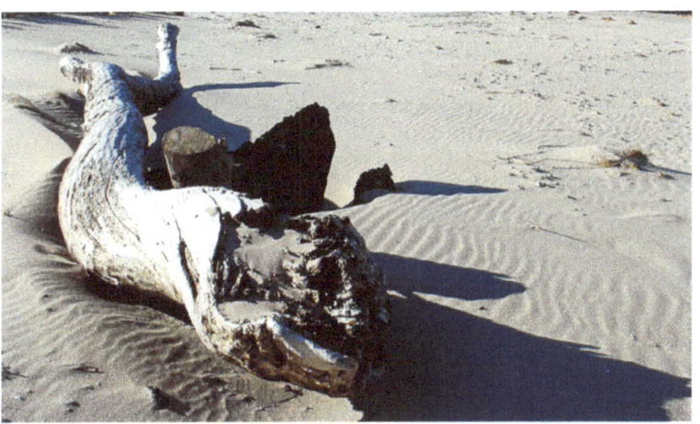
A log on the beach in Onekama.

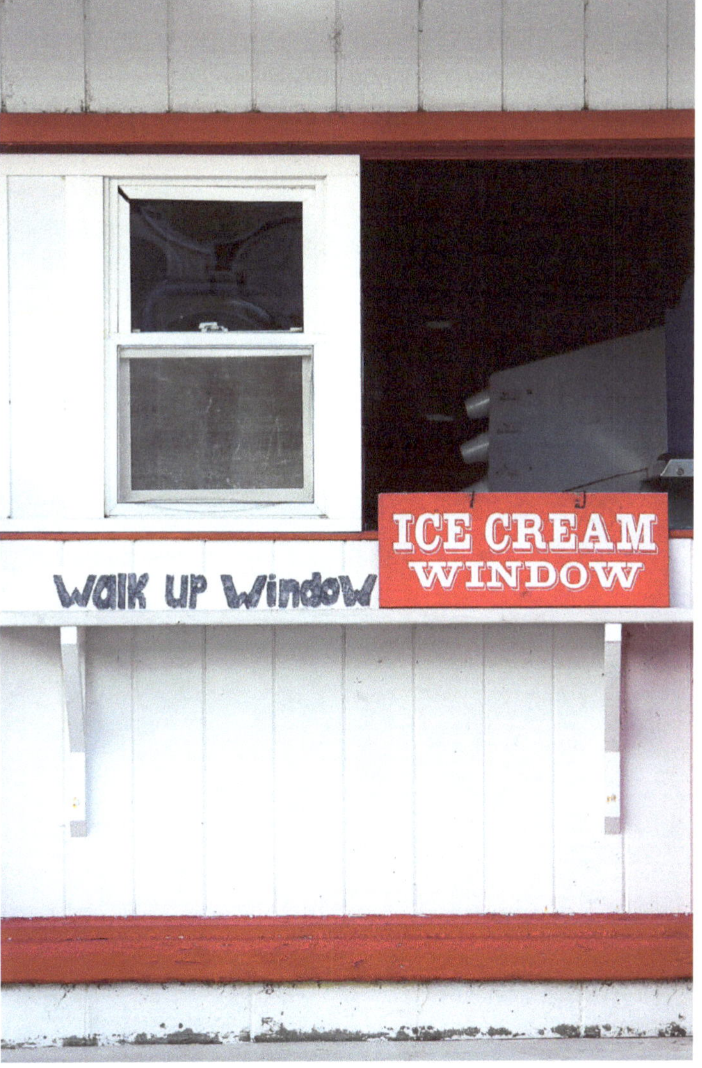

An ice cream shop in Onekama.

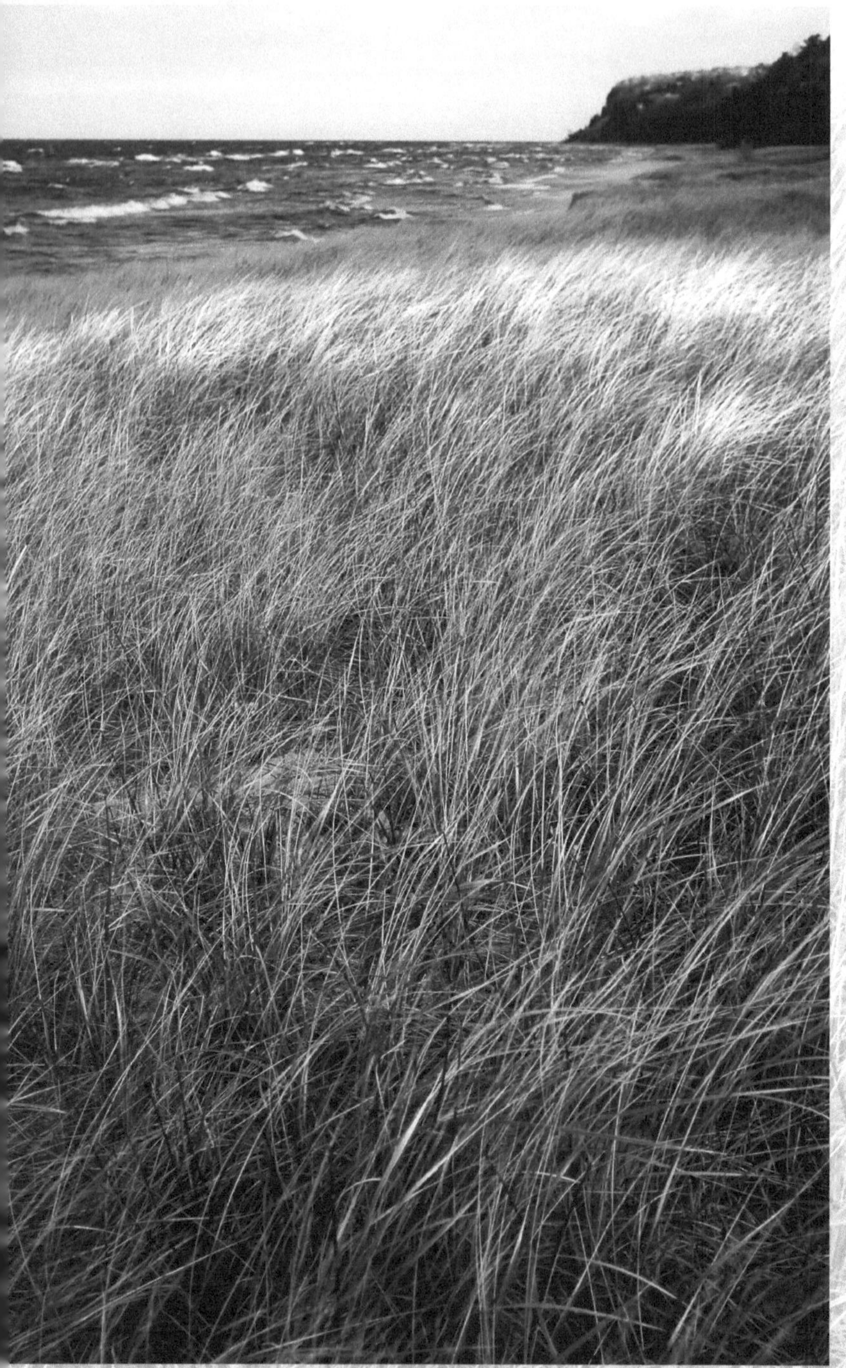

Dune grasses along Lake Michigan at Pierport.

Pierport

Pierport is one of the best kept secrets along the Northwest Shore. It once had its own post office and own pier from which local lumber was shipped to the world. Today, Pierport is an unincorporated community within Onekama Township, with no businesses, town, or pier. Pierport is marked only by a lone road sign along M-22, and consists merely of a small parking lot which opens to miles of beach. It remains one of the most secluded, uncrowded, and pristine areas along the Lake Michigan shoreline. Even at the height of Summer, tourists number in the dozens (at most) around Pierport, compared to the hundreds that flock to more popular nearby beaches in Manistee, Onekama, and Frankfort. After a day taking in the sun, be sure to have a drink from "Old Faceful," a spring-fed fountain just off the beach that has run continuously since 1931.

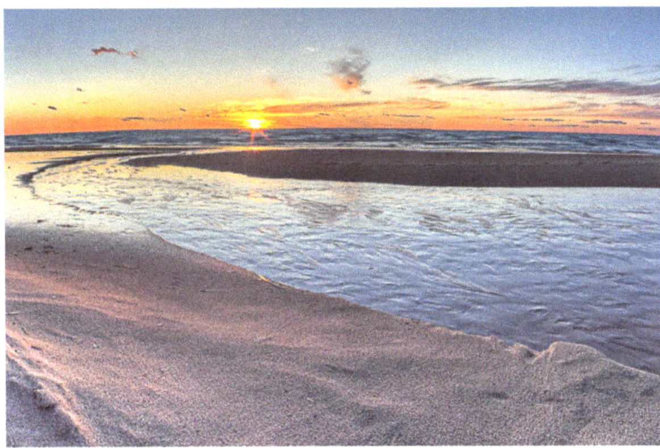

Sunset over Pierport Beach.

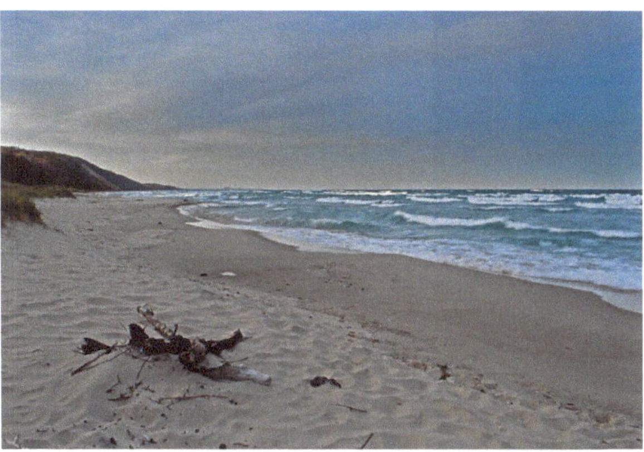

Remnants of a bonfire at Pierport.

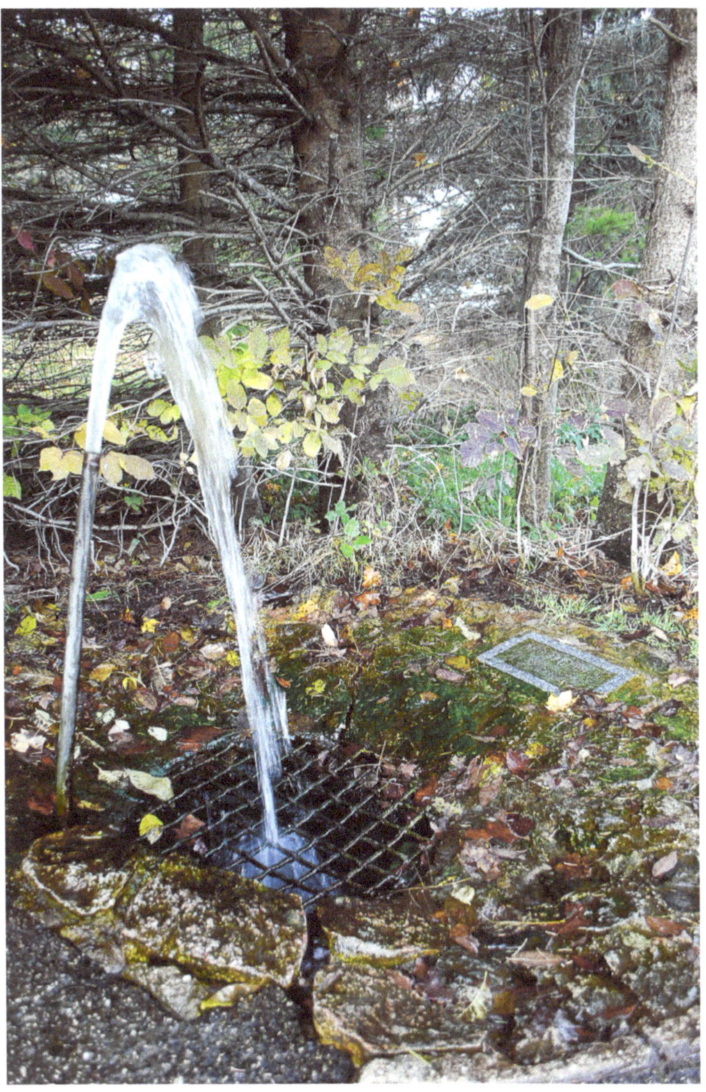

Old Faceful flowing just feet from Pierport Beach.

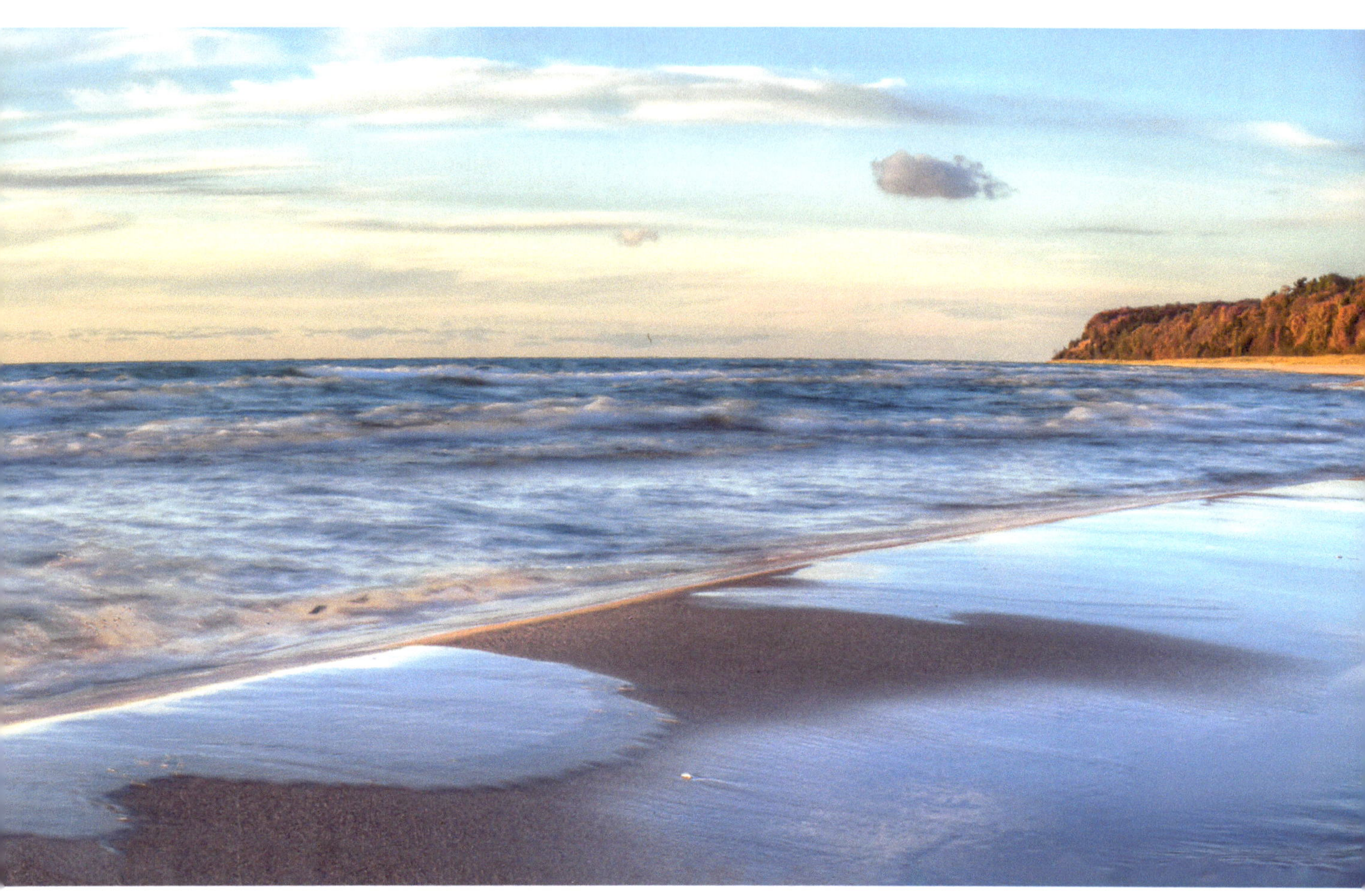

Fall colors along Pierport. The beach extends
for miles uninterripted, and is lined
with dune grasses, forest, and large dunes.

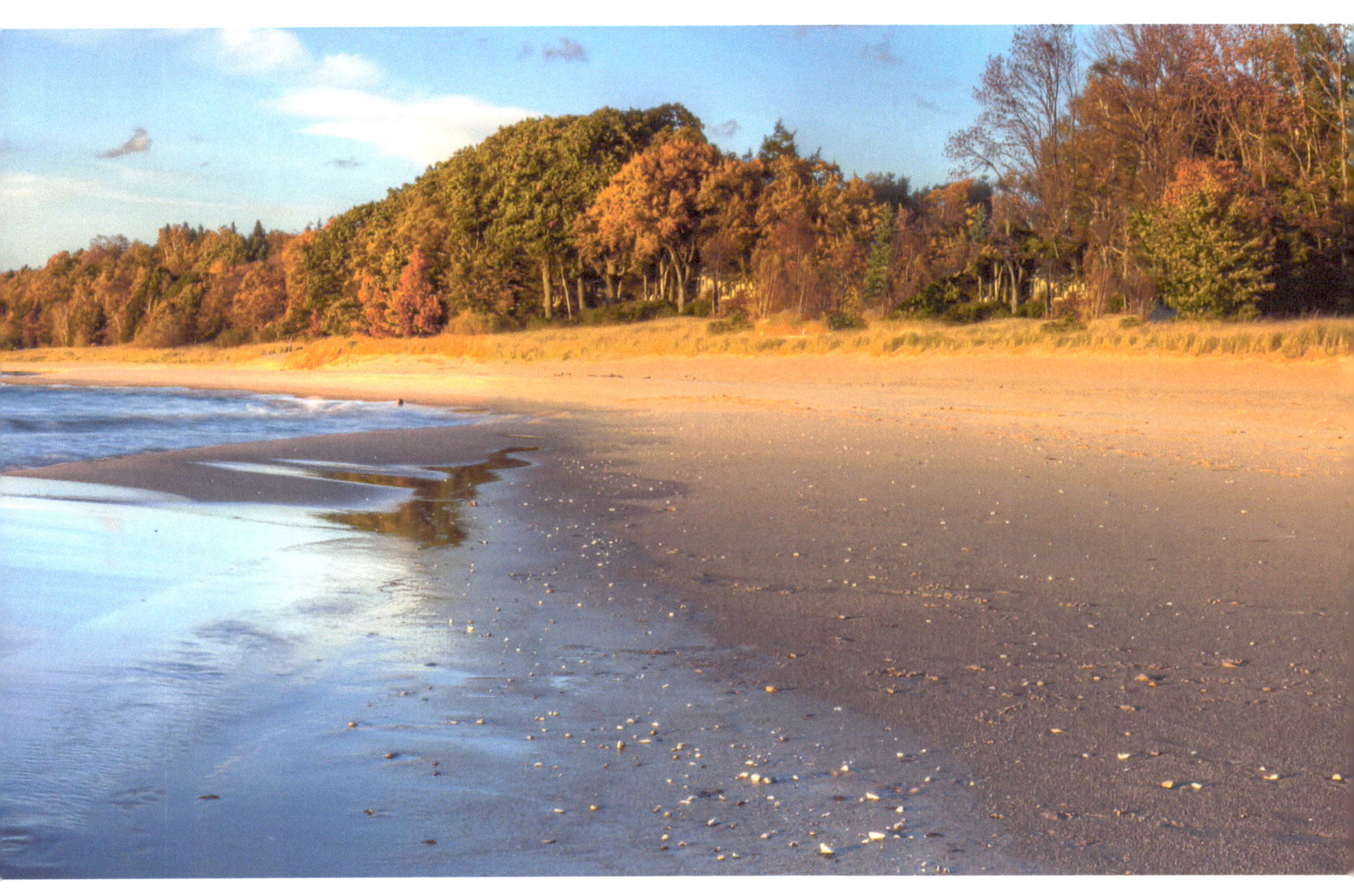

Arcadia

Arcadia is a small beach town sitting along Arcadia Lake on M-22. Arcadia Lake has a channel to Lake Michigan and a marina near downtown. The marina bustles with fishing boats launching into Lake Michigan in the Spring, Summer, and Fall.

Arcadia's downtown is sparse, but a drive north up the hill brings travelers to the Arcadia Overlook roadside park. It provides one of the greatest views of Lake Michigan available anywhere. Along the Northwest Shore, the views from the Arcadia Overlook are rivaled only by those available further north along the Pierce Stocking Scenic Drive in Sleeping Bear Dunes.

A short drive south of downtown Arcadia brings one to Arcadia Bluffs Golf Club, which is the youngest course in Golf Digest's top-50. The patio and lawn outside of Arcadia Bluffs' clubhouse is open to the public and a great place to enjoy the sunset with a glass of wine. On weekend nights in the Summer, Arcadia Bluffs even hires a Scottish bagpiper to entertain guests on the lawn and patio.

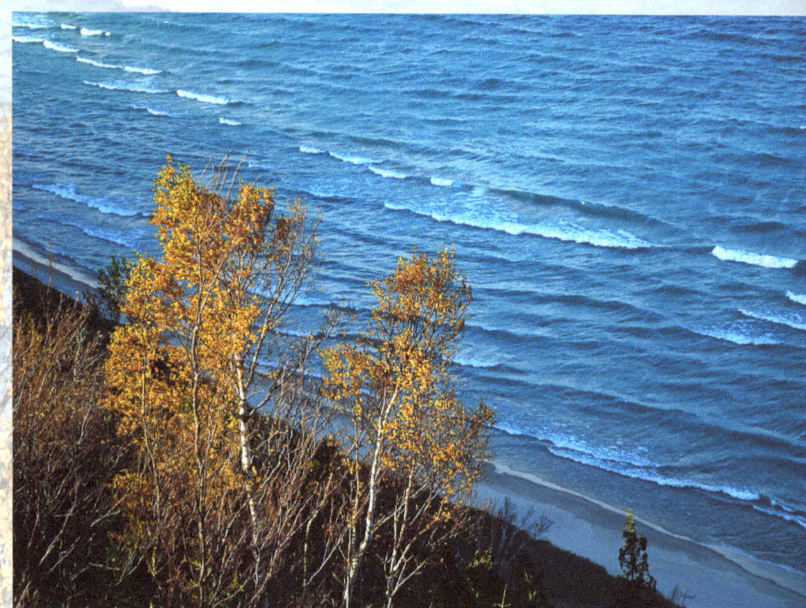

Birch trees over Lake Michigan at Arcadia.

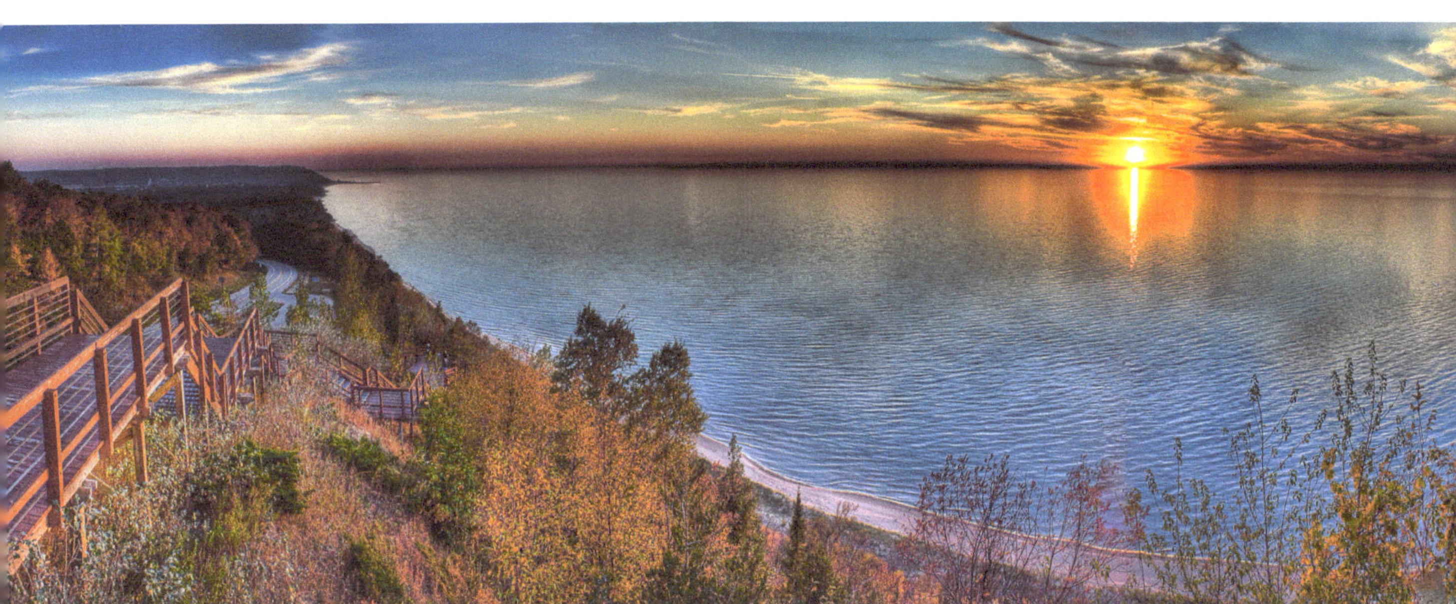

Sunset from the Arcadia Overlook about two miles north of downtown Arcadia. The overlook sits huundreds of feet above the lake and is one of the highest points along the shoreline in Michigan. It provides 180 degree panorama views of Lake Michigan to the west and Arcadia to the south. There is a small roadside park on the site with a long stairway to multiple viewing decks.

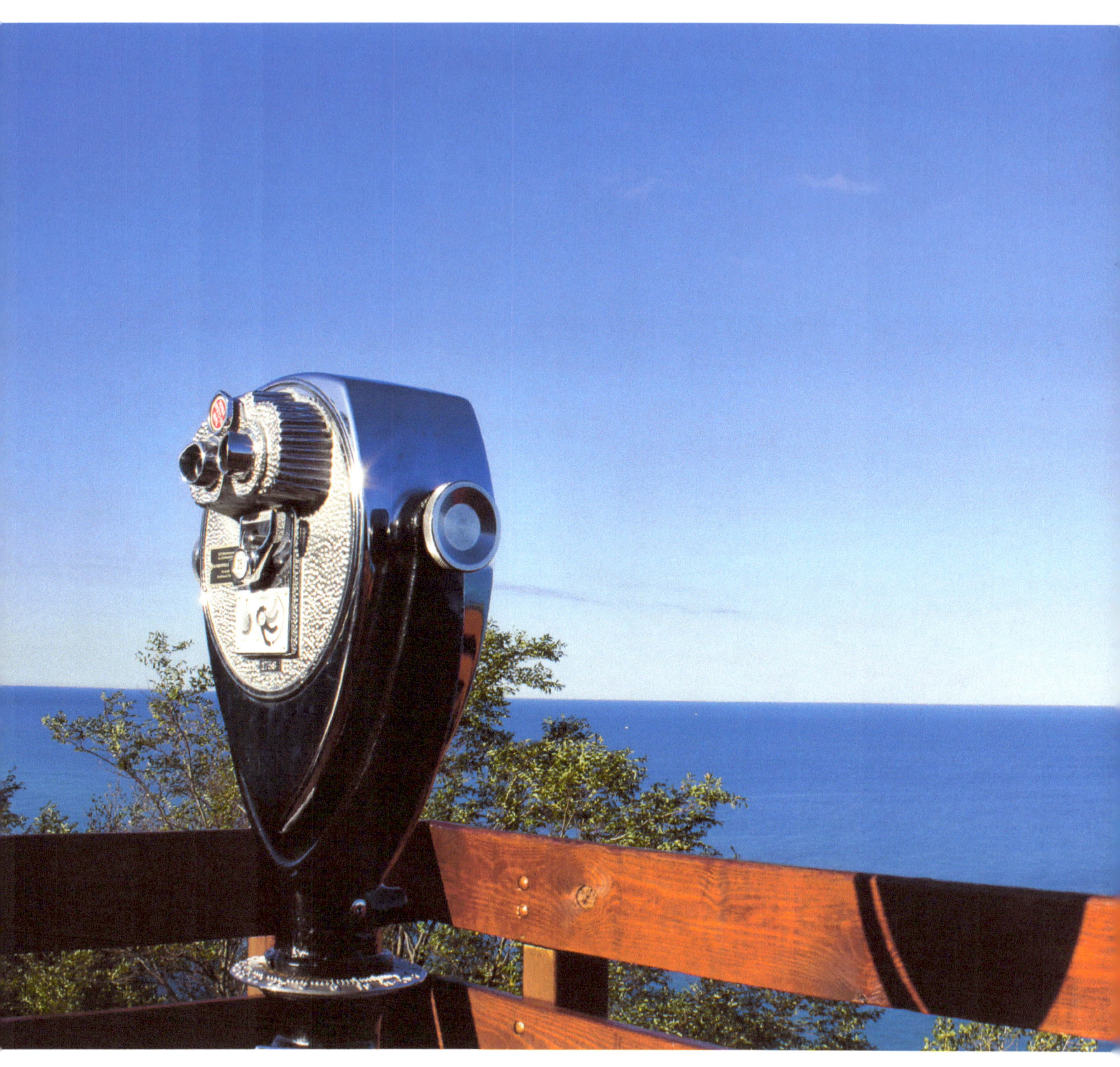

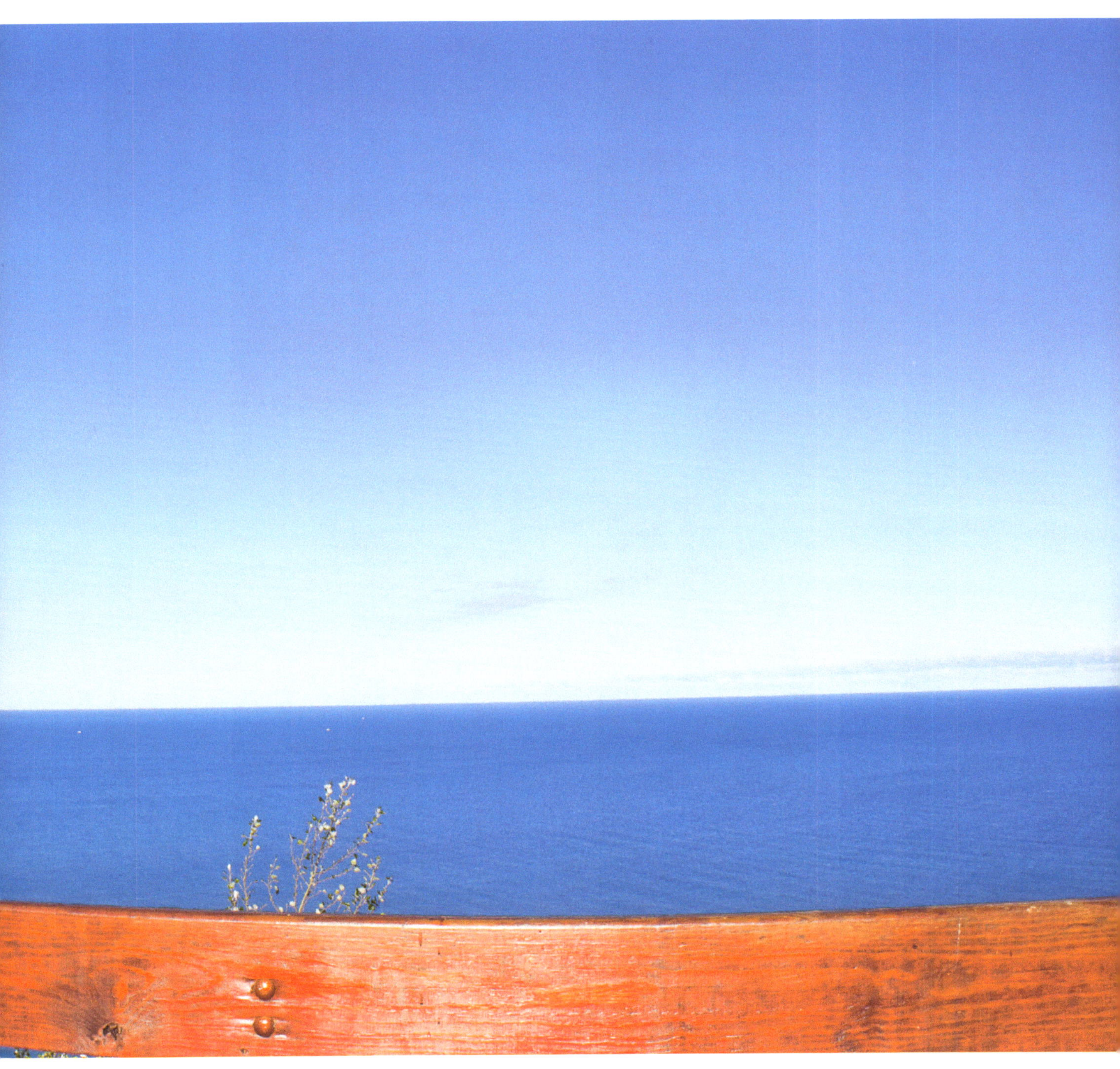

Telescope at the Arcadia Overlook. On a clear day, one can see twenty to thirty miles into Lake Michigan and clear south to Manistee along the shoreline.

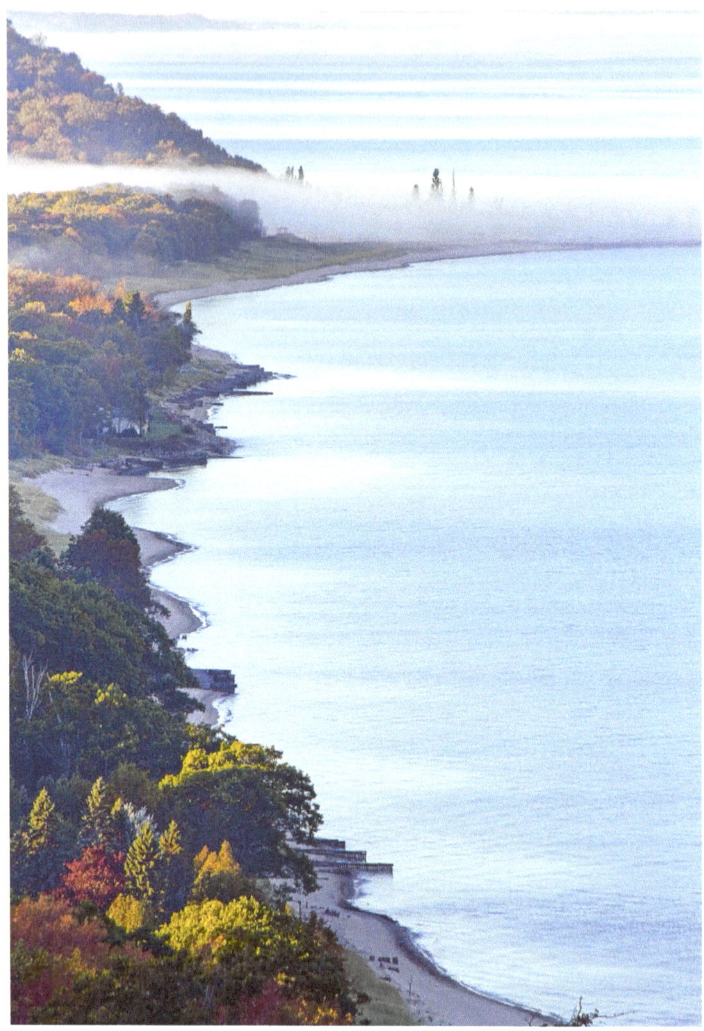

Arcadia shoreline from the Arcadia Overlook.

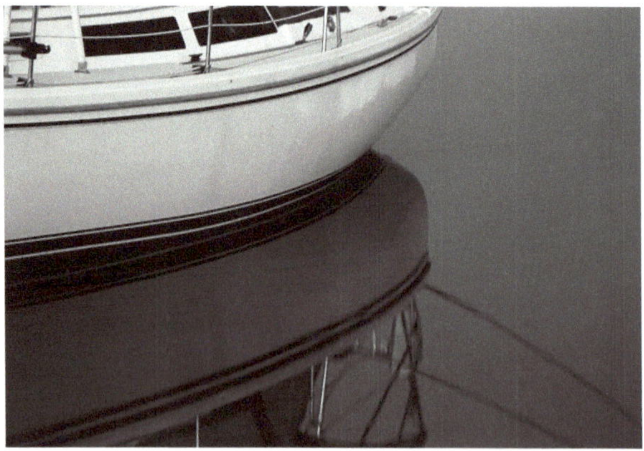

The hull of a sailboat in Arcadia Harbor.

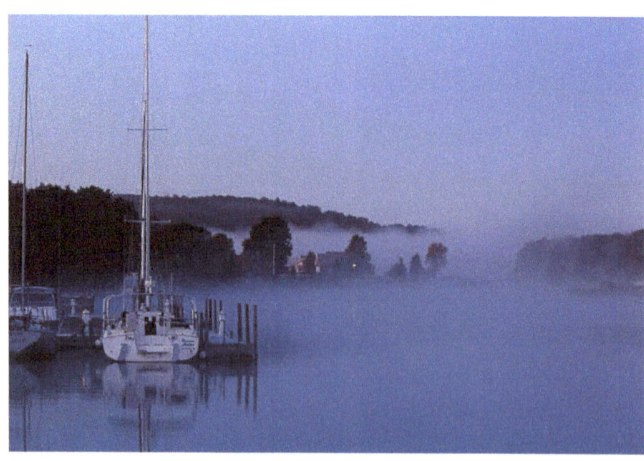

Arcadia Harbor at dawn.

Sunset over Lake Michigan from Arcadia Overlook. The Arcadia Overlook is one of the most popular destinations along the shore for sunset watchers.

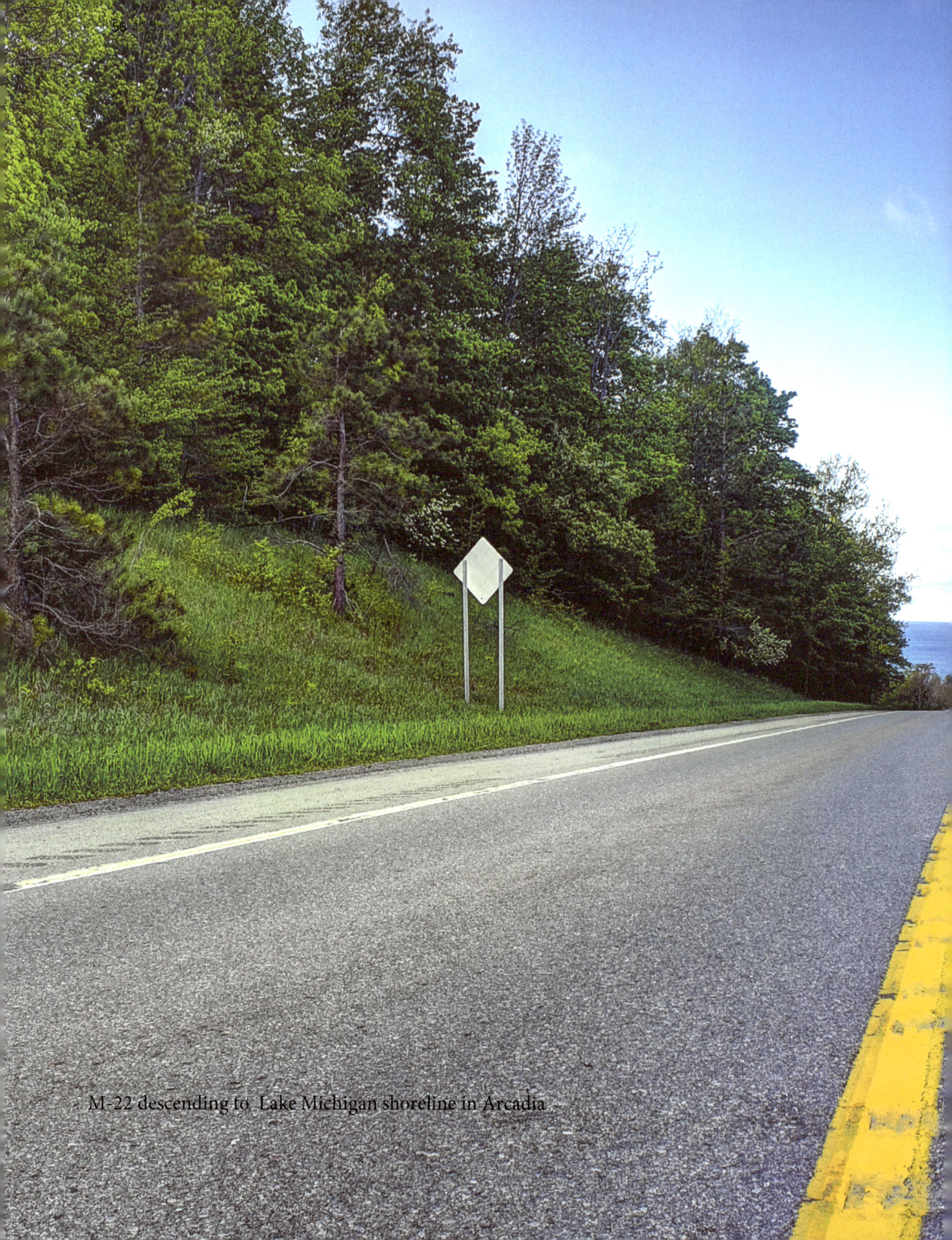

M-22 descending to Lake Michigan shoreline in Arcadia

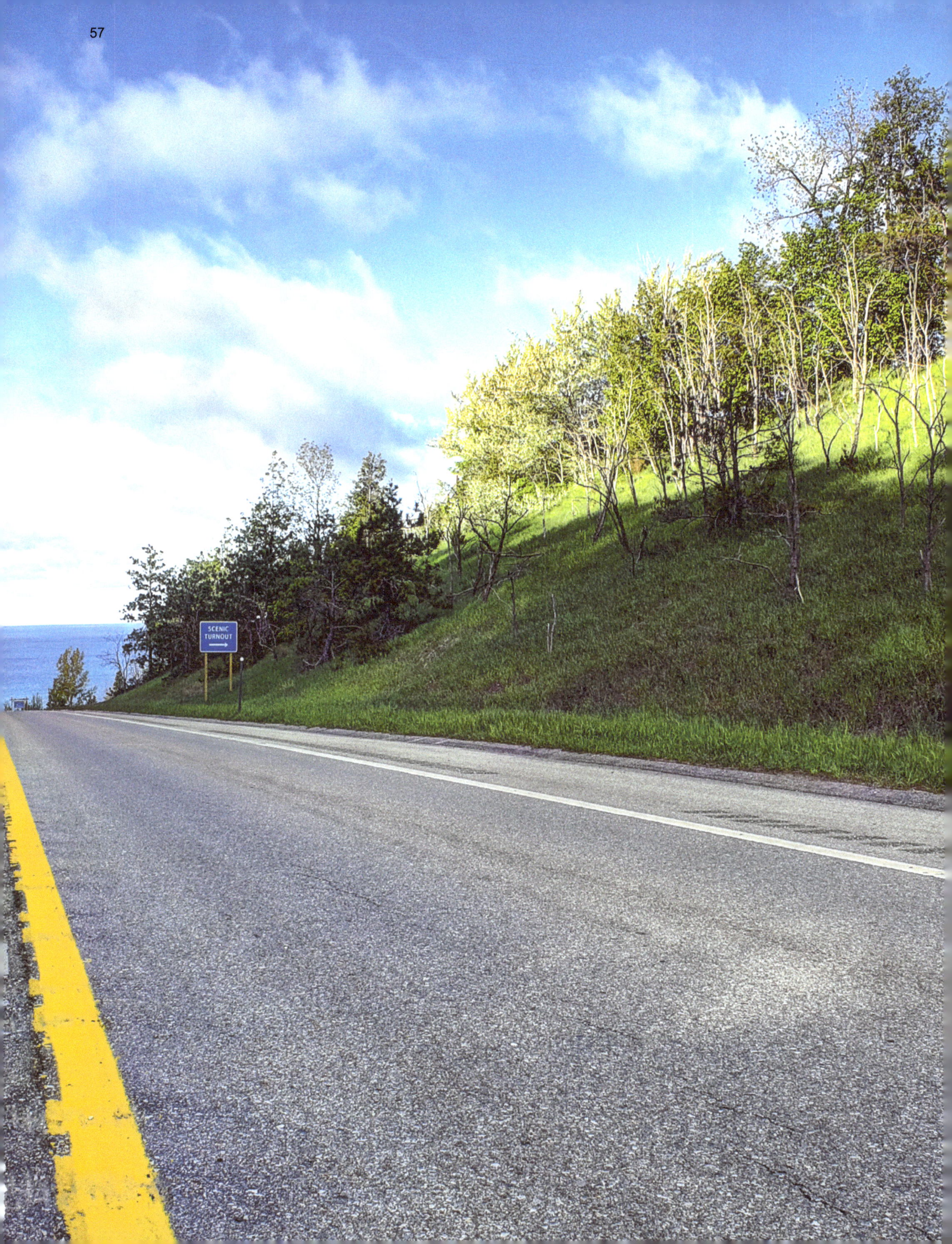
SCENIC
TURNOUT

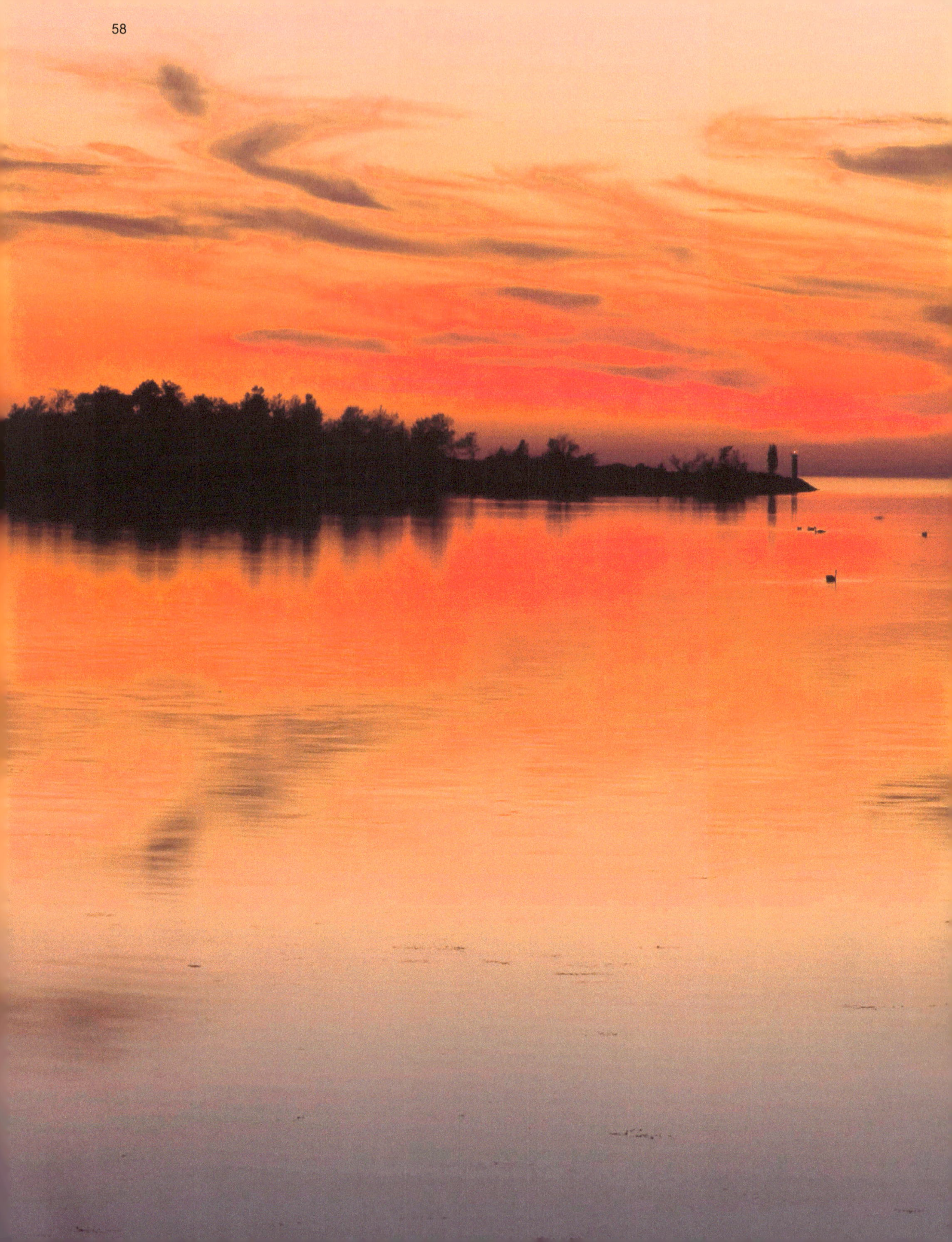

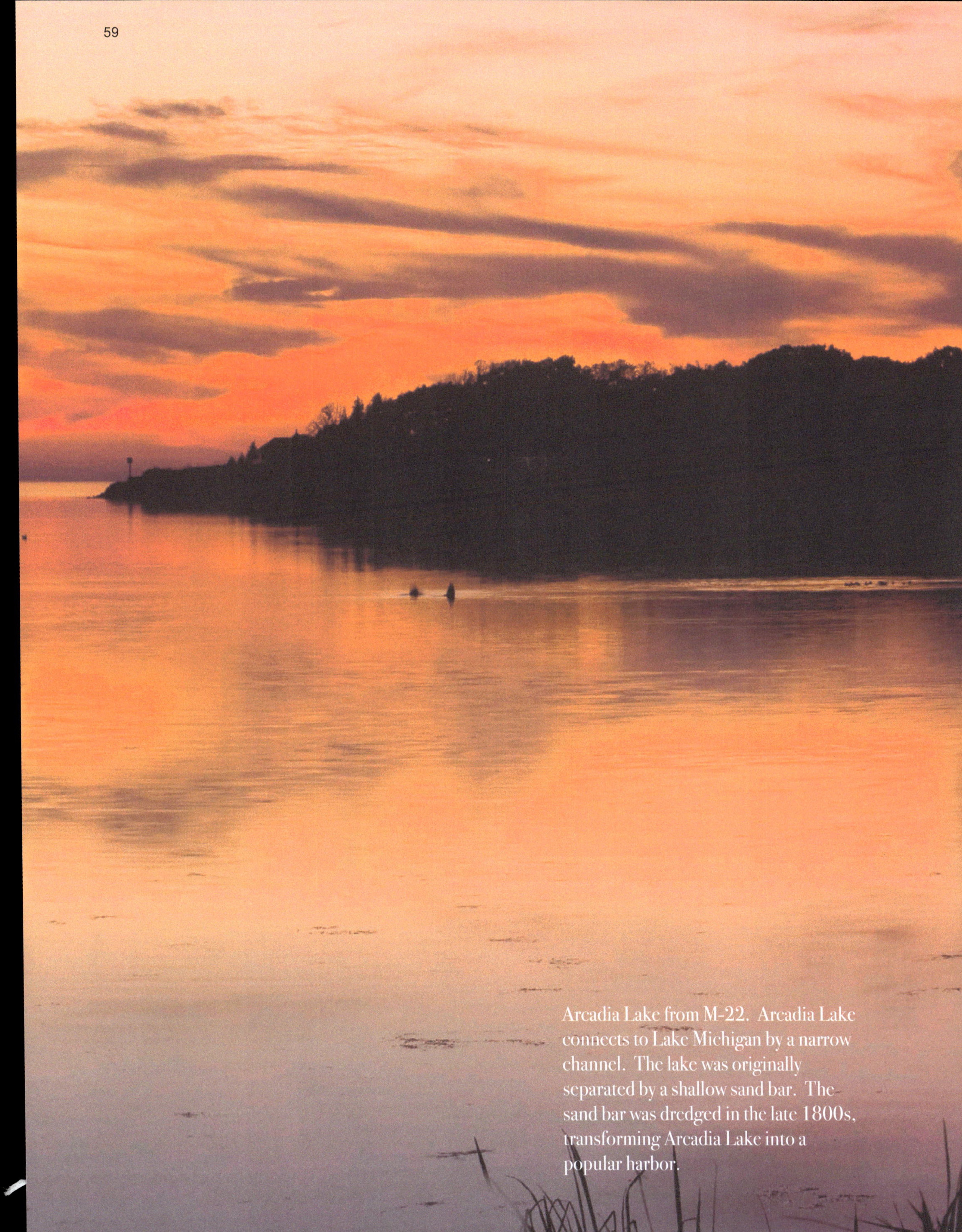

Arcadia Lake from M-22. Arcadia Lake connects to Lake Michigan by a narrow channel. The lake was originally separated by a shallow sand bar. The sand bar was dredged in the late 1800s, transforming Arcadia Lake into a popular harbor.

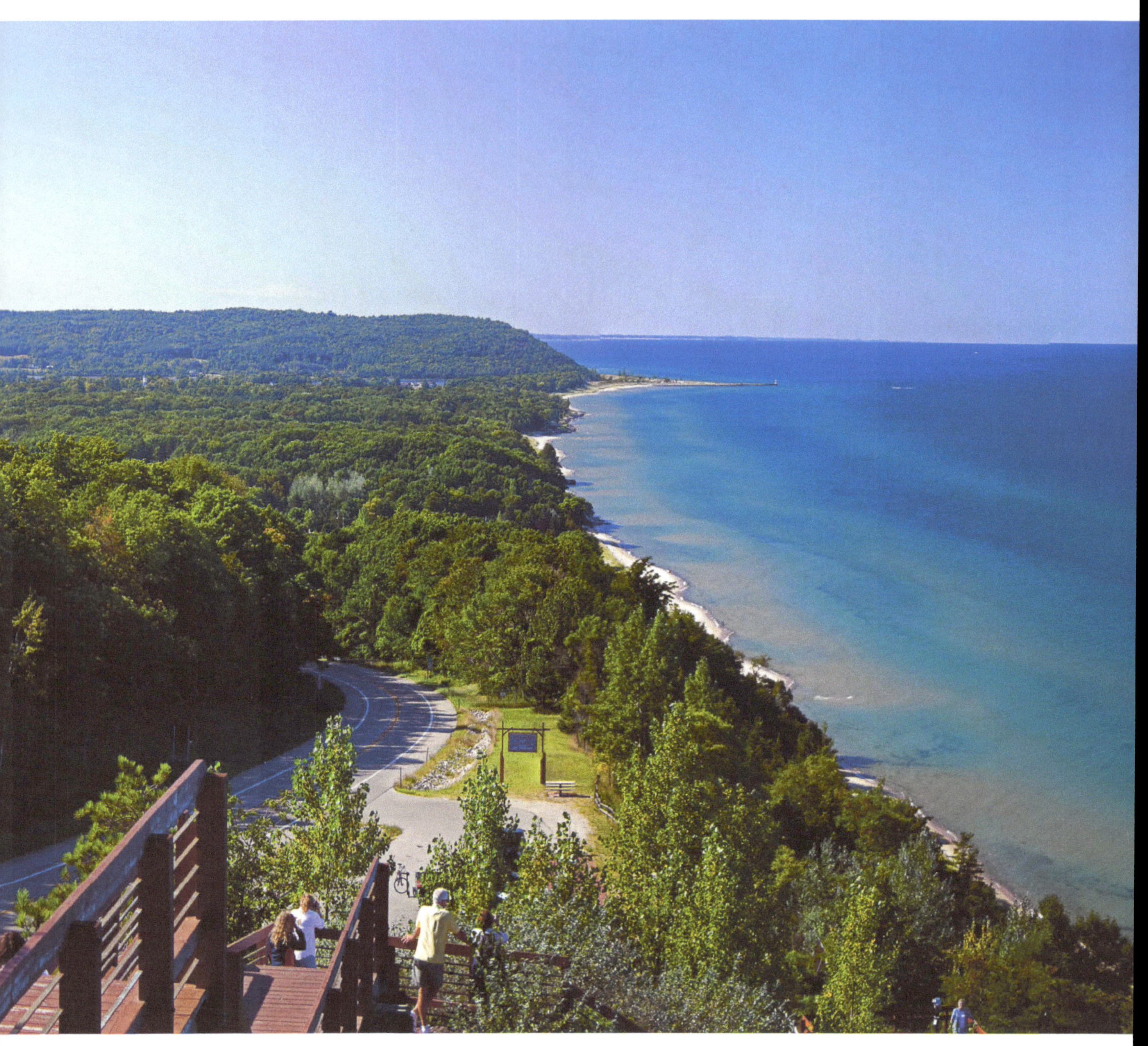

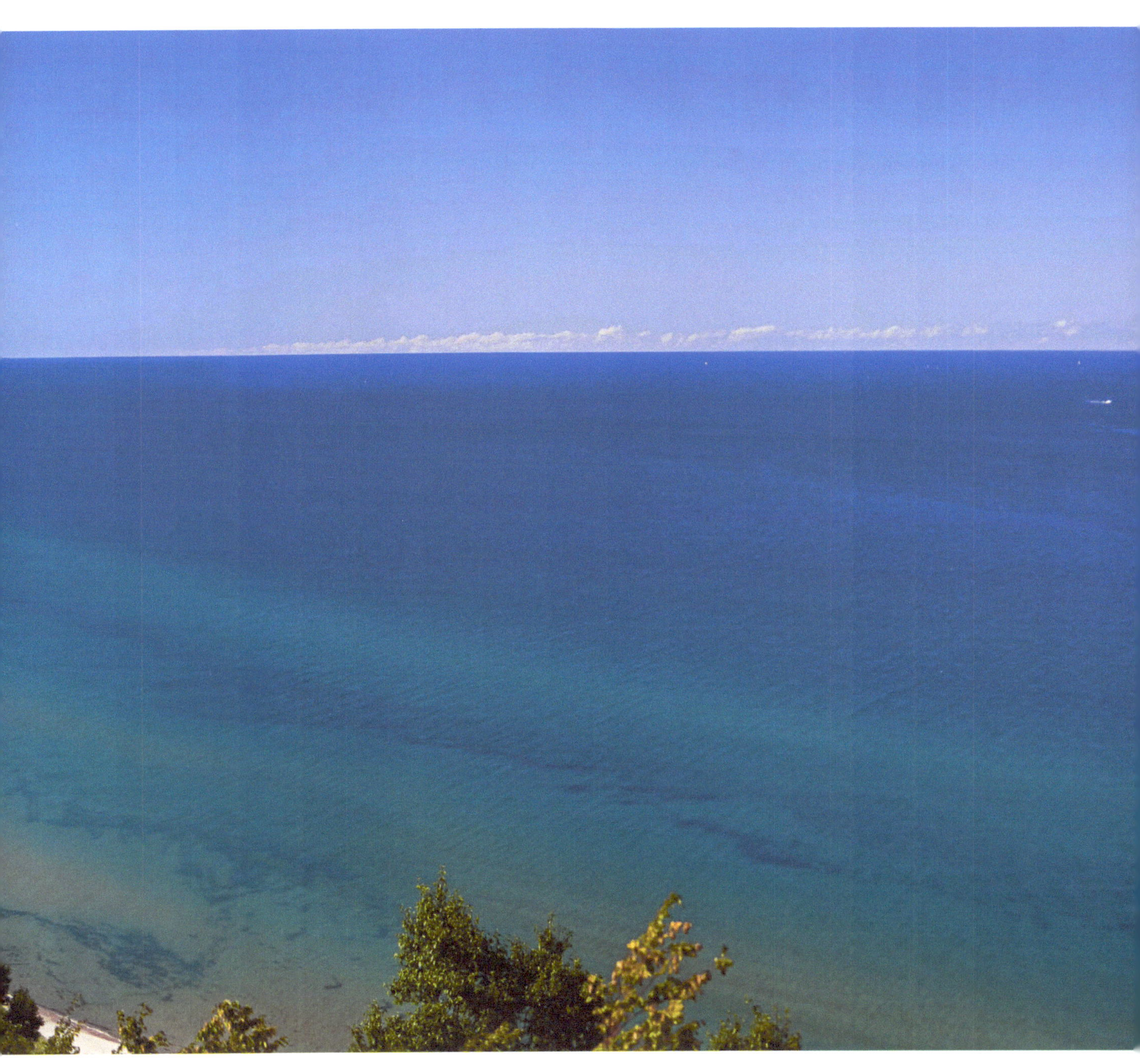

Lake Michigan from Arcadia Overlook roadside park

Frankfort/Elberta

Frankfort and Elberta sit on the north and south side of Betsie Lake at the mouth of the Betsie River, about twelve miles north of Arcadia. Elberta was once the end of the Ann Arbor Railroad, which connected cargo and passengers from southern Michigan with ferry service to multiple locations in Wisconsin. Both towns were at the heart of the logging boom in the late 1800s.

Frankfort and Elberta are now popular tourist destinations. Downtown Elberta is the smaller of the two, featuring a few shops and cafes, and access to the beach at Lake Michigan. Frankfort bills itself as the "Gateway to the Dunes," as it is the last town along M-22 before the Sleeping Bear Dunes National Lakeshore. Its downtown occupies three city blocks along Betsie Lake and is an easy walk to the beach, pier, and lighthouse. Frankfort's pier is a popular tourist destination, stretching hundreds of yards into Lake Michigan. The Frankfort North Breakwater Lighthouse towers over the shoreline at the end of the pier.

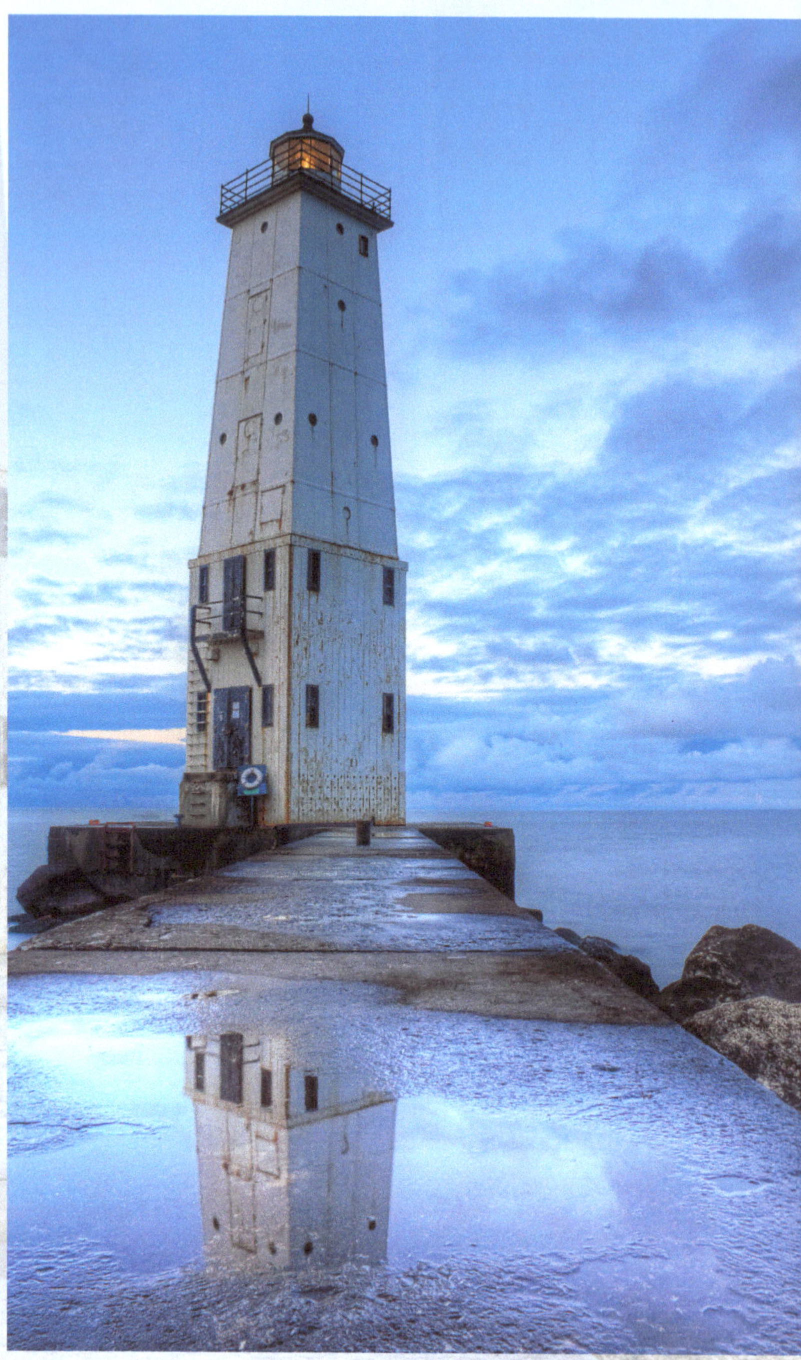

Frankfort North Breakwater Lighthouse at sunrise.

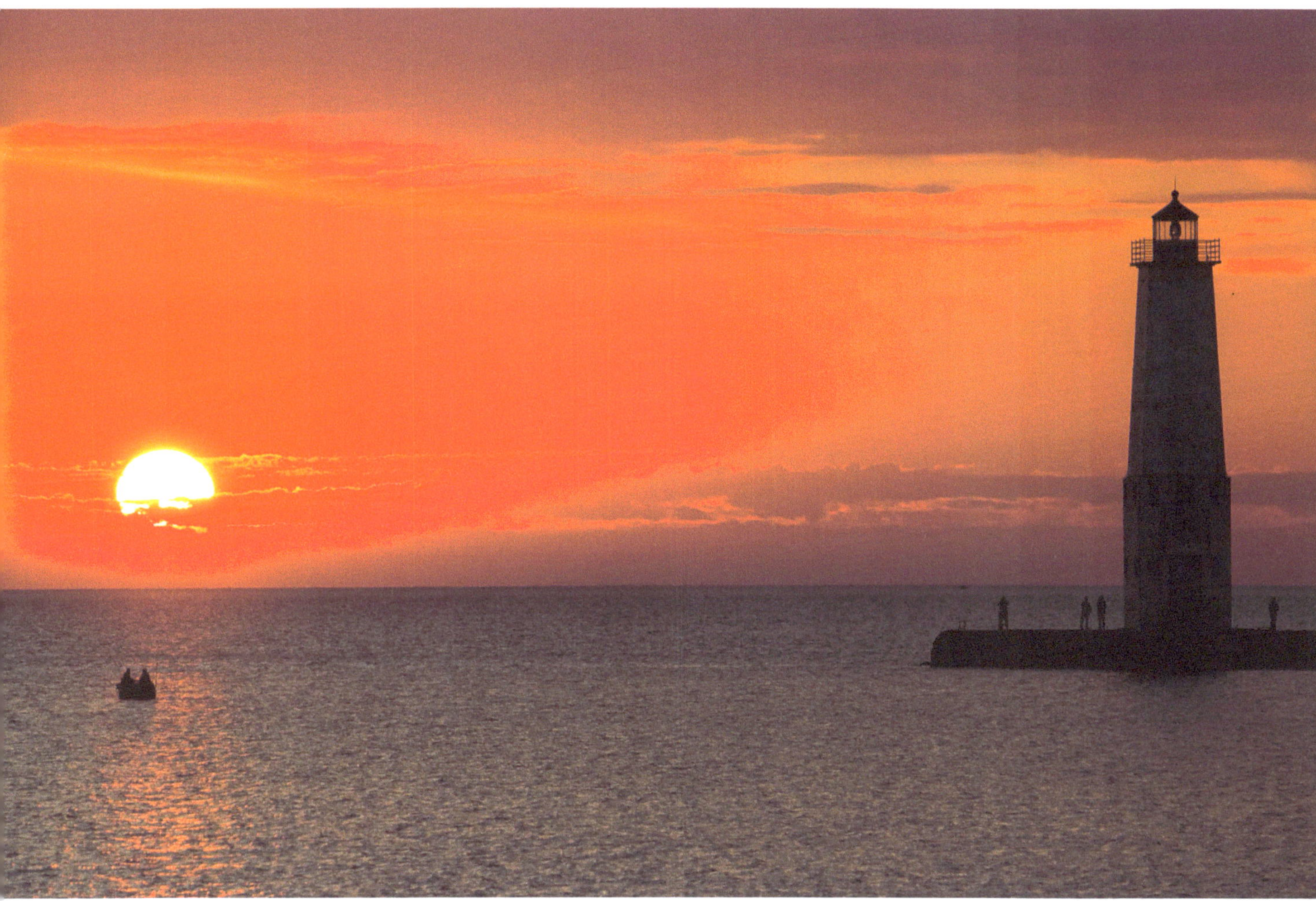

Sunset from Frankfort's beach. The beach and pier are within easy walking distance from Frankfort's downtown. The beach and pier are popular among tourists, fishermen, and boaters. In summer months, the area is among the busiest along the shoreline.

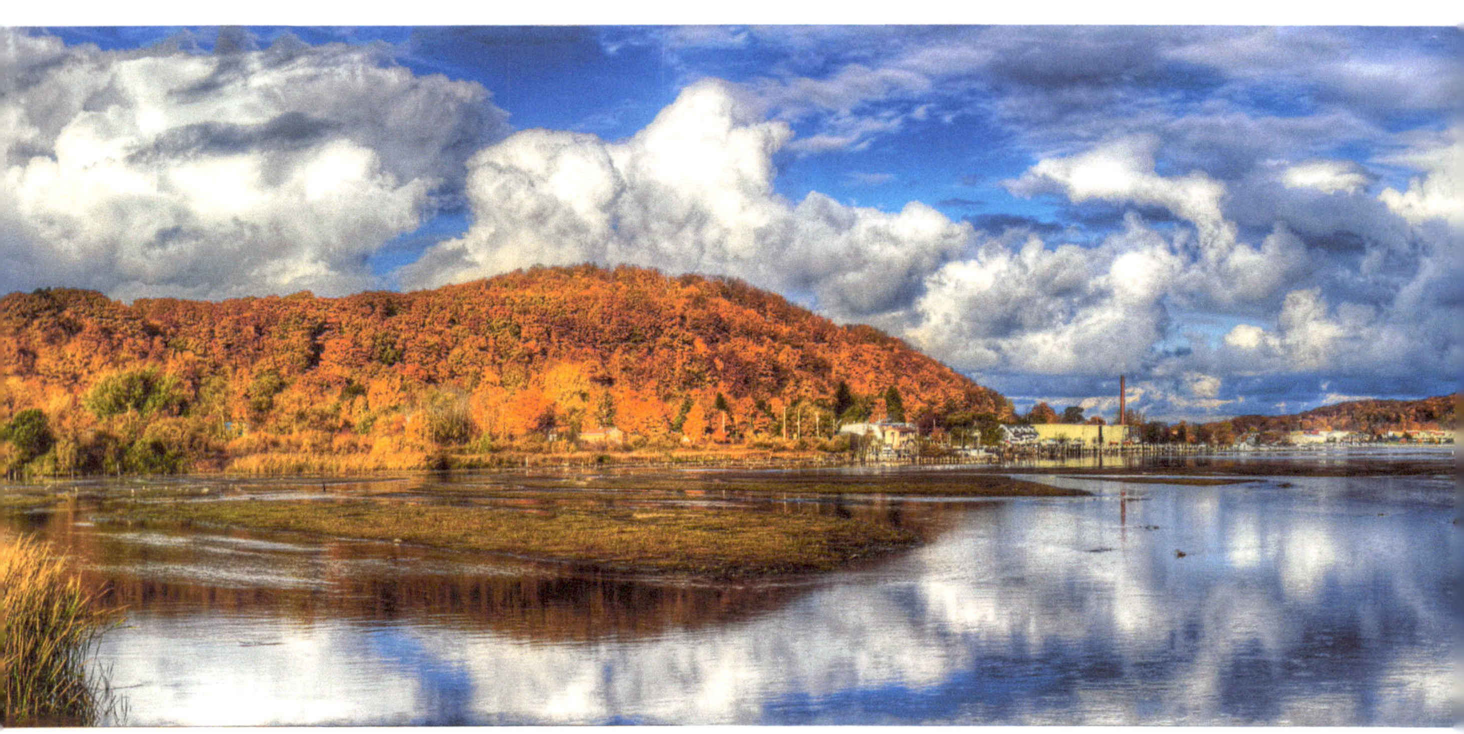

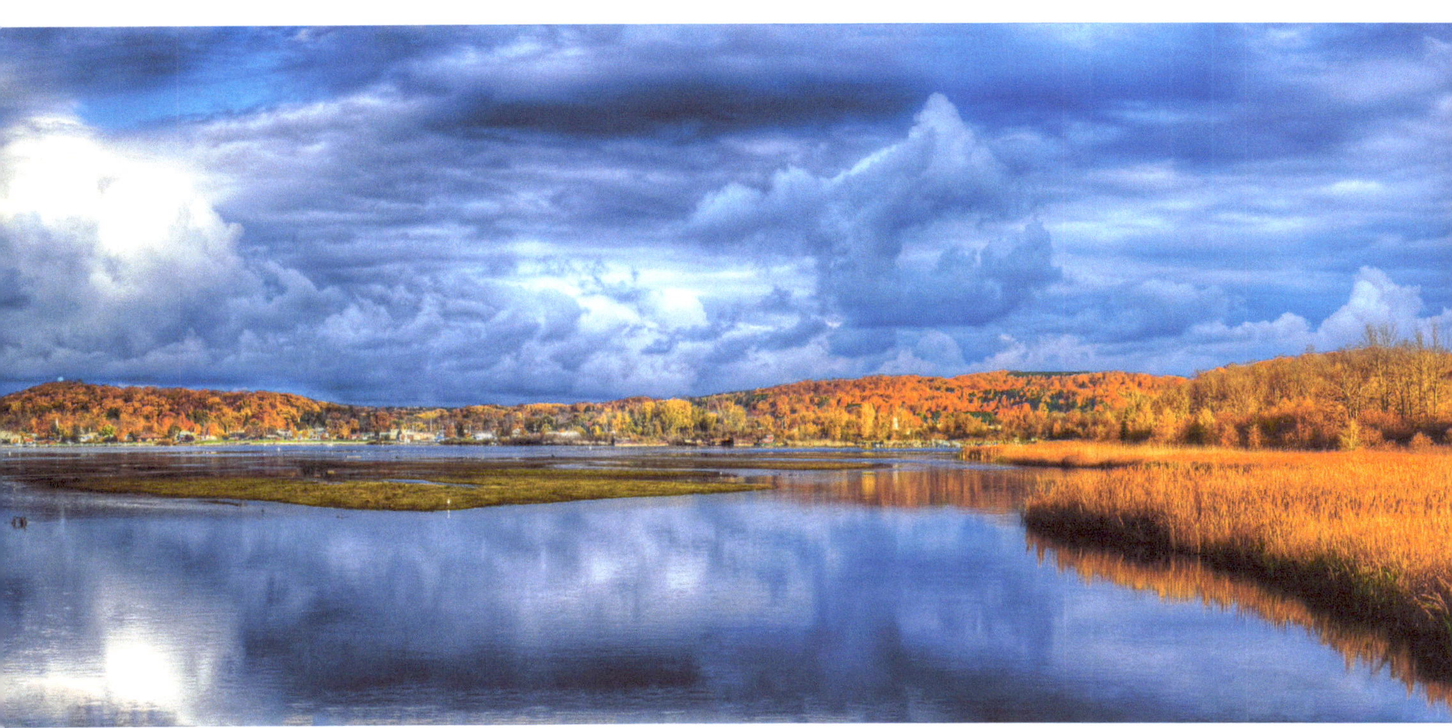

Betsie Lake in the Fall. Betsie Lake sits between Frankfort and Elberta, and is formed by the flow of the Betsie River into Lake Michigan. Betsie Lake can accomodate commercial freighters from Lake Michigan, but is more commonly home to pleasure boats and charter fishing boats.

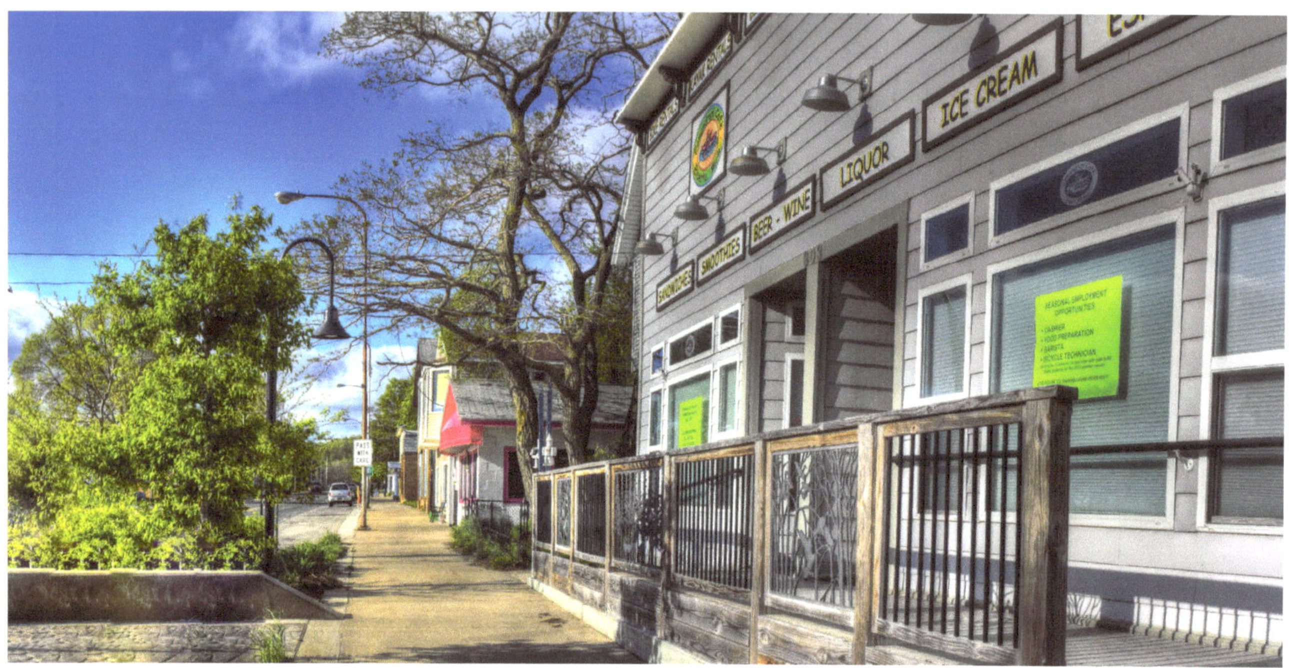

Shops in downtown Elberta

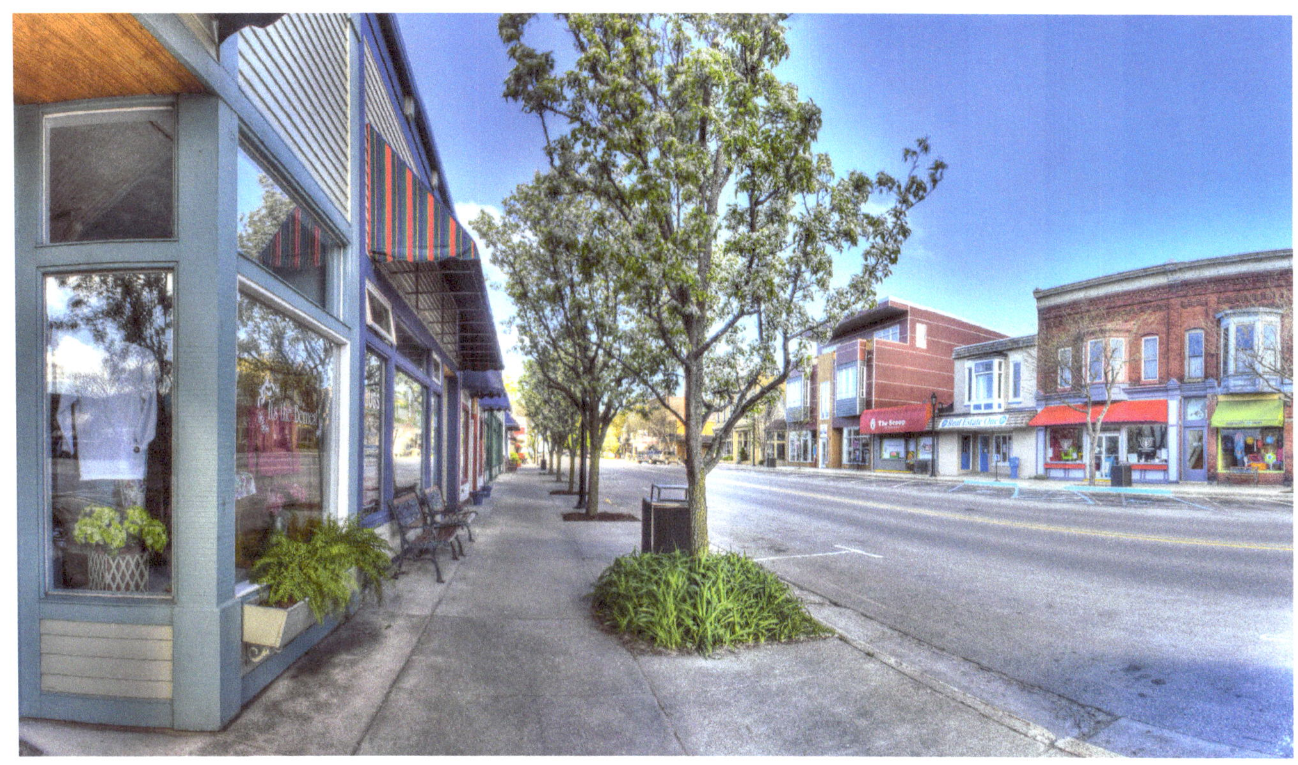

Shops in downtown Frankfort

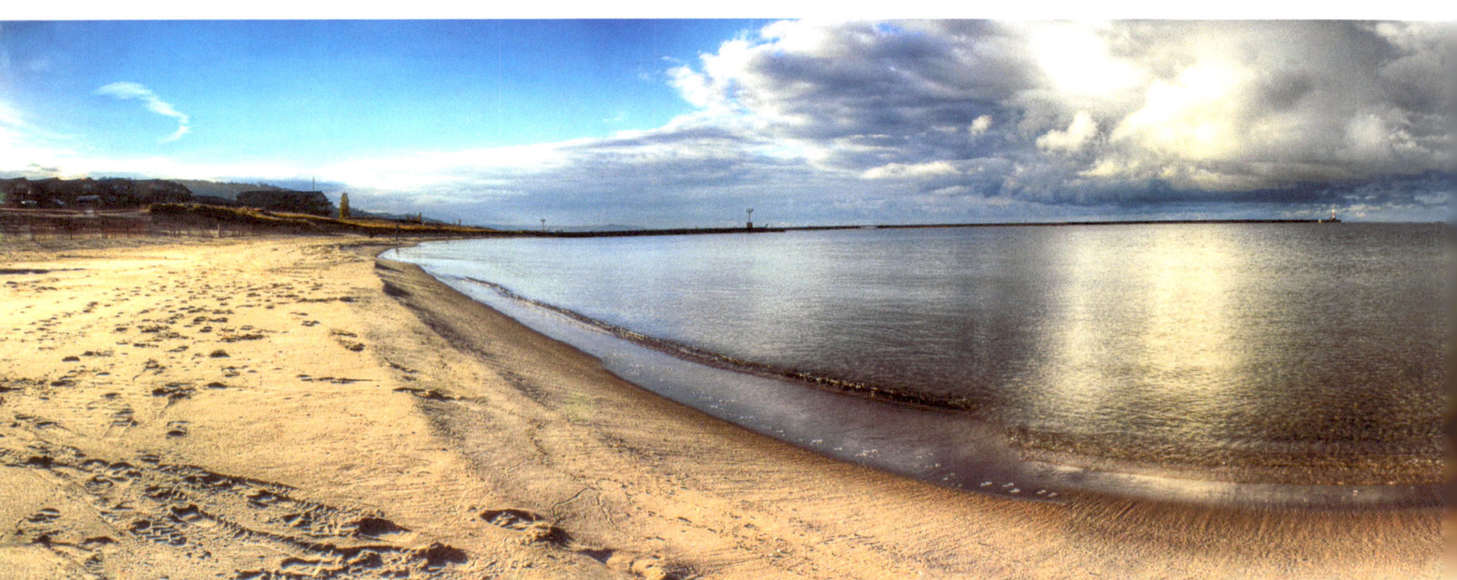

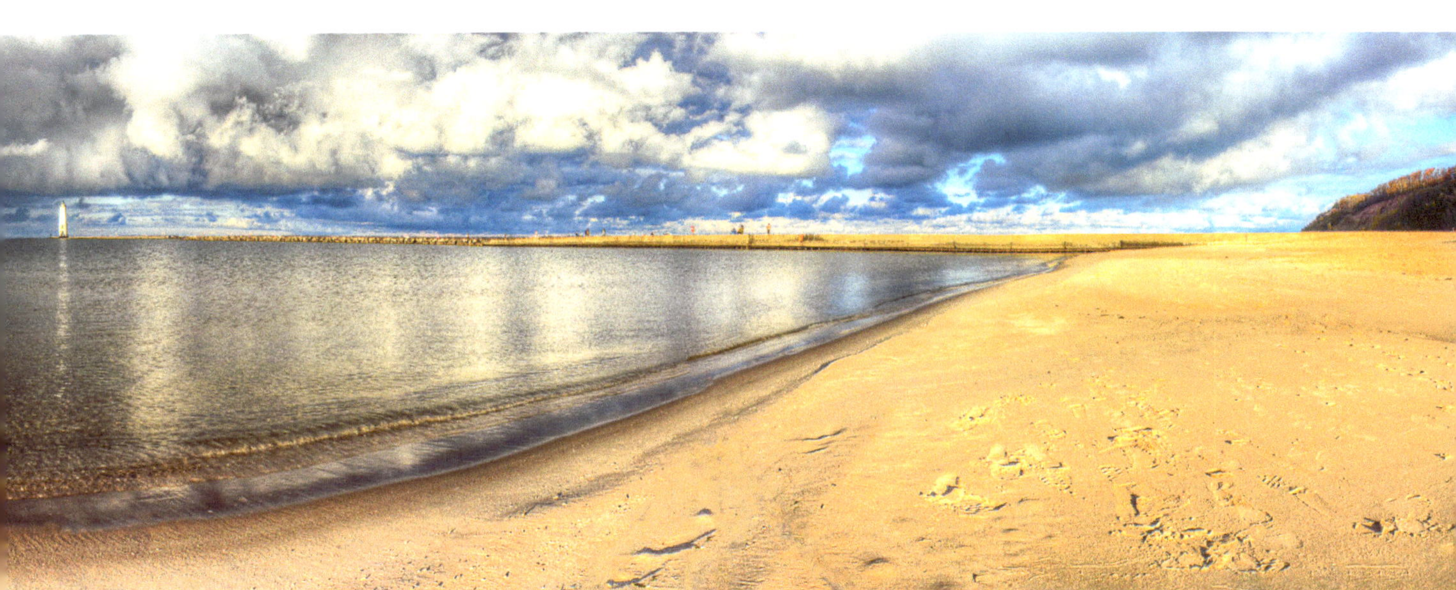

Frankfort's beach with pier and North Breakwater Lighthouse in the distance.

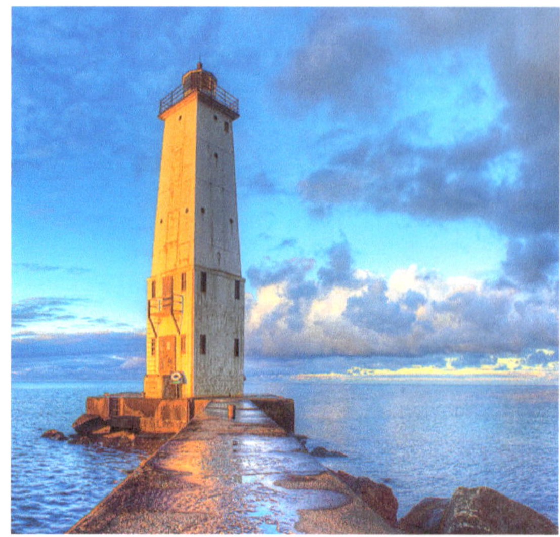

Frankfort North Breakwater Lighthouse at sunrise.

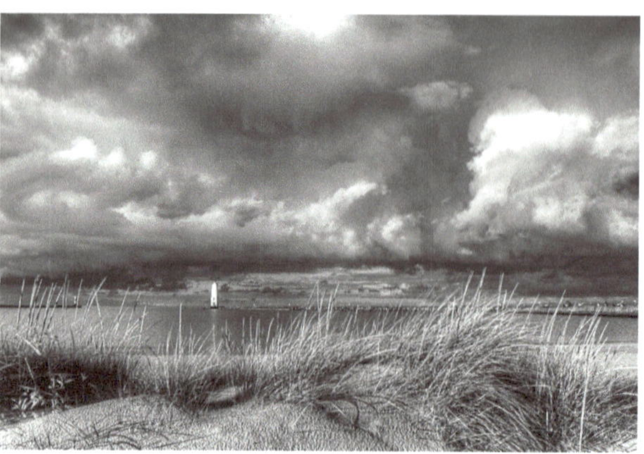

Frankfort North Breakwater Lighthouse from beach.

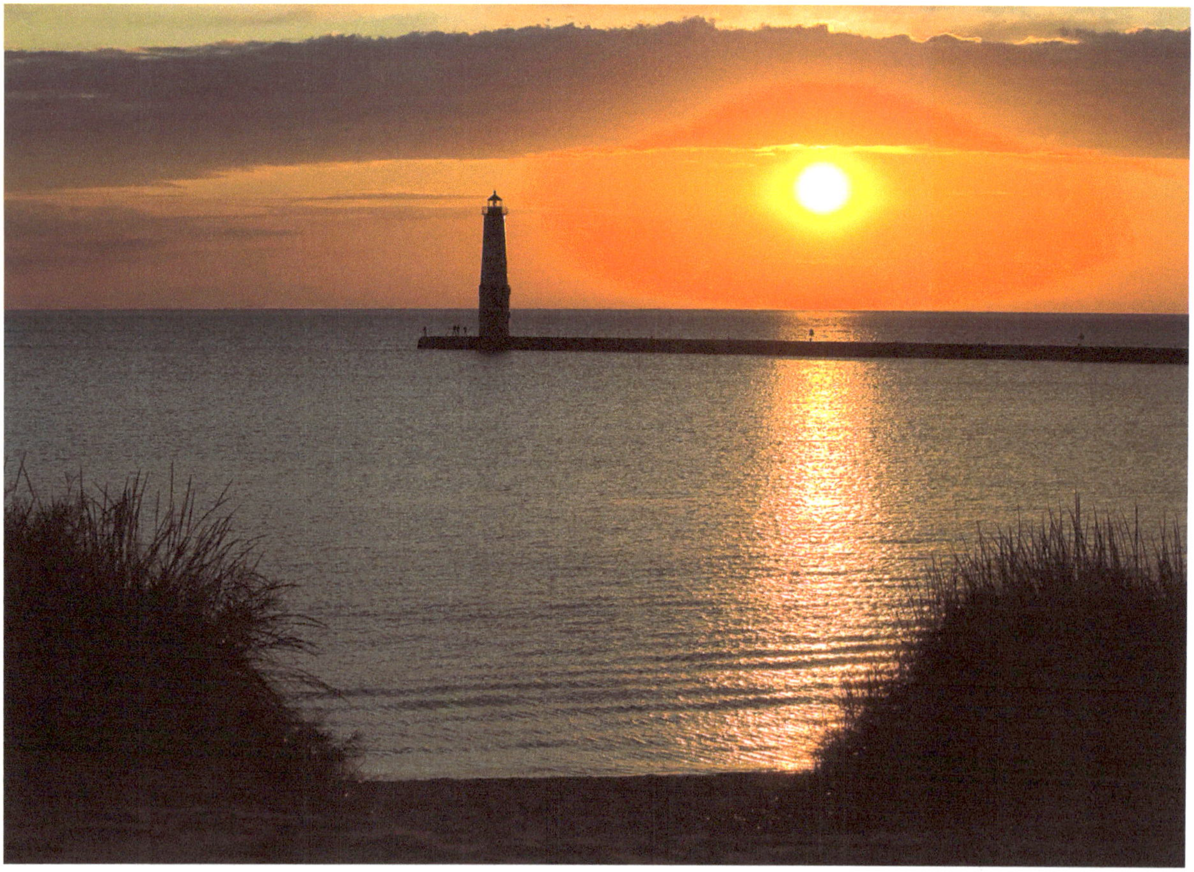

Frankfort North Breakwater Lighthouse with sunrise in distance.

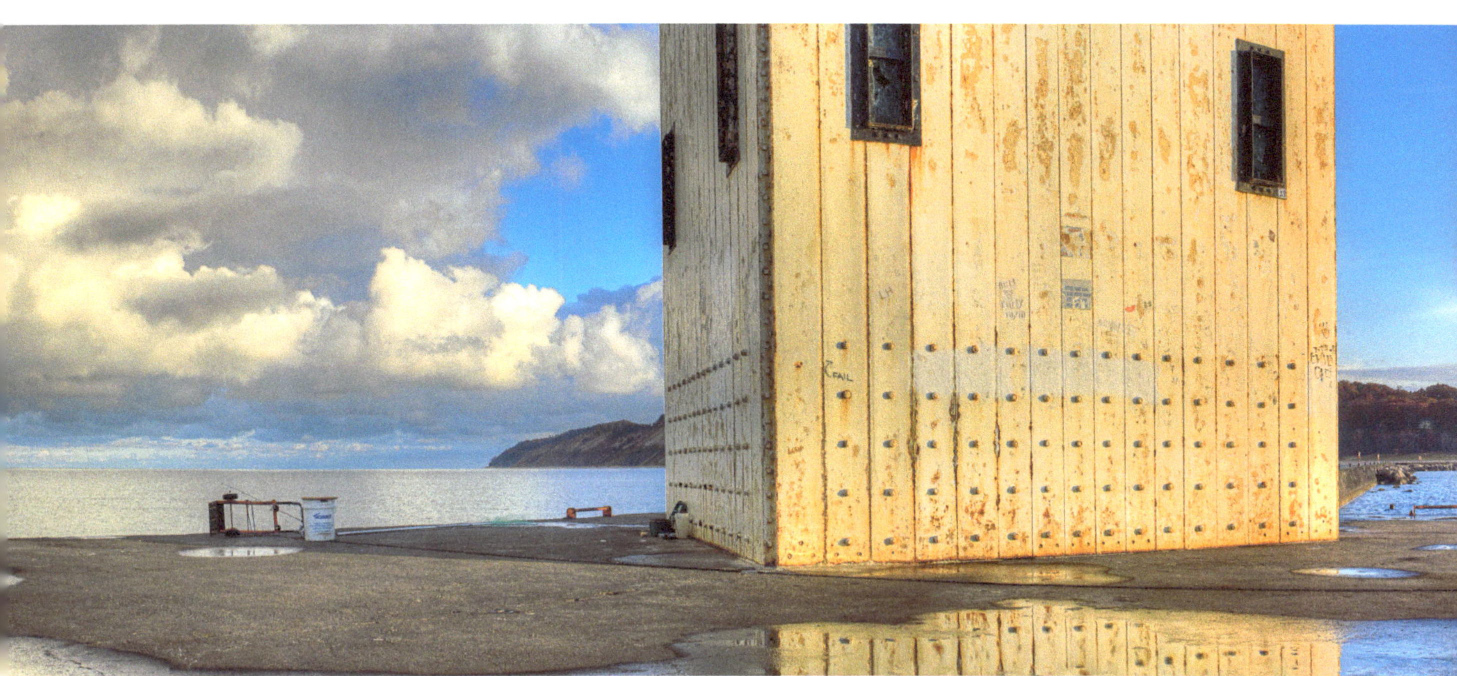

The base of Frankfort North Breakwater Lighthouse. The lighthouse was first lit in 1873 and still serves as an active aid in navigation today. The lighthouse illuminates nightly just after sunset.

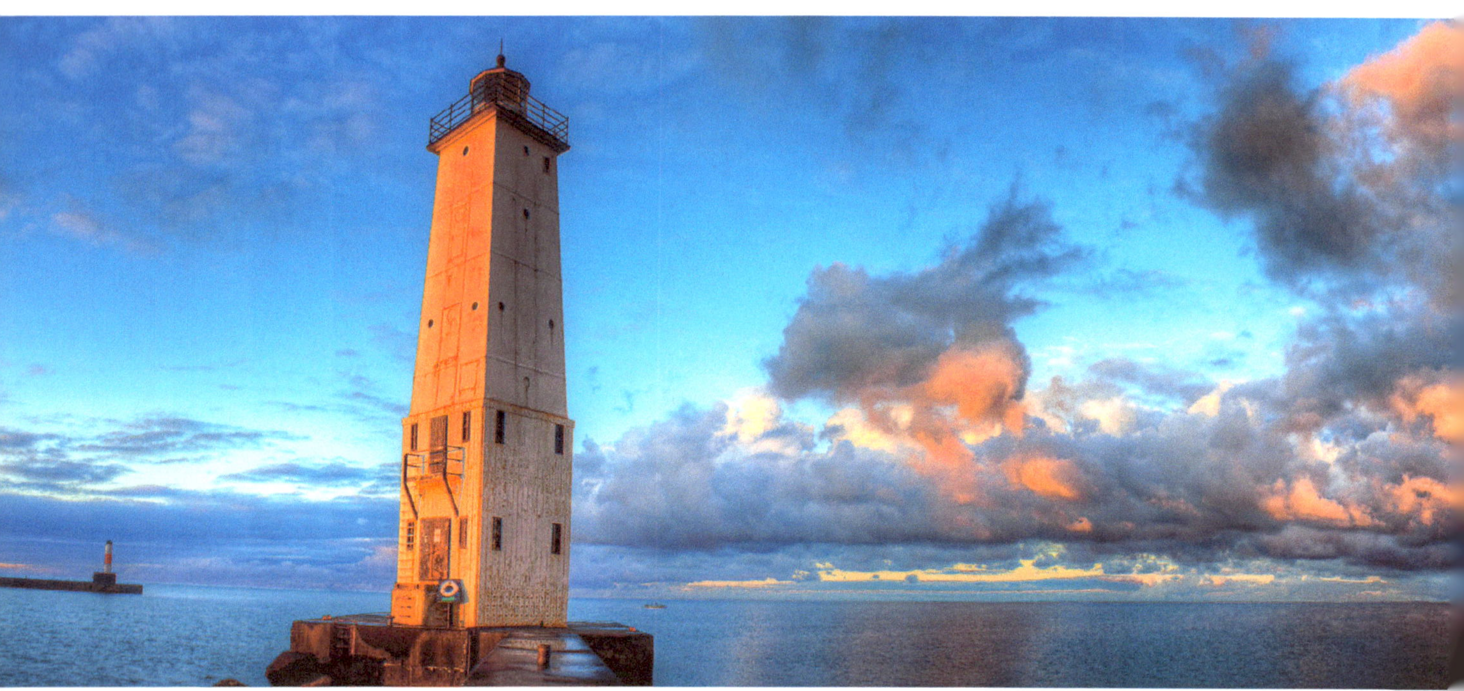

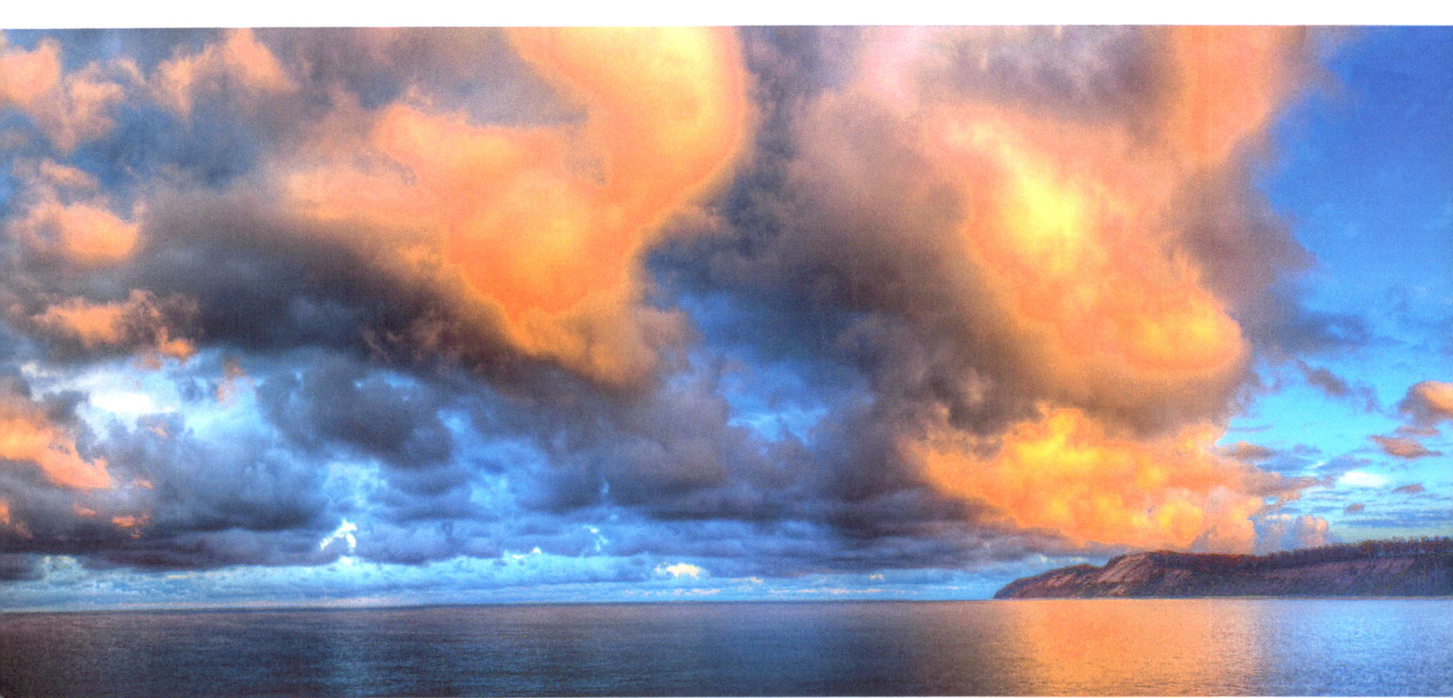

Early morning from the Frankfort pier. Even though the beach and pier face the sunset, it is also a great area to watch the sunrise. From the end of the pier, the sun rises over downtown and illuminates the lighthouse with brilliant orange light every morning.

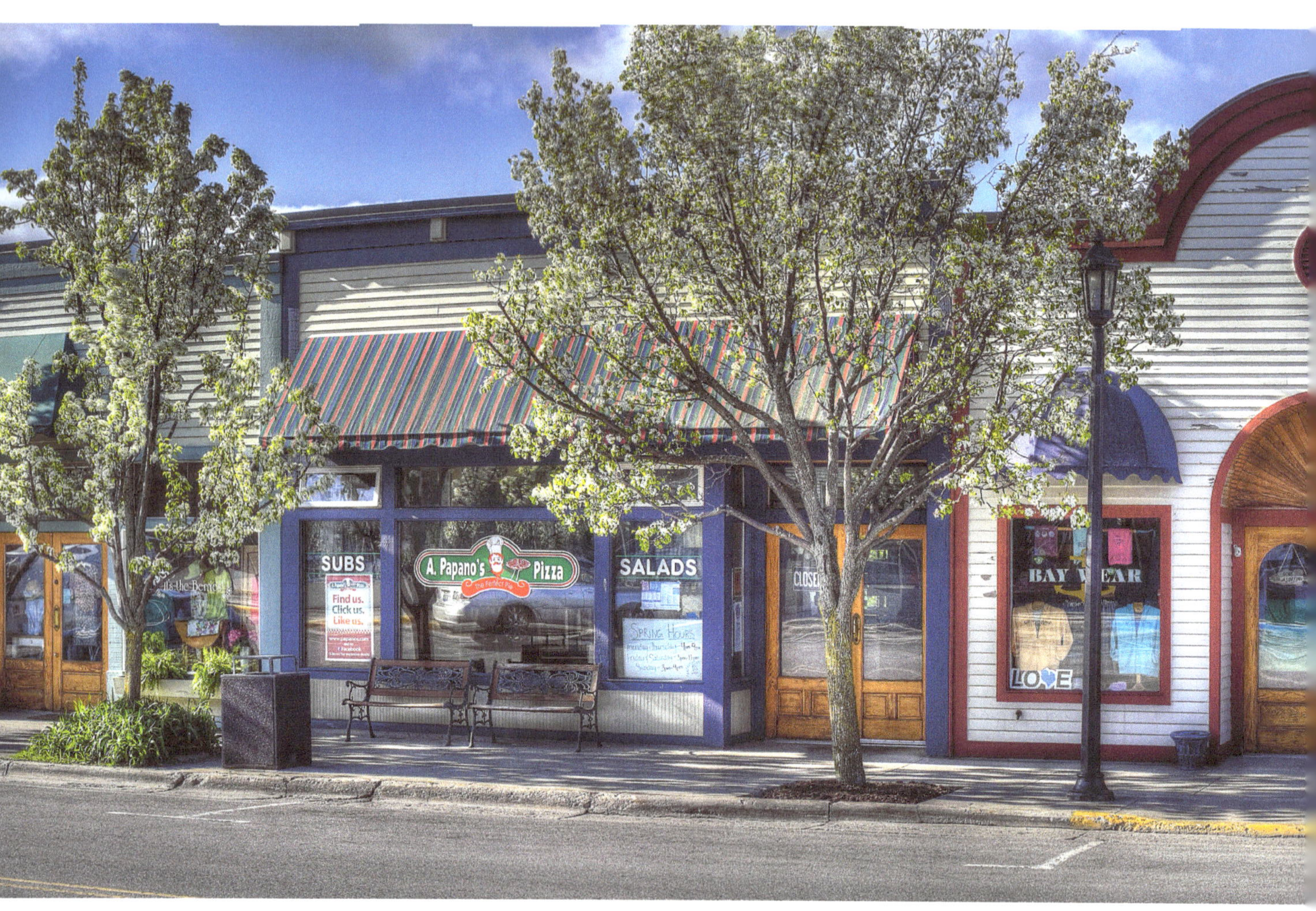

SUBS
A. Papano's Pizza
The Perfect Pie
SALADS
Find us.
Click us.
Like us.
SPRING HOURS

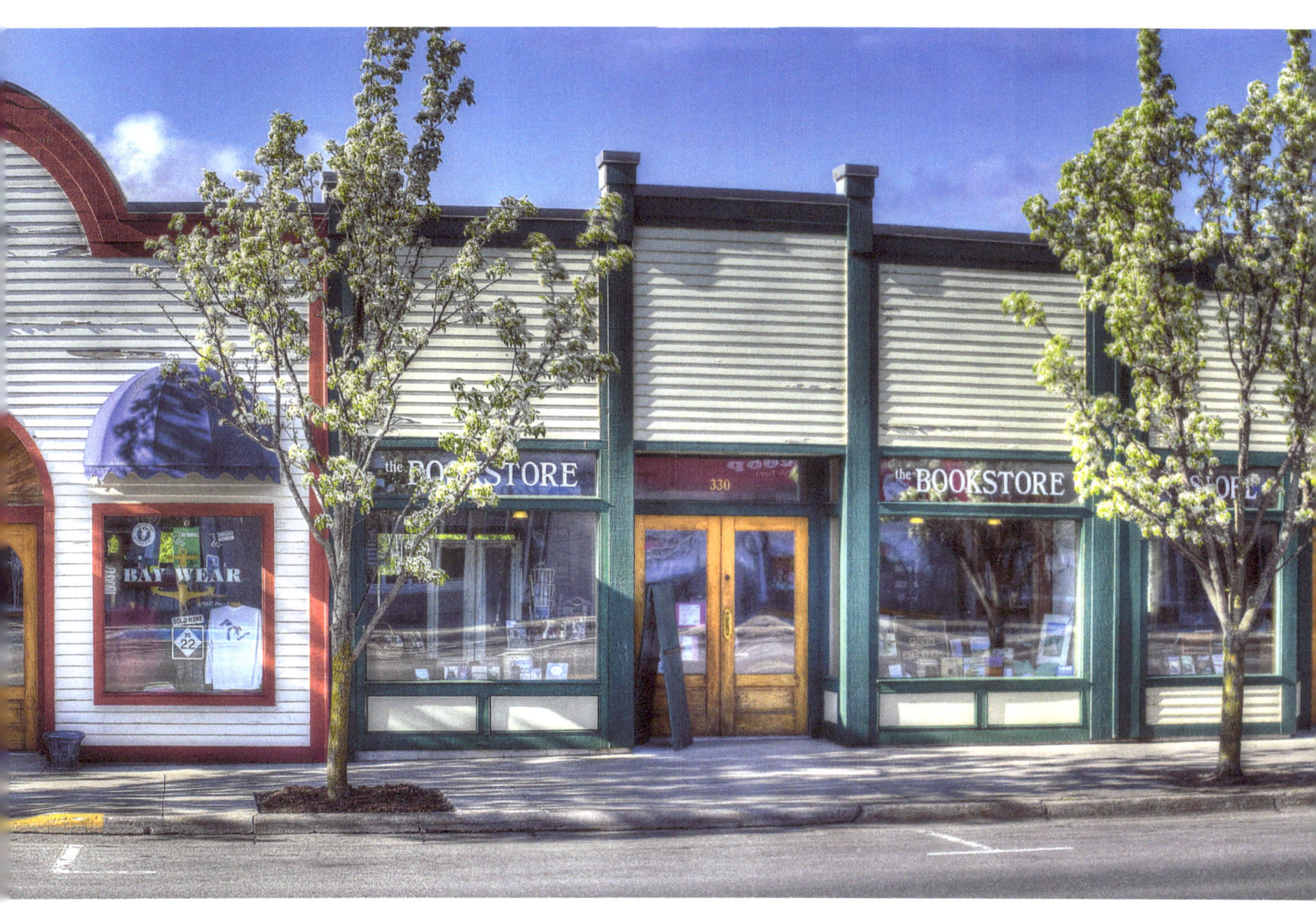

Shops in Frankfort

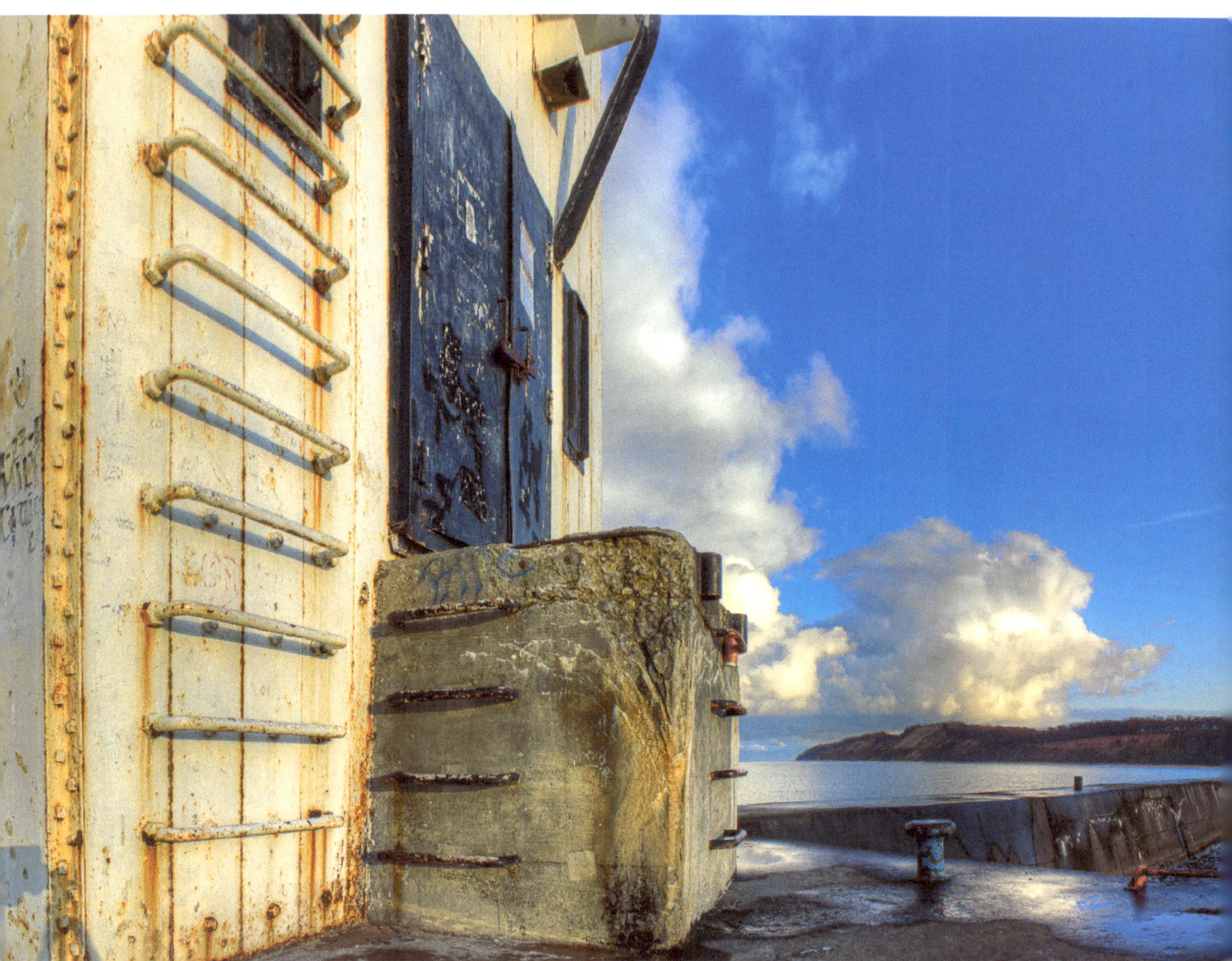

Frankfort North Breakwater Lighthouse with sunrise in distance.

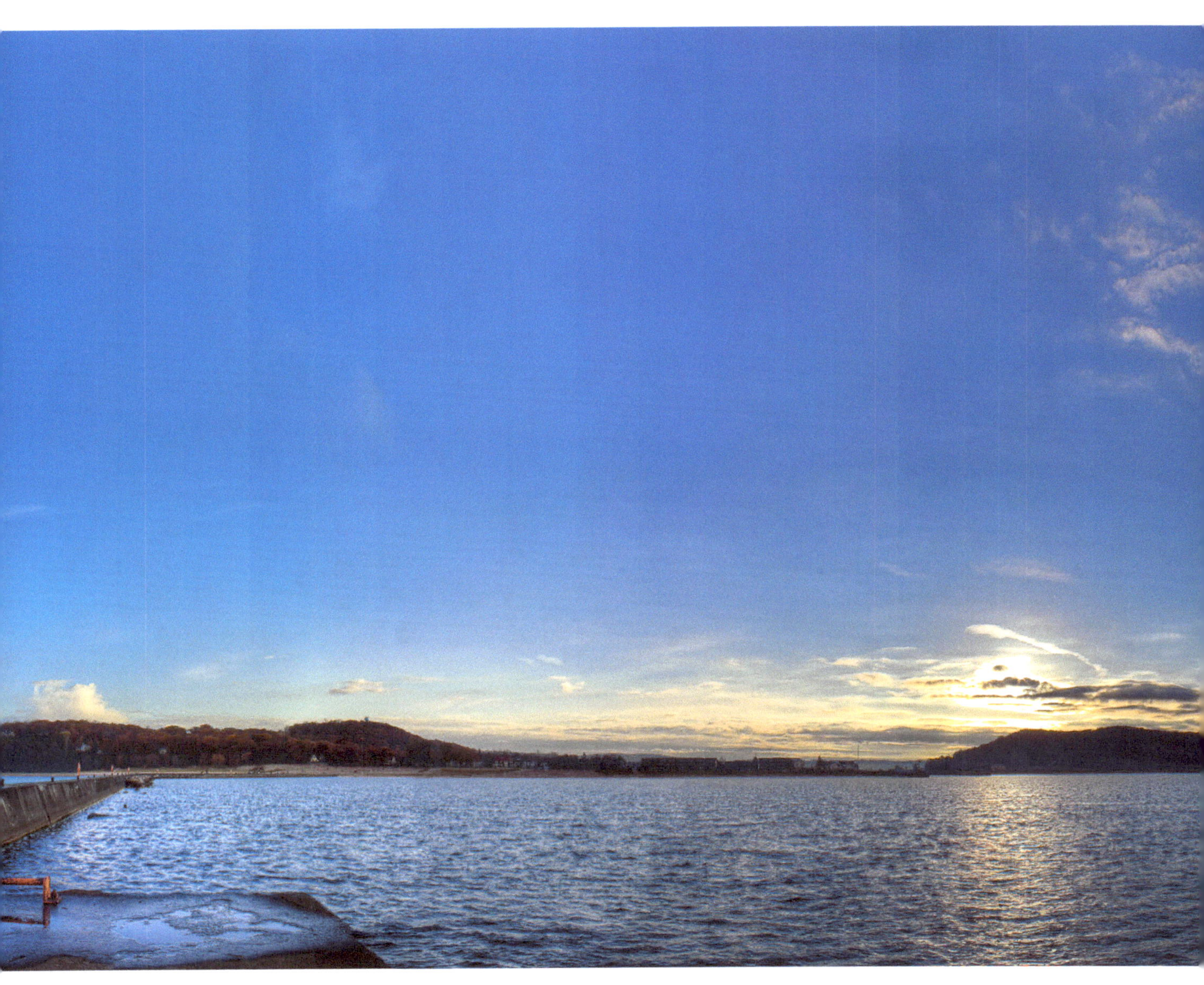

Point Betsie

The Point Betsie Lighthouse is one of the oldest continuously operating lighthouses in Michigan. Construction began in 1854. The lighthouse was first illuminated in 1859 and was visible 27 miles from shore. It is unique among the area's lighthouses because it includes an adjacent life saving station and a residence for the lightkeeper. The residence was occupied until 1989, when the Point Betsie Lighthouse became the final lighthouse in Michigan to automate.

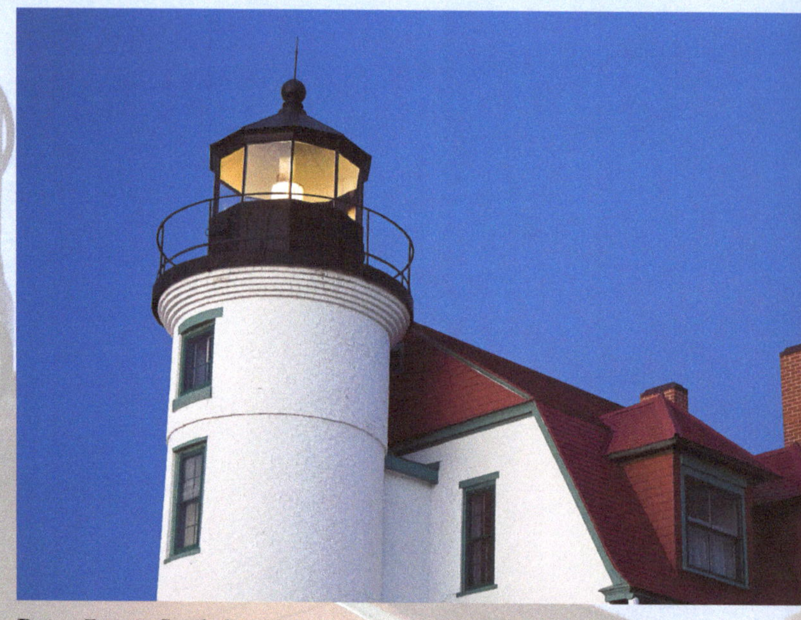

Point Betsie Lighthouse.

Located just a few miles north of Frankfort, Point Betsie is easily accessible from M-22. The lighthouse is an architectural attraction in its own right, and the miles of beaches north and south of the lighthouse make Point Betsie one of the most beautiful areas in Northern Michigan. Point Betsie is also one of the few lighthouses that is still accessible both outside and inside, with tours operating daily during the summer. Its beauty and accessibility make it one of the most photographed lighthouses in the United States.

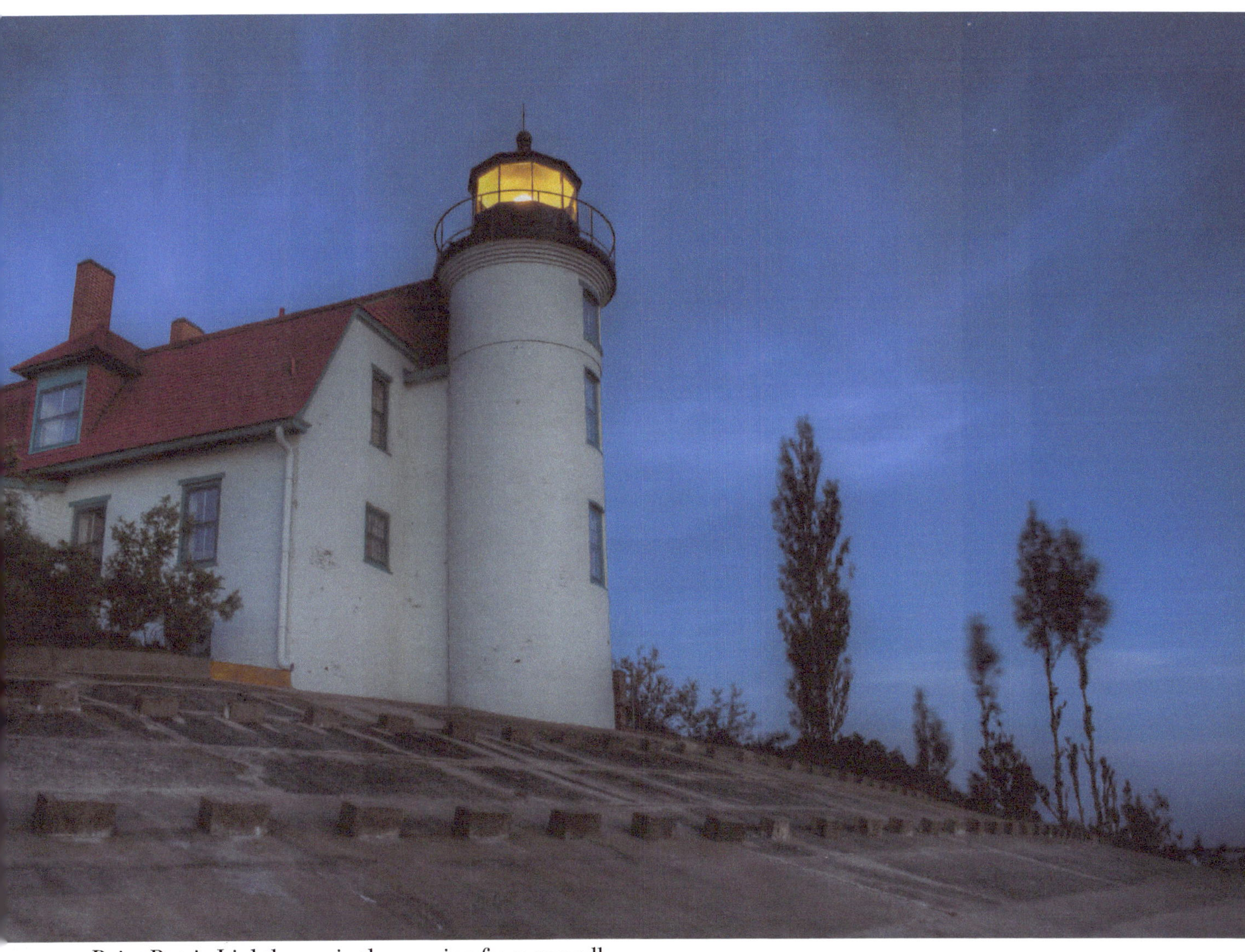

Point Betsie Lighthouse in the evening from seawall. The lighthouse is one of the most popular in Michigan. It illuminates nightly just after sunset.

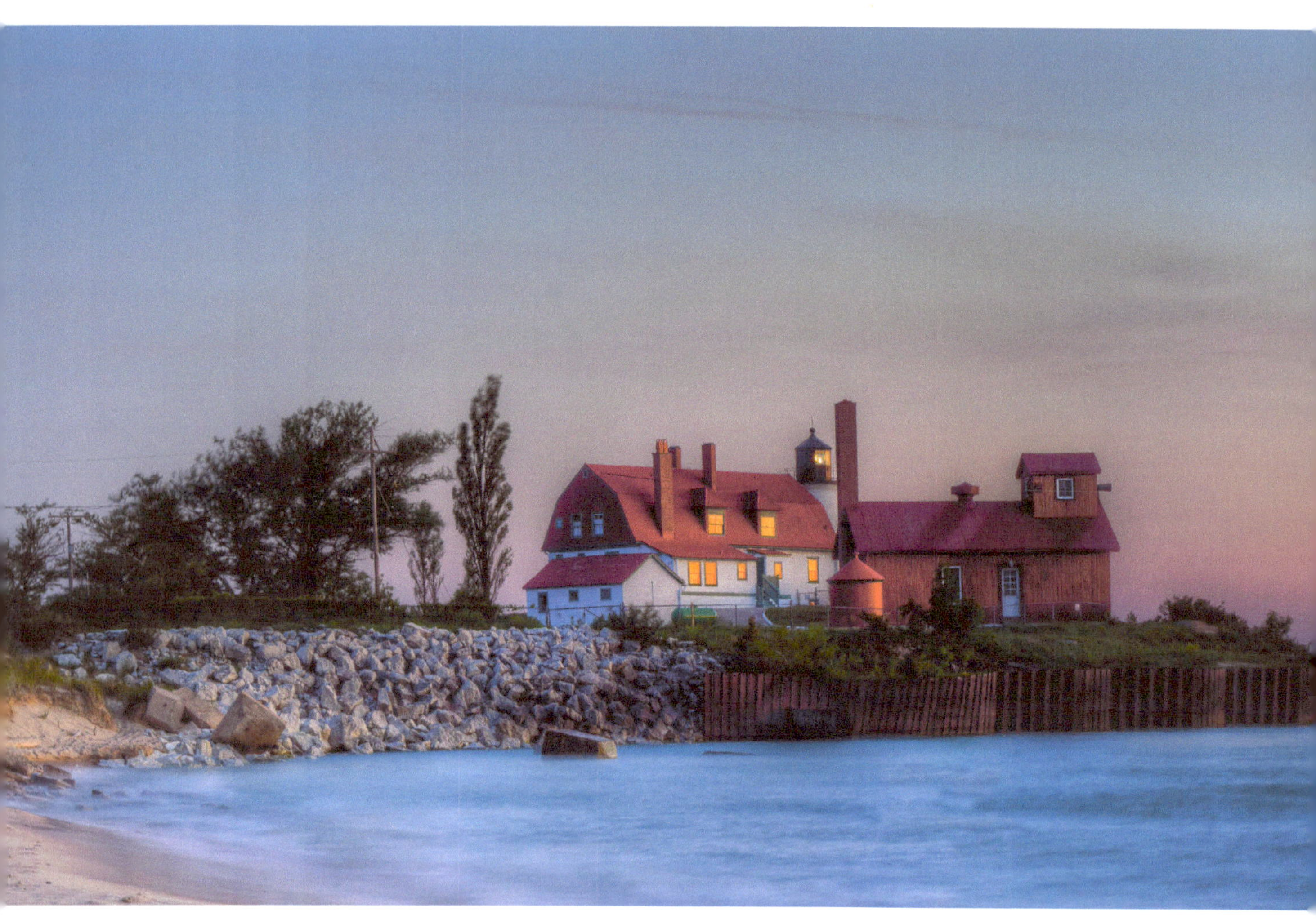

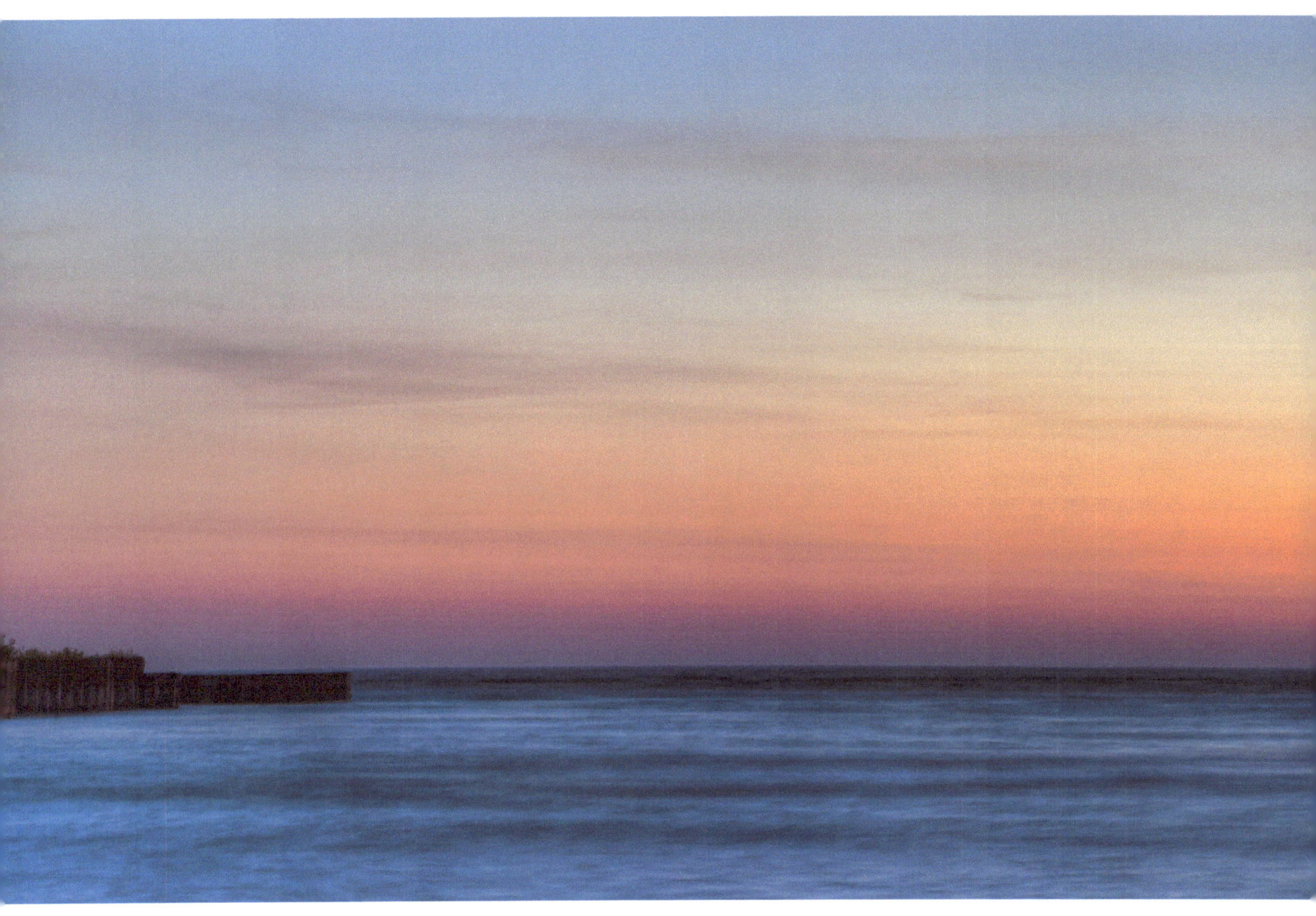

Point Betsie Lighthouse and life-saving station at sunset. Point Betsie is unique among area lighthouses because it includes an attached residence and the bright red life saving station next door.

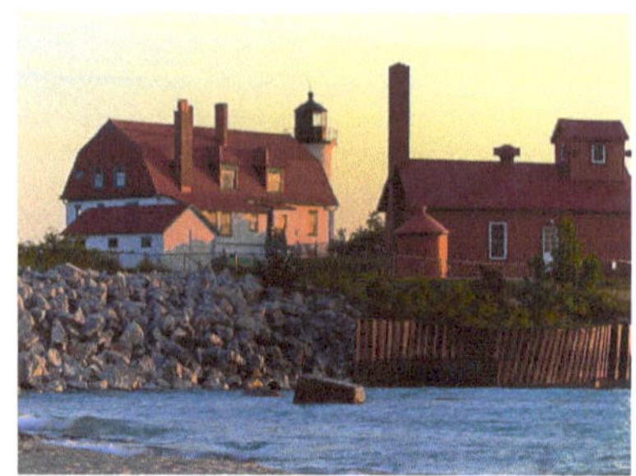

Lighthouse and life-saving station.

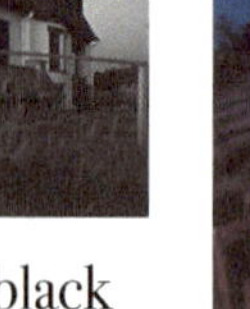

Point Betsie at sunrise in black and white.

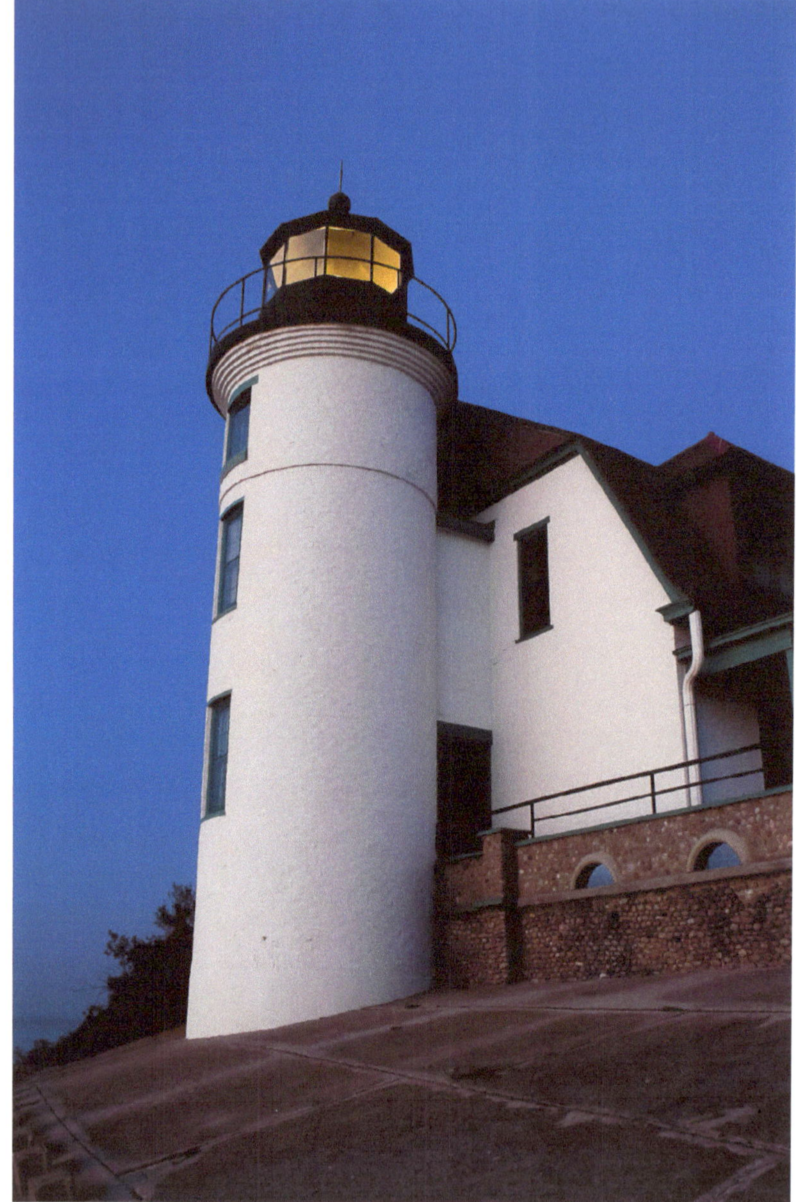

Point Betsie Lighthouse at dusk.

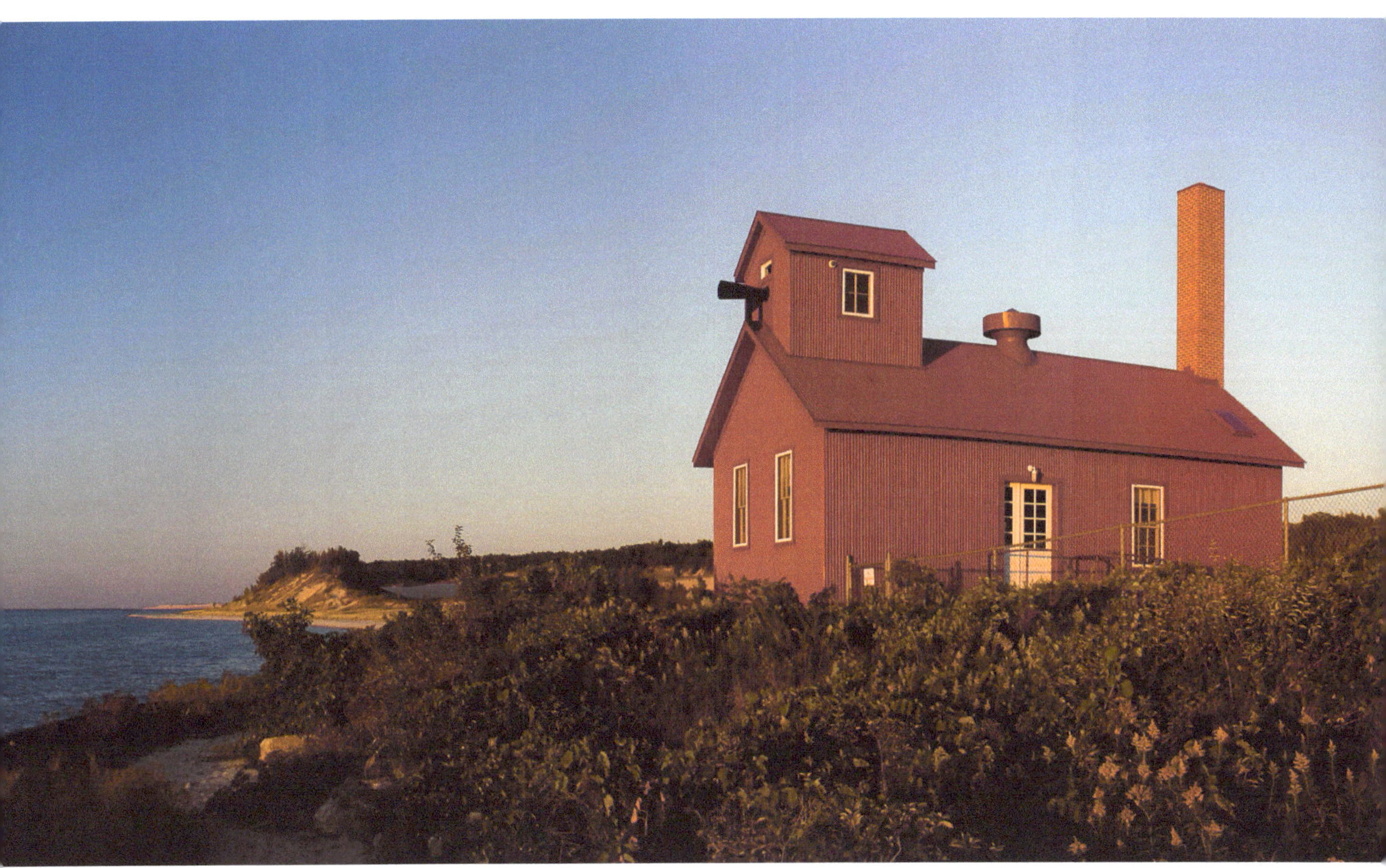

Point Betsie life-saving station. The station was built in 1876, about twenty years after the lighthouse was completed. The life-saving station was closed in 1937, however, amid budgetary pressures facing the U.S. Coast Guard.

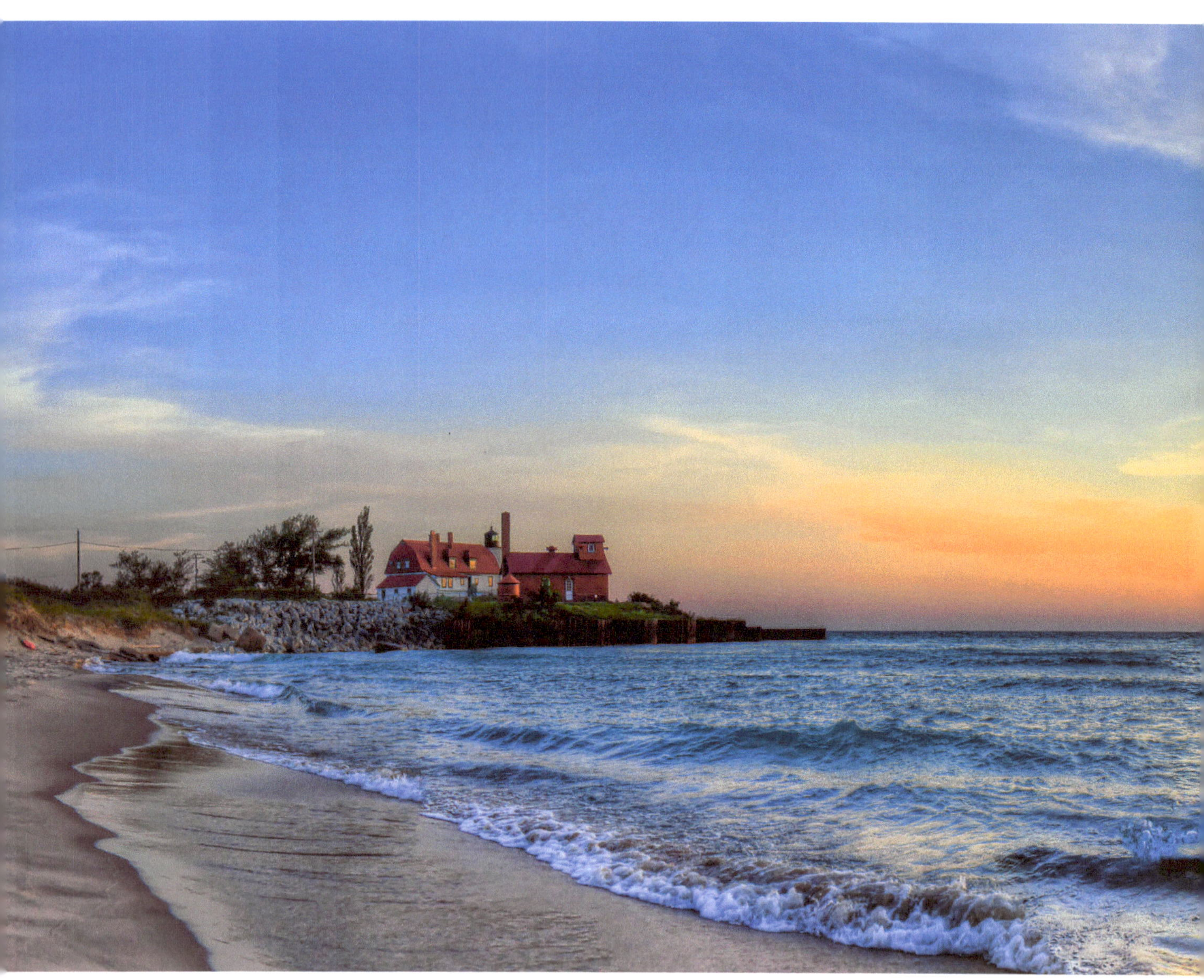

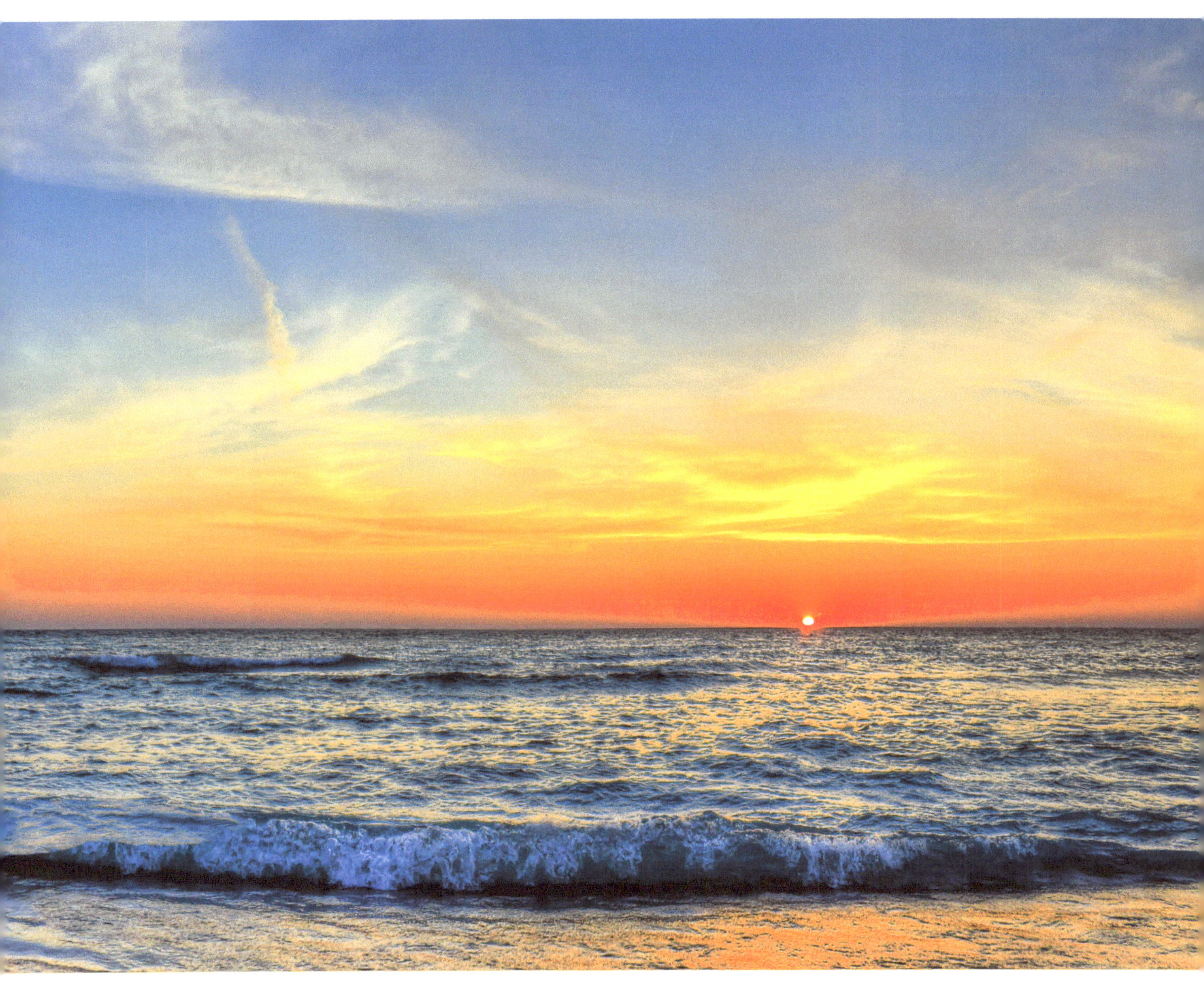

Sunset over Lake Michigan from the shoreline north of Point Betsie Lighthouse. There are miles of beaches north and south of the Point Betsie Lighthouse. The beaches are easily accessible from the parking lot by the lighthouse.

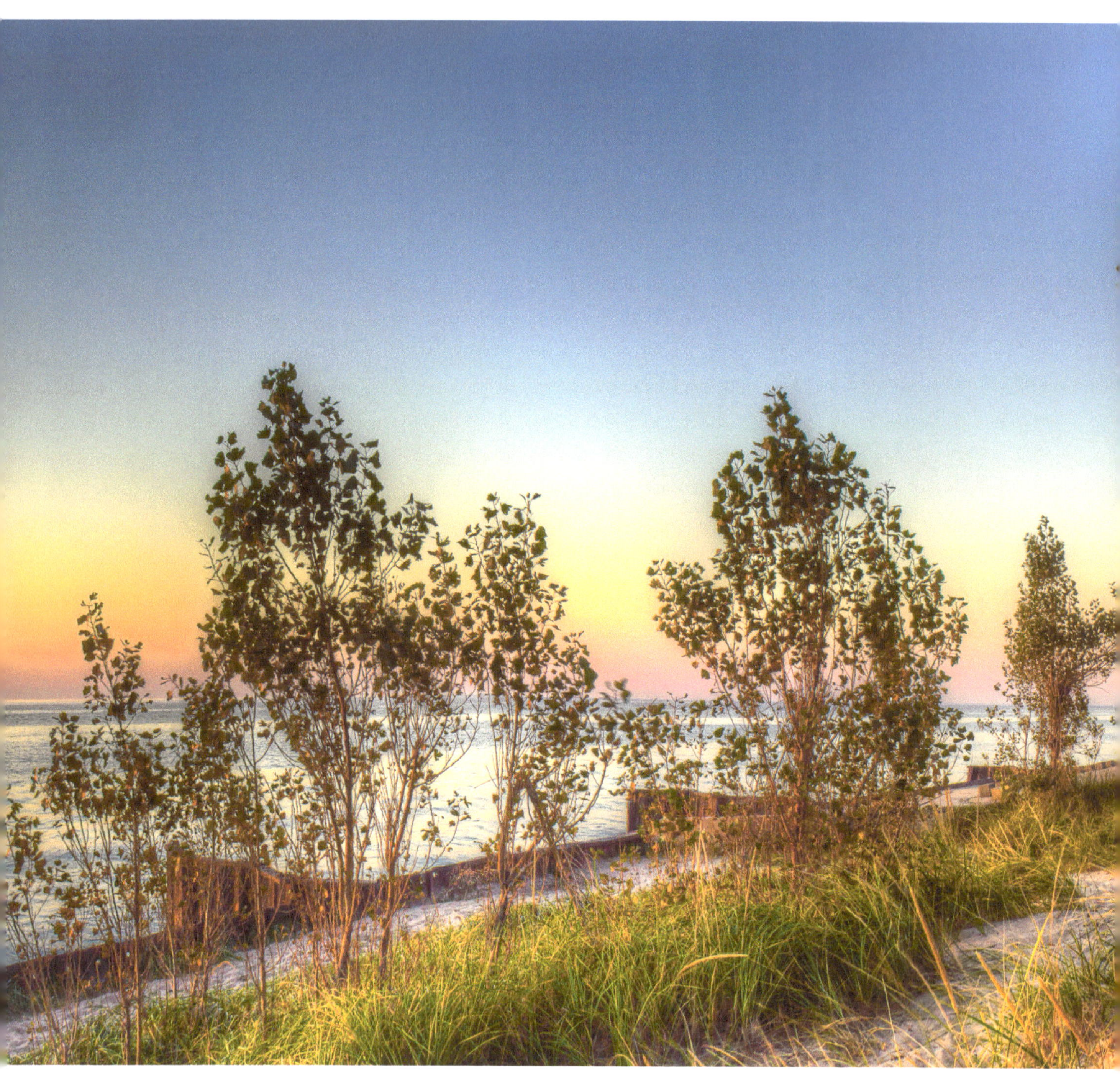

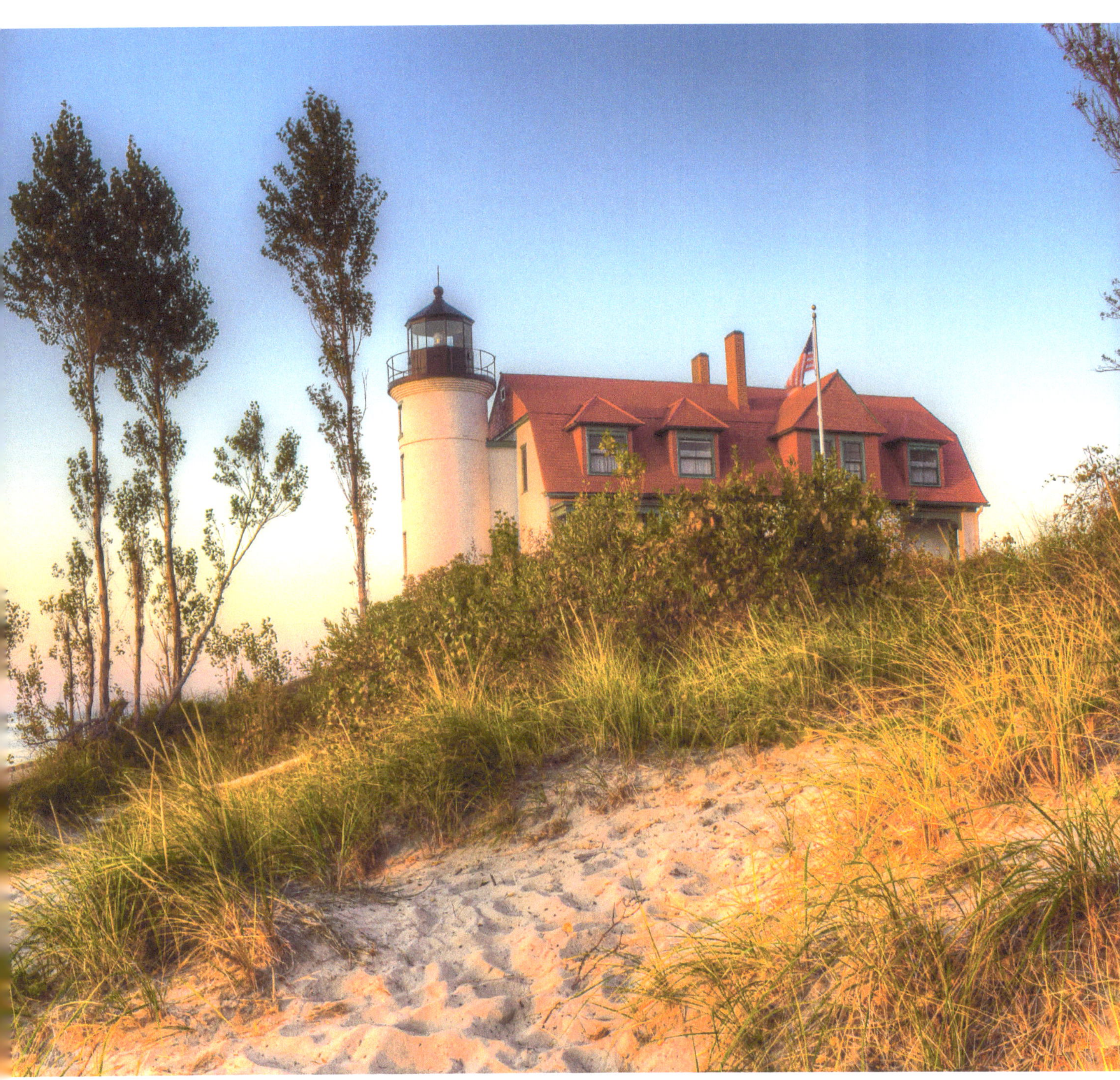

Point Betsie dunes and lighthouse. Point Betsie's popularity is due in part to the scenery surrounding the lighthouse. Unlike the concrete piers surrounding lighthouses in Manistee and Frankfort, there are beaches and dunes surrounding Point Betsie for miles.

Sleeping Bear Dunes

Sleeping Bear Dunes stretches for thrity-five miles along Lake Michigan starting just north of Frankfort and ending about ten miles south of Leland. It also includes North and South Manitou Islands, which sit a few miles off of the shore. Sleeping Bear Dunes is one of two federally protected lakeshores in Michigan under the management of the National Park Service.

Sleeping Bear Dunes with South Manitou Island in distance.

Sleeping Bear Dunes has something for everyone. There are thirty-five miles of lakeshore along Lake Michigan, thousands of acres of forest, hundreds of miles of hiking trails, and quick access to the towns of Frankfort, Glen Arbor, and Empire. Once one of the best kept secrets among national parks and lakeshores, Sleeping Bear Dunes has recently skyrocketed in popularity after Good Morning America named it the Most Beautiful Place in America.

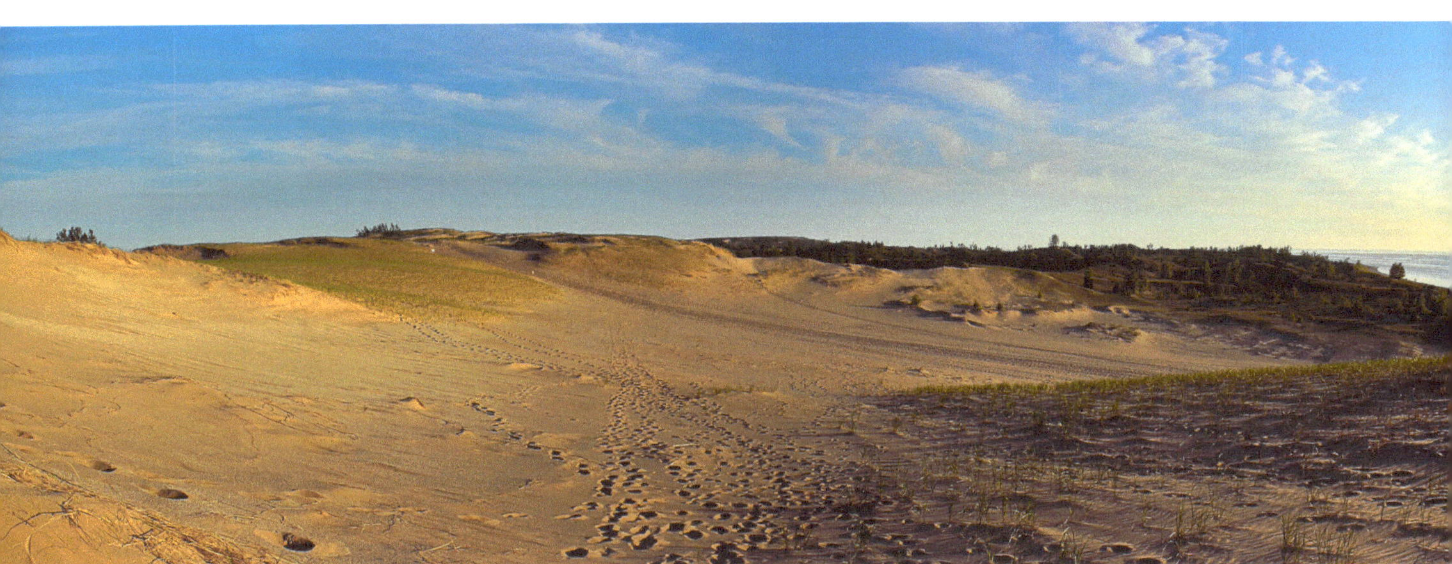

Sleeping Bear Dunes near Glen Haven. The tiny village of Glen Haven sits within the Sleeping Bear Dunes and consists of a few restored logging buildings owned by the National Park Service. It also provides free access to the dunes at the Sleeping Bear Point Trailhead. From the trailhead, it is a short walk to some amazing views of the dunes and of Lake Michigan.

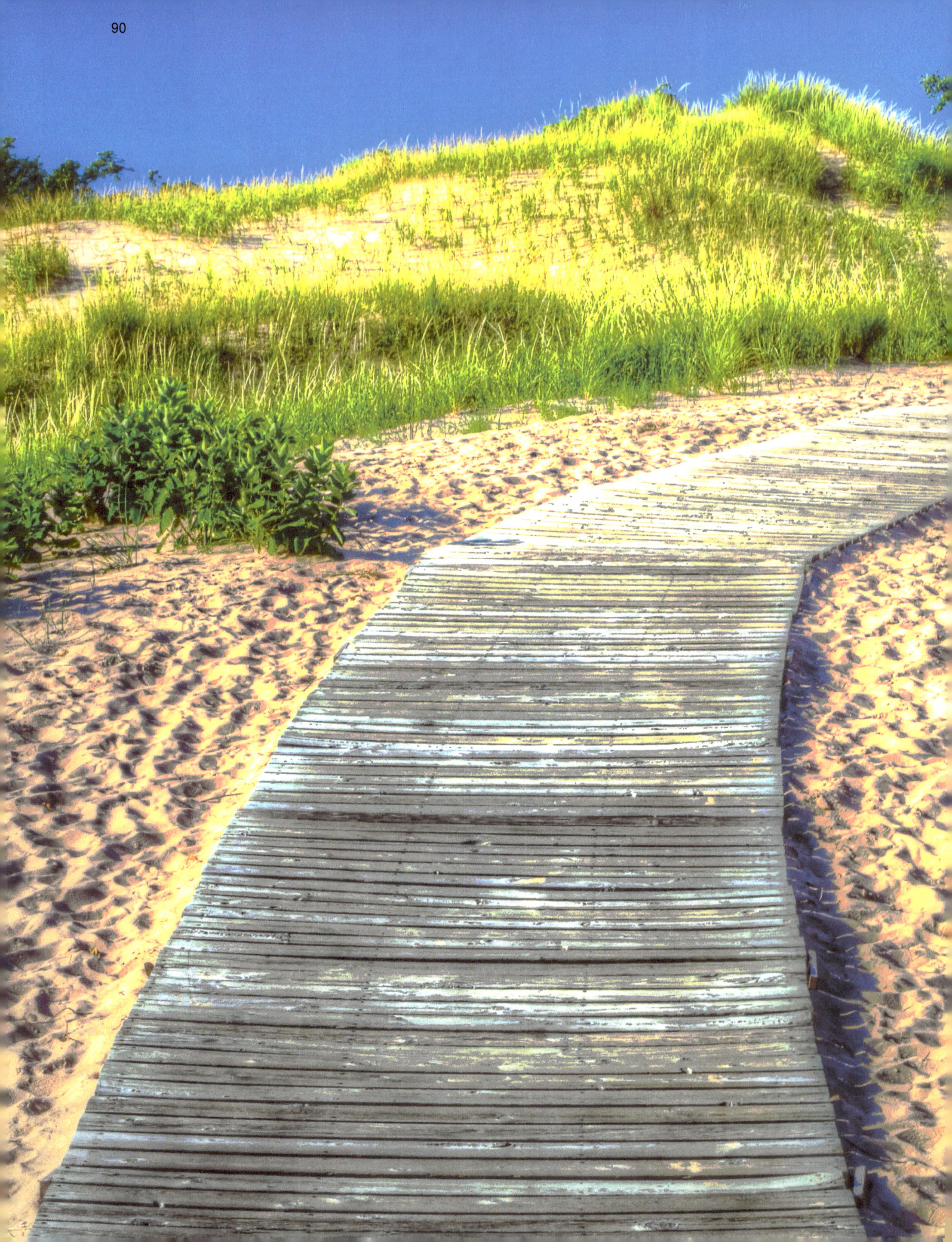

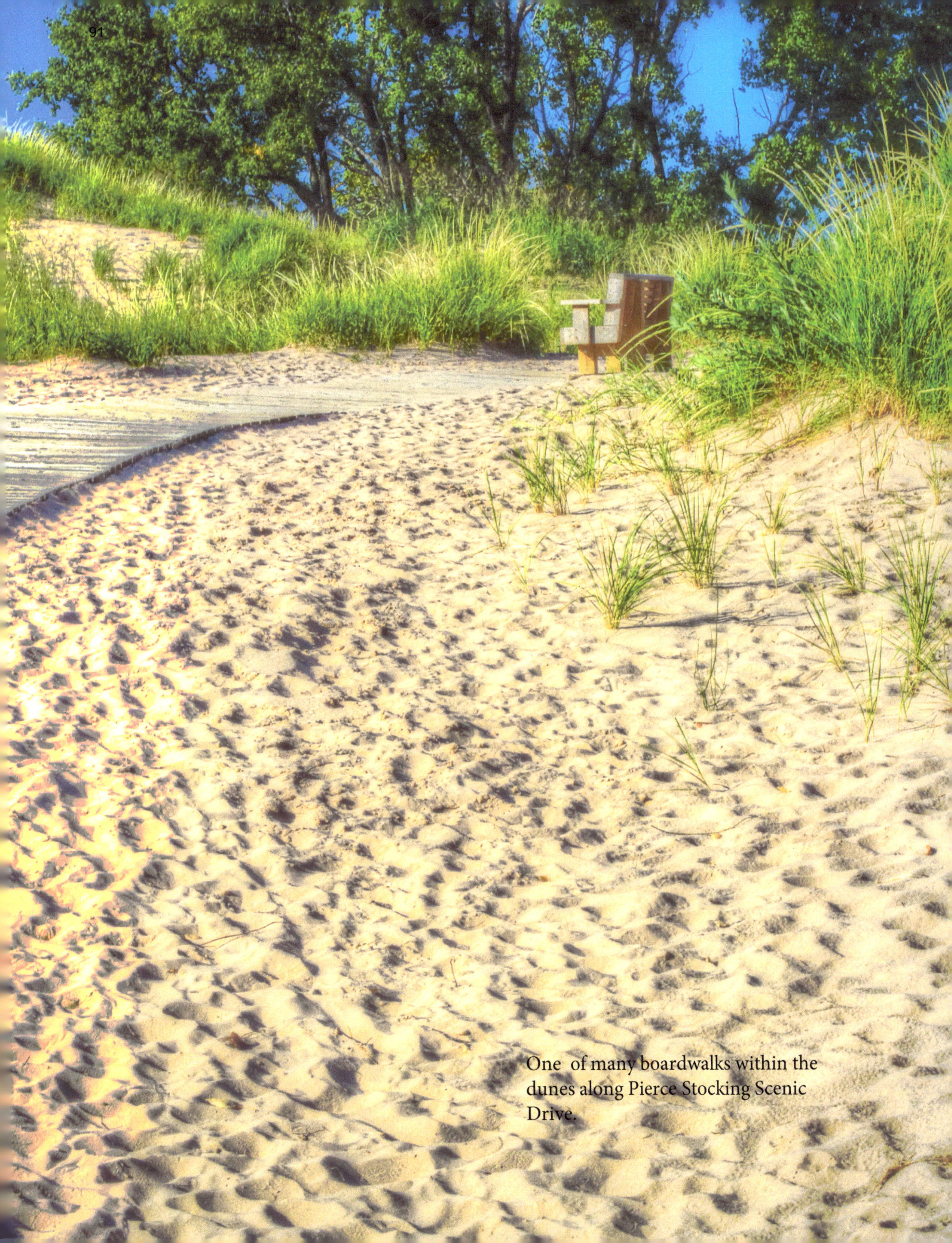

One of many boardwalks within the dunes along Pierce Stocking Scenic Drive.

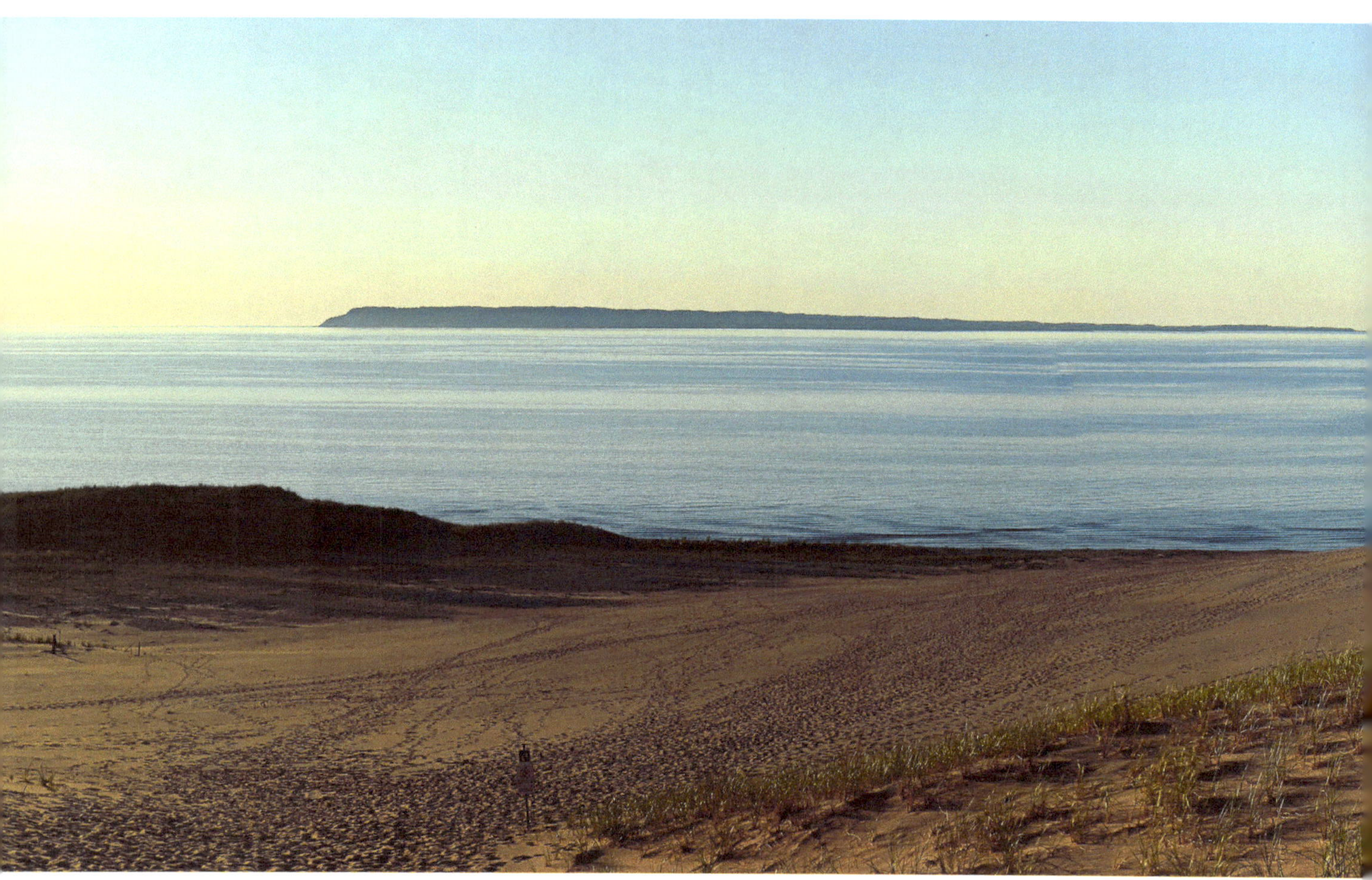

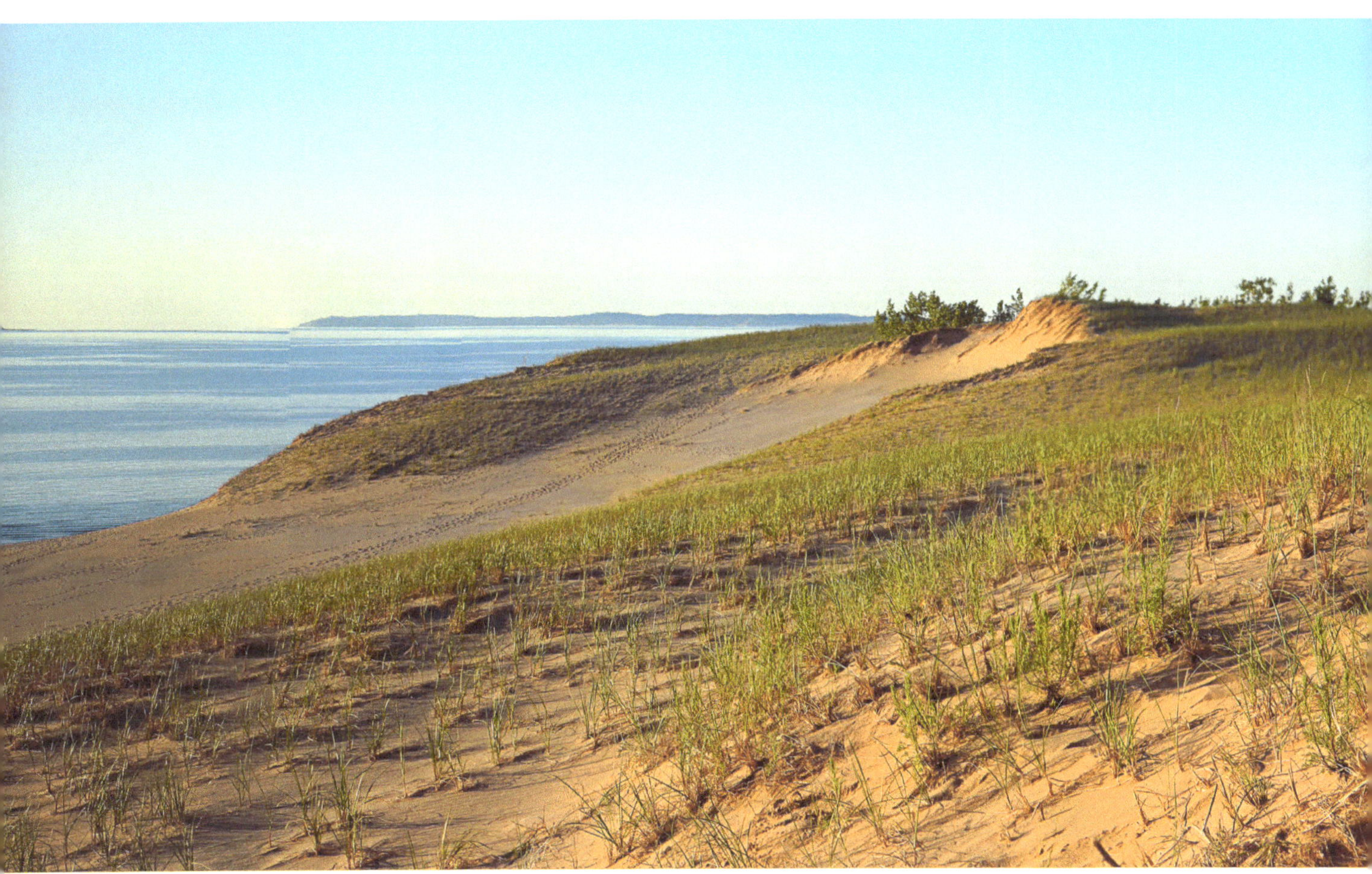

The dunes overlooking South Manitou Island. North and South Manitou Island sit within the federally protected national lakeshore and are accessible by ferry from Leland. The islands are largely uninhabited and are excellent places for hiking and camping. The islands can be seen from the mainland for miles around. The Pierce Stocking Scenic Drive provides some of the most dramatic views of the islands.

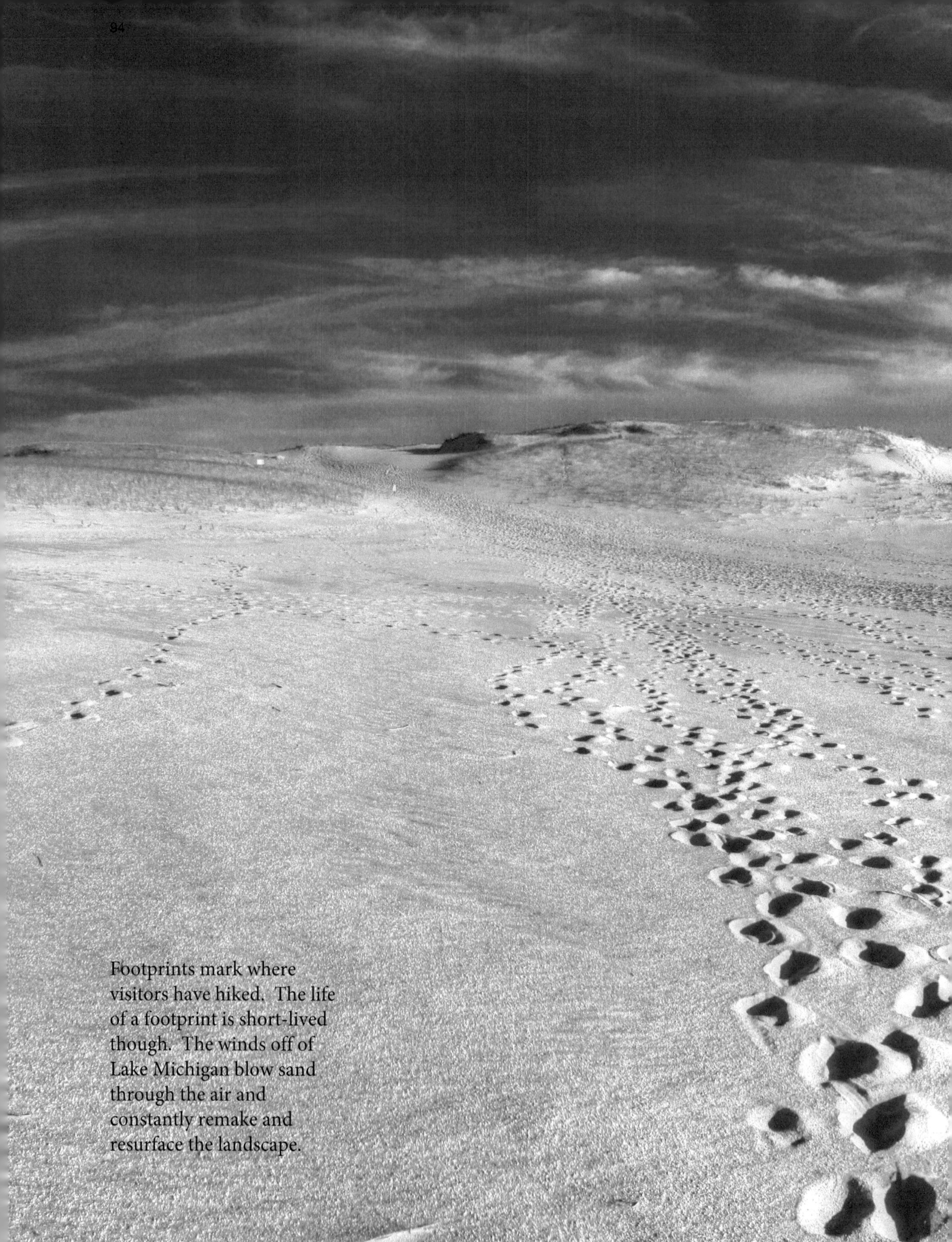

Footprints mark where visitors have hiked. The life of a footprint is short-lived though. The winds off of Lake Michigan blow sand through the air and constantly remake and resurface the landscape.

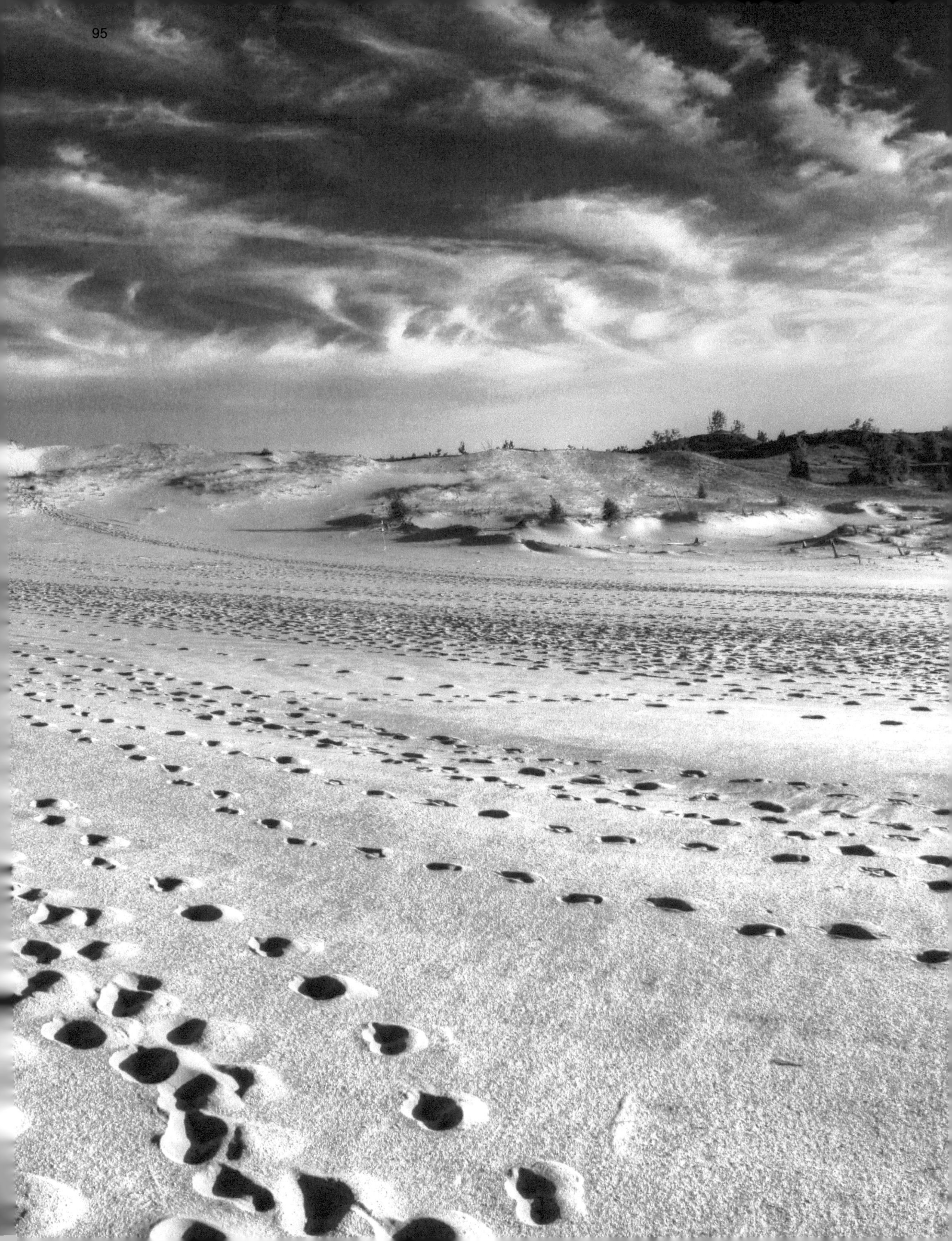

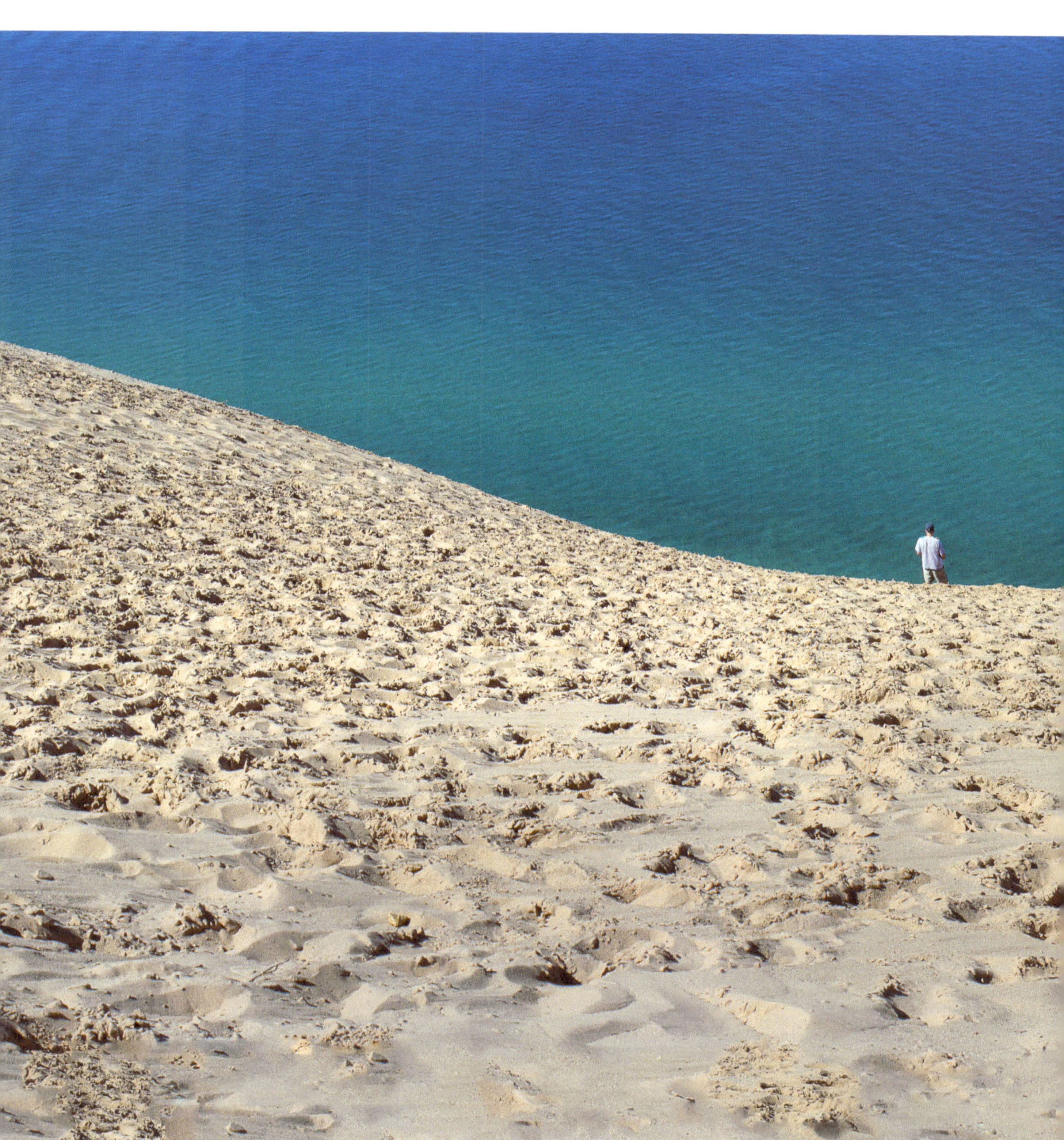

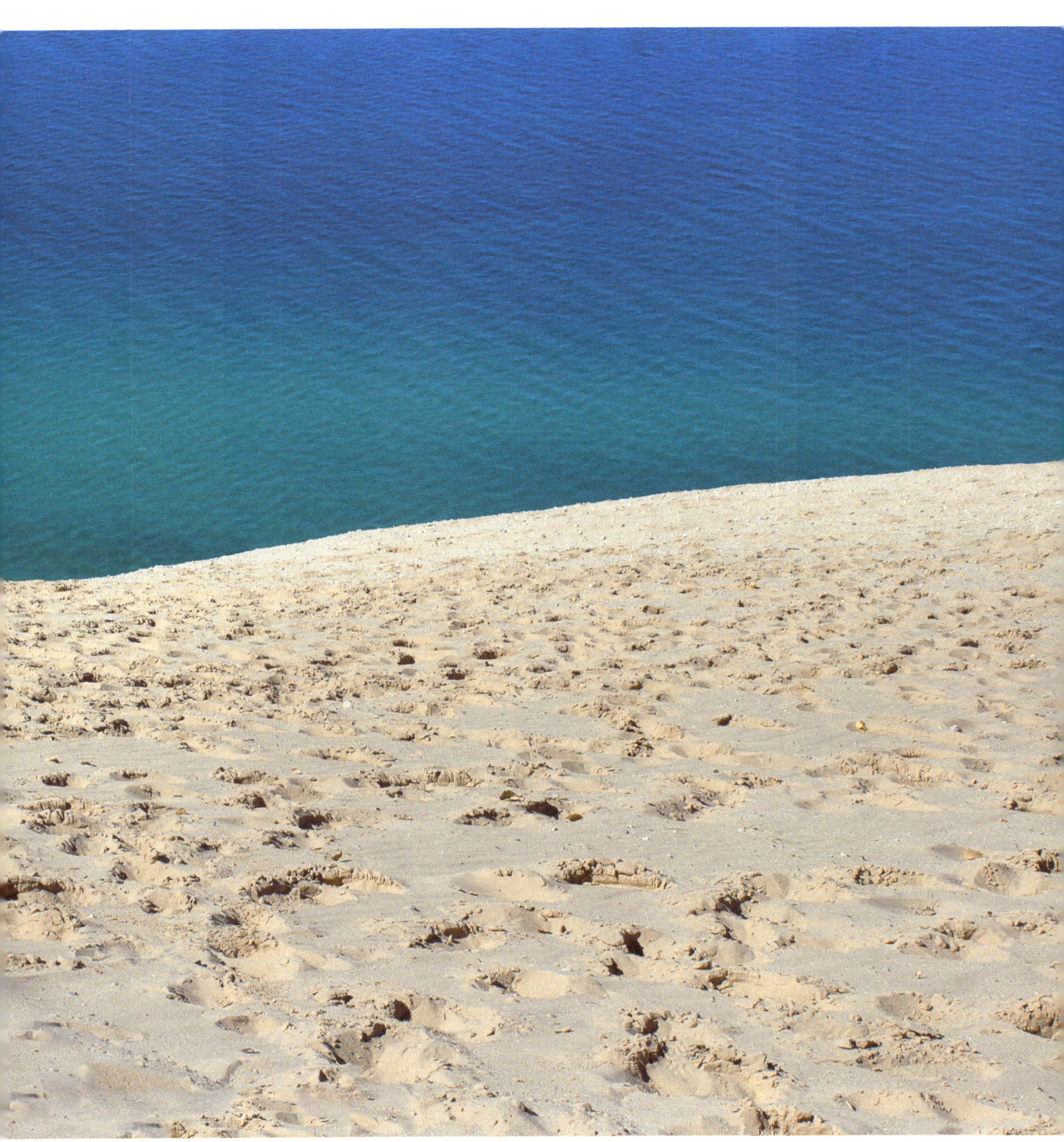

A lone hiker descends the dunes toward Lake Michigan.

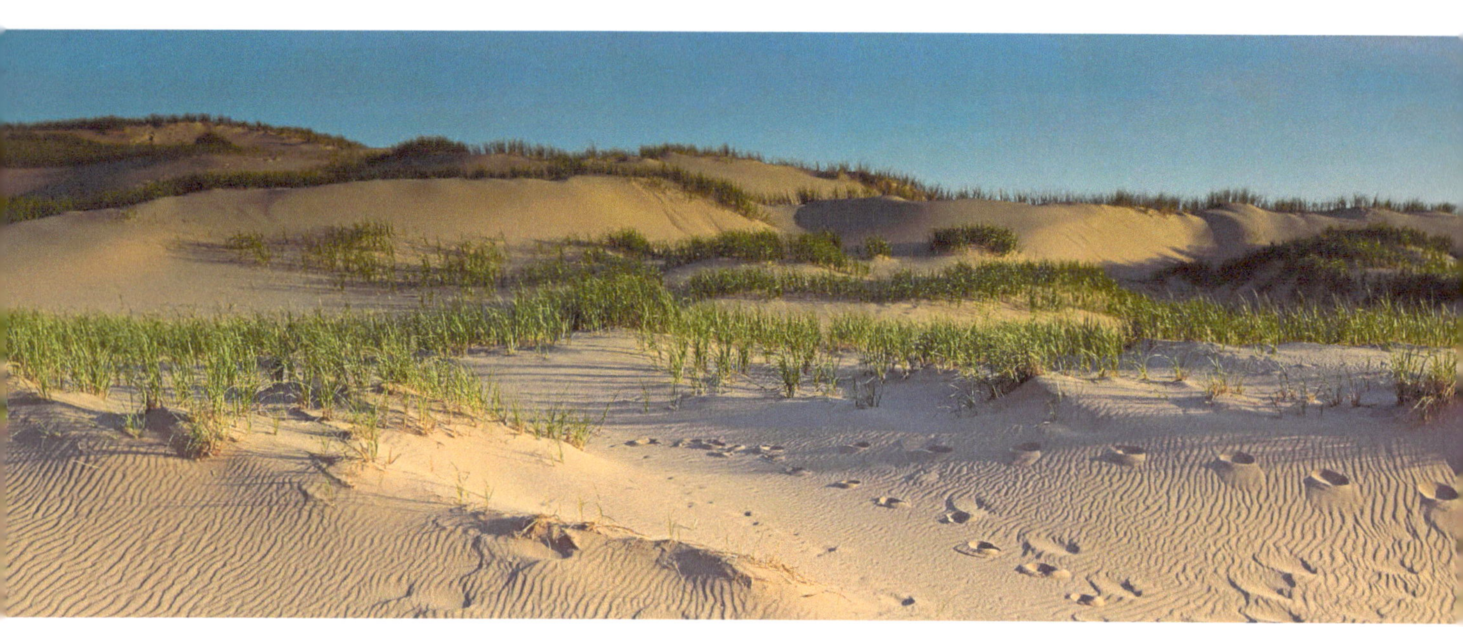

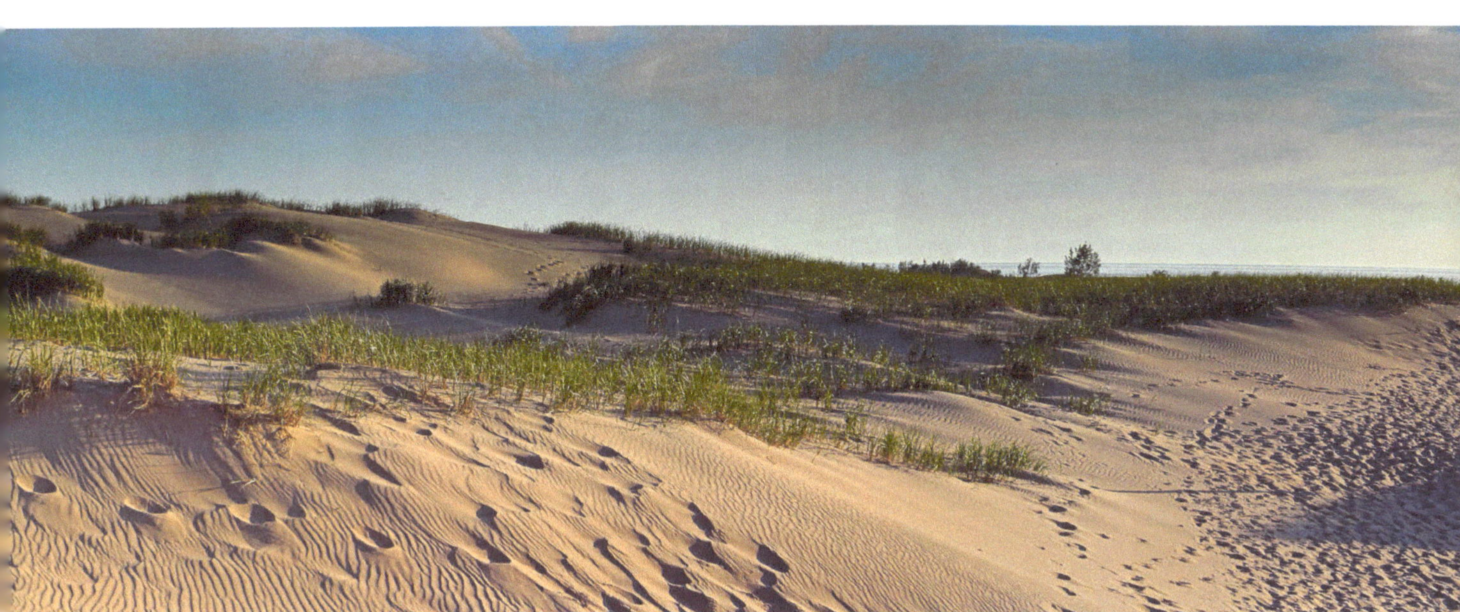

Panorama of the dunes before sunset. Sunrise and sunset are great times of day in the dunes, not only because of the beauty of the sun rising and setting over the dunes and the lake, but also because of the texture of the terrain that is brought out by the low angle of sunlight.

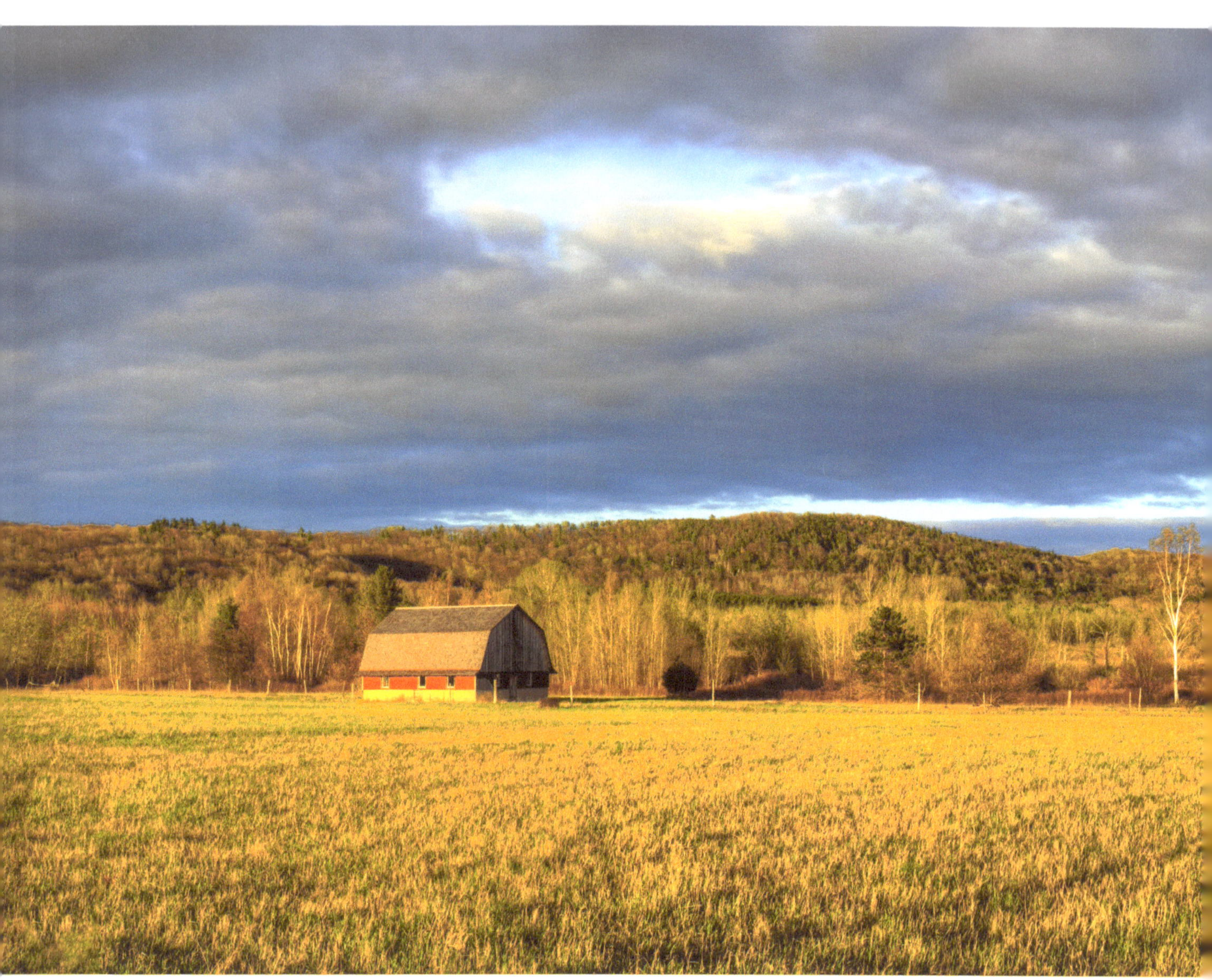

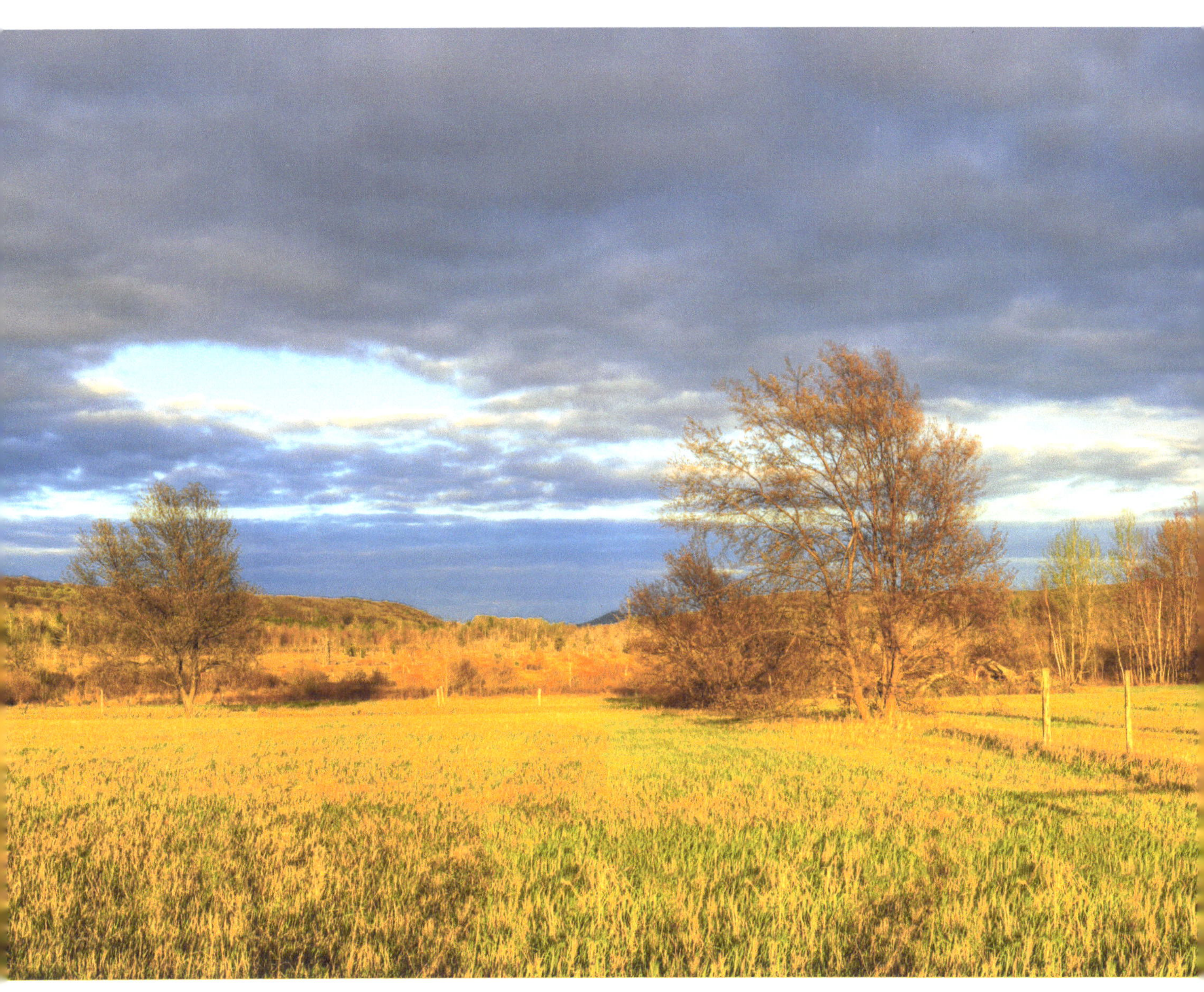

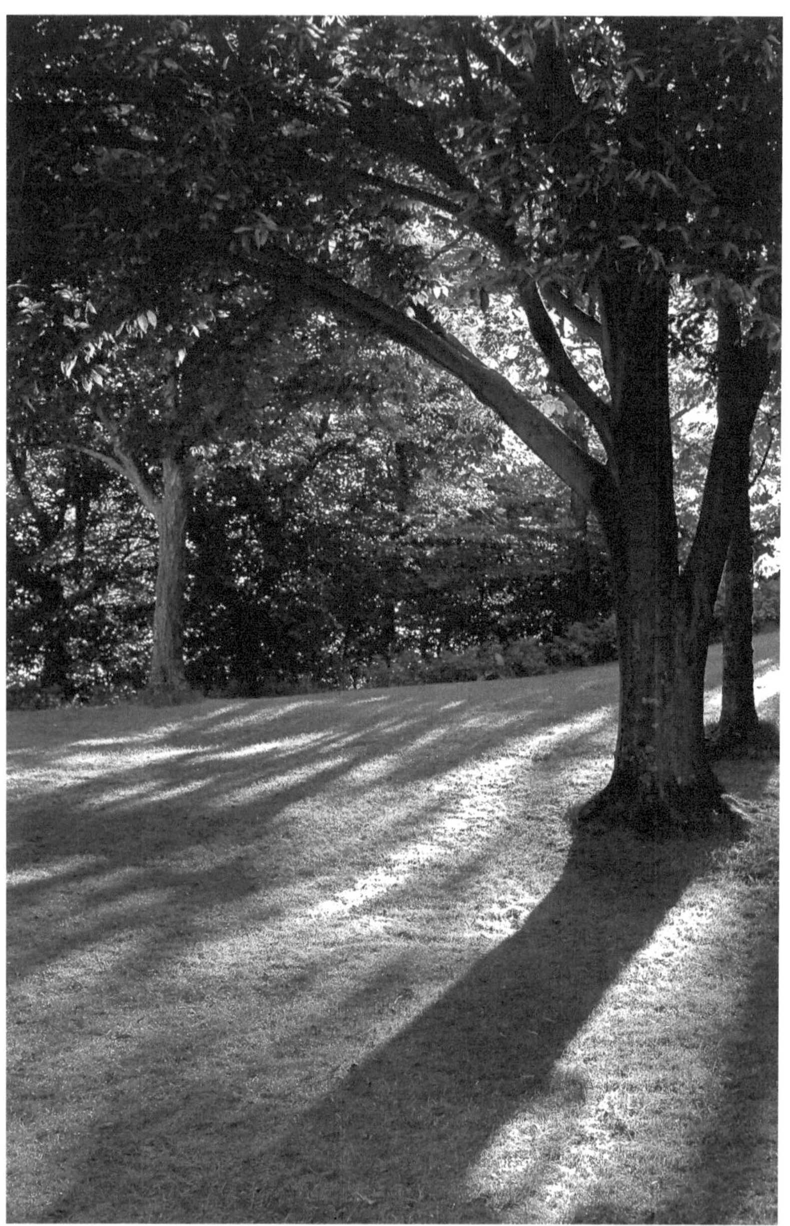

A maple tree along Pierce Stocking Scenic Drive.

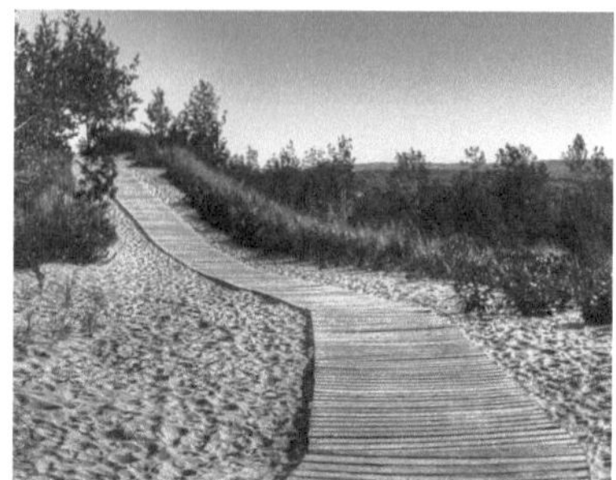

Boardwalk through the dunes.

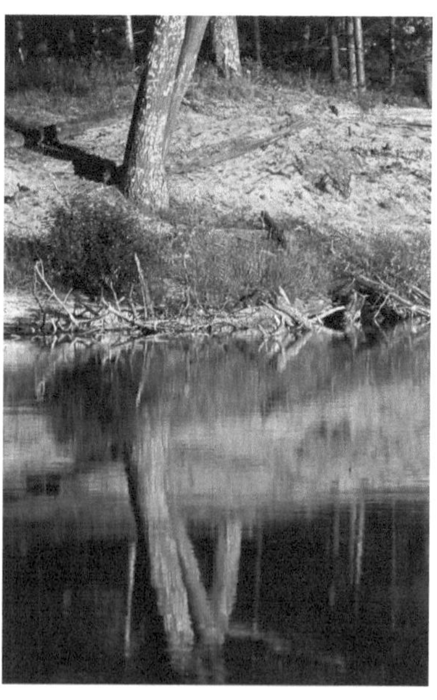

Reflection on the Platte River.

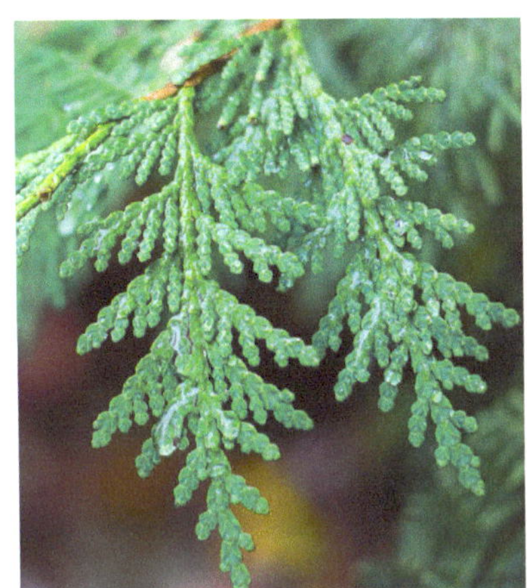

Rain drops on pines.

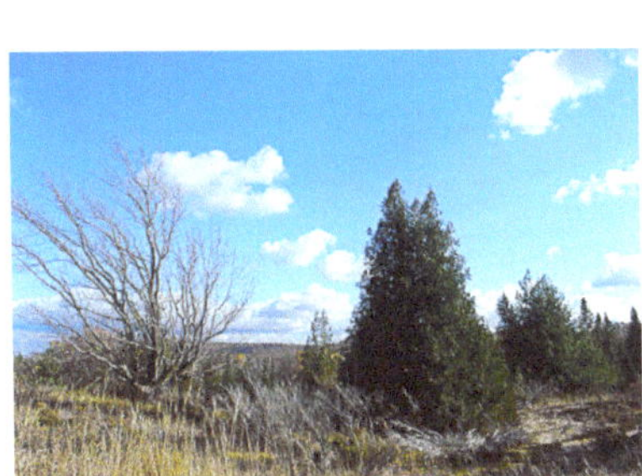

Late Fall along dune trails.

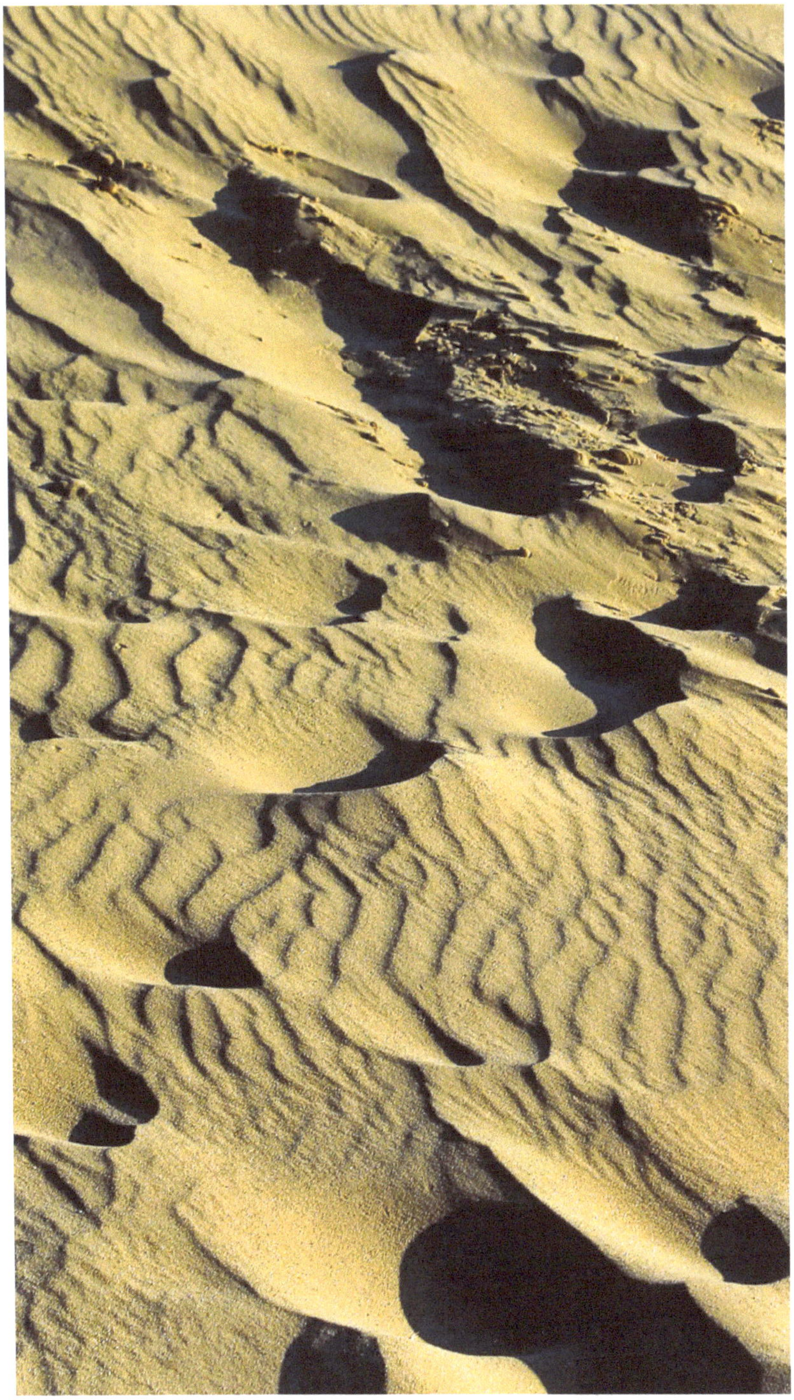

The wind-swept surface of the dunes.

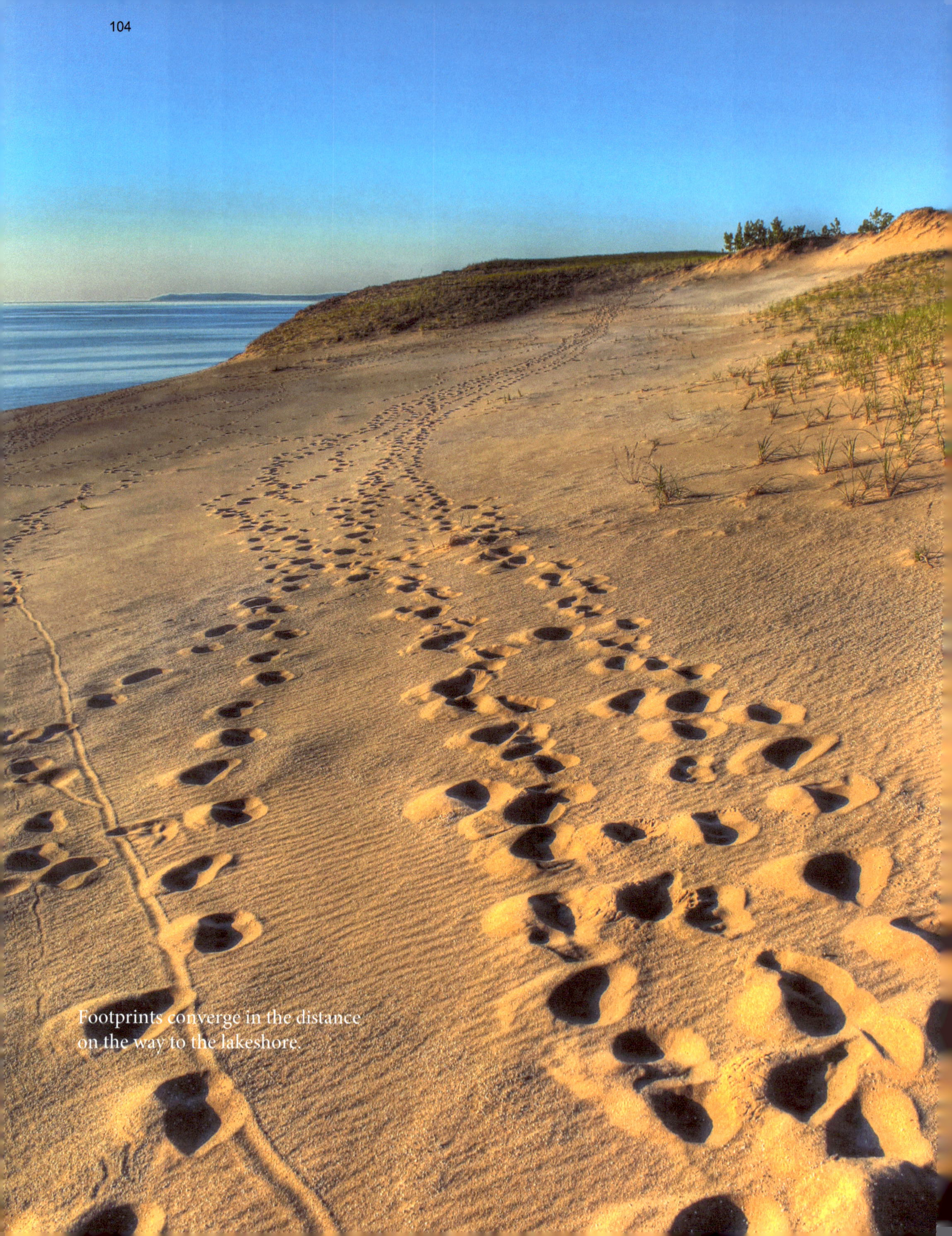

Footprints converge in the distance on the way to the lakeshore.

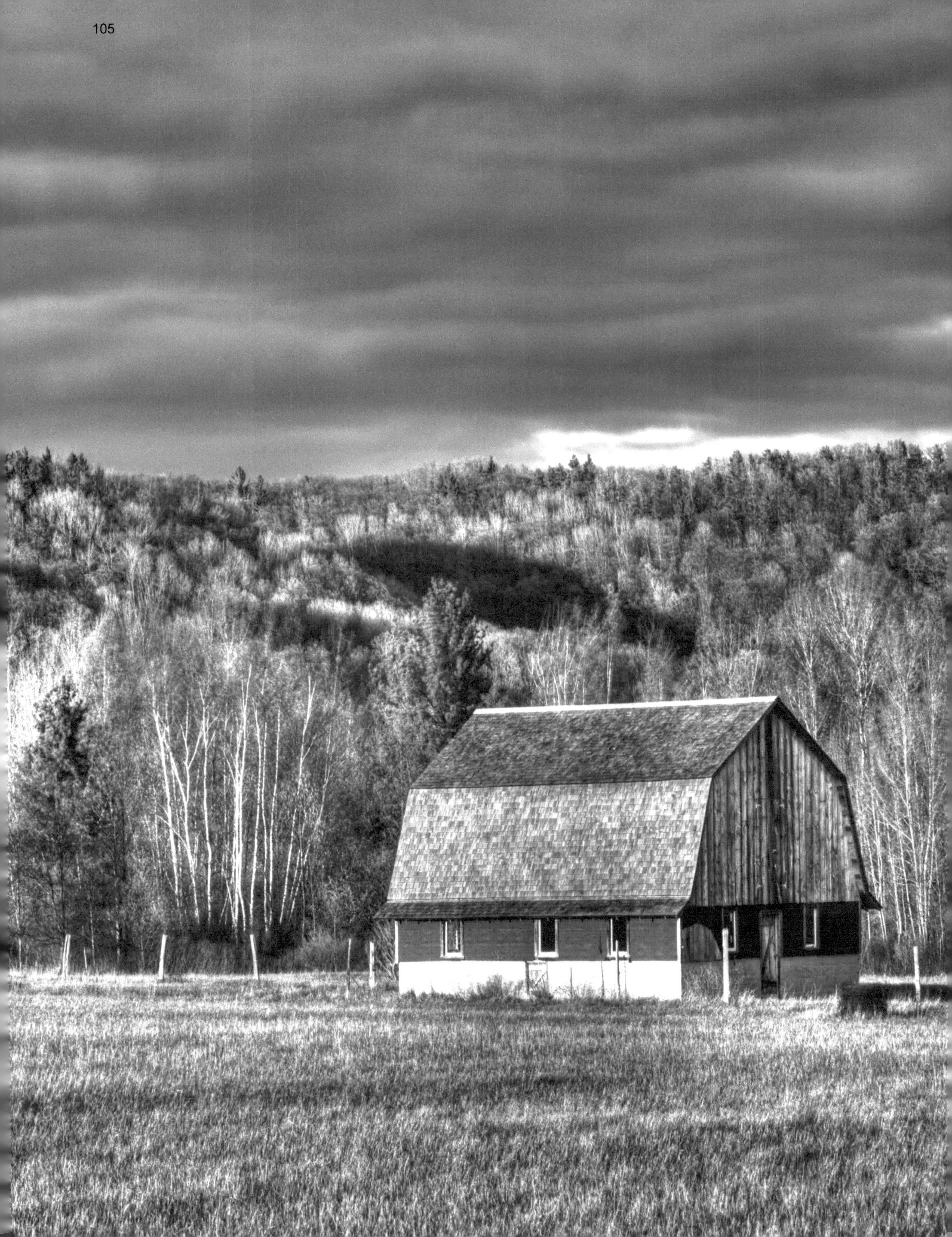

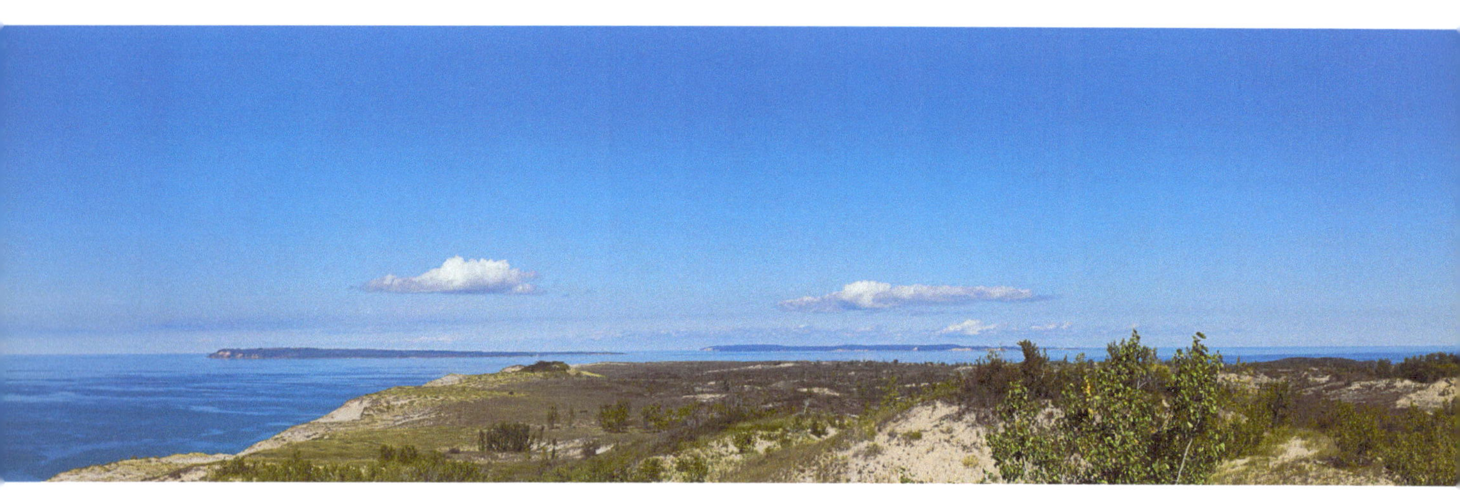

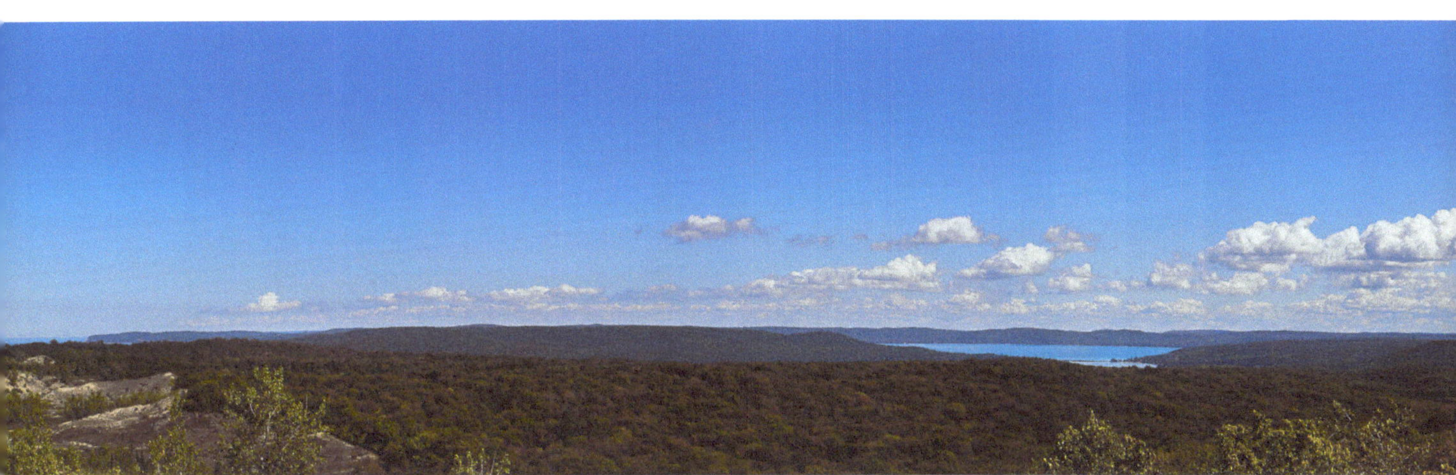

180 degree panorama from Glen Lake to South Manitou Island from Pierce Stocking Scenic Drive. The drive winds through native forest and along the shoreline for seven miles. It provides numerous 360 degree views of the dunes, Glen Lake, North Manitou Island, and South Manitou Island.

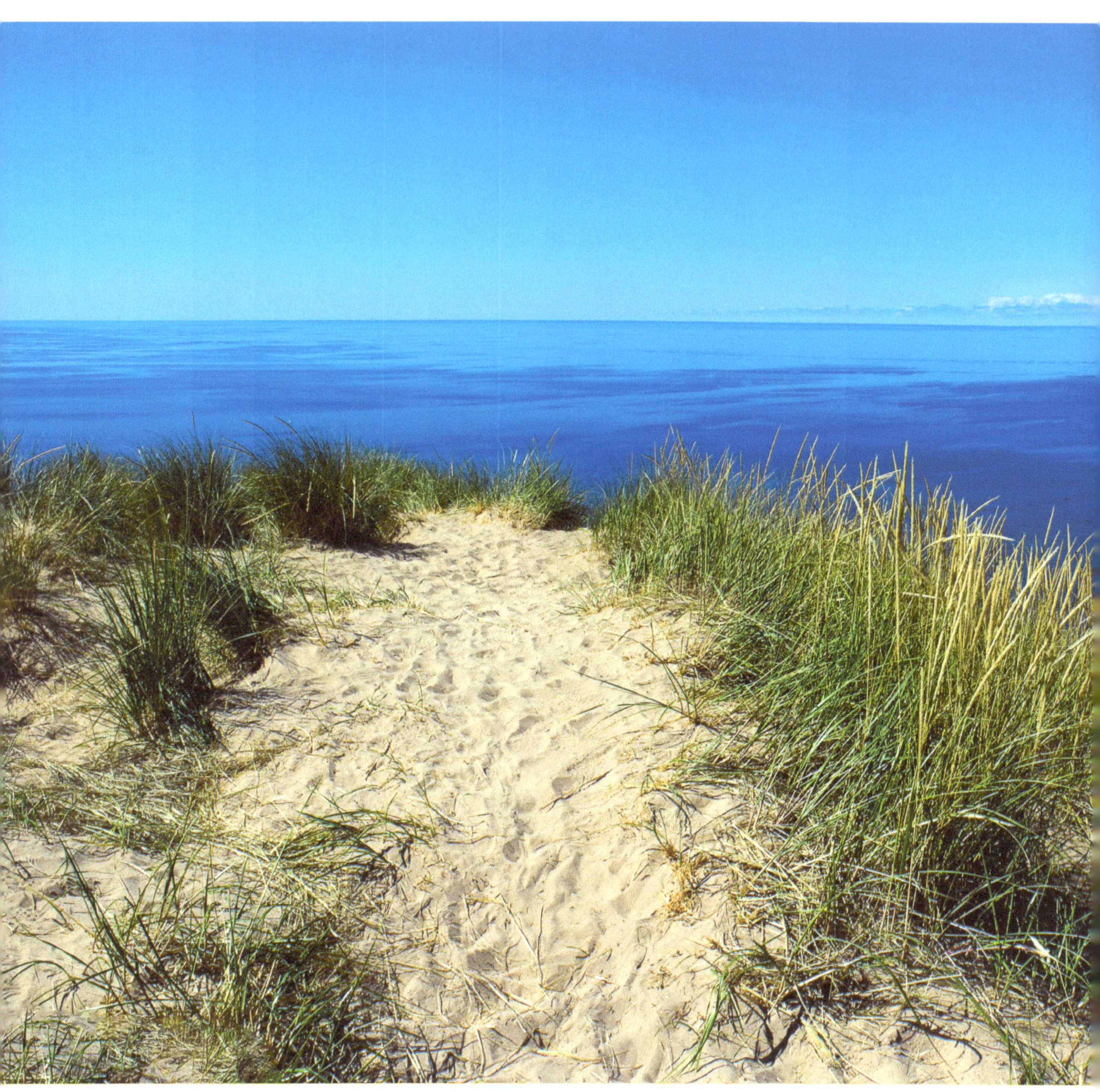

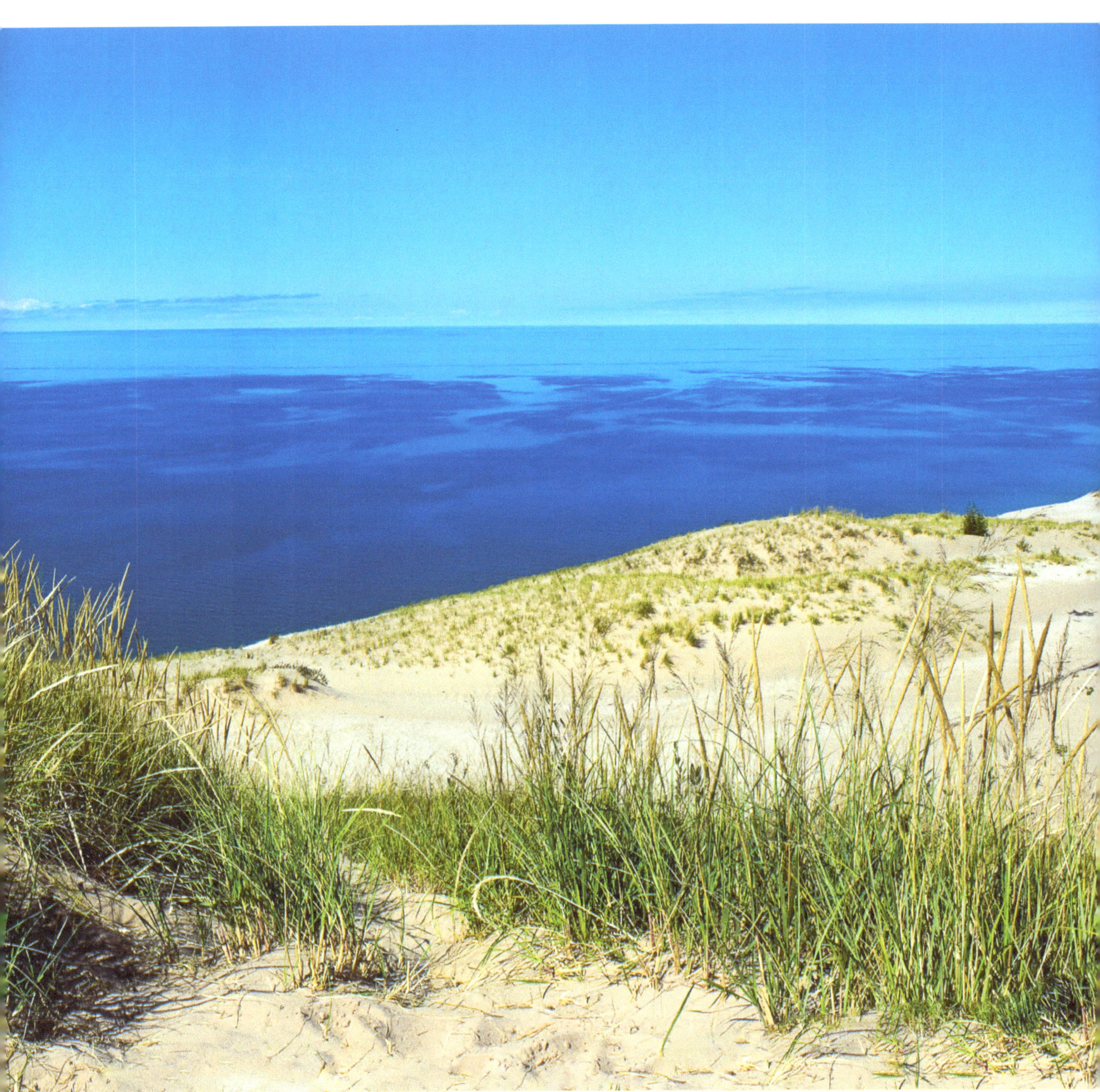

Bluffs overlooking Lake Michigan at Sleeping Bear Dunes.

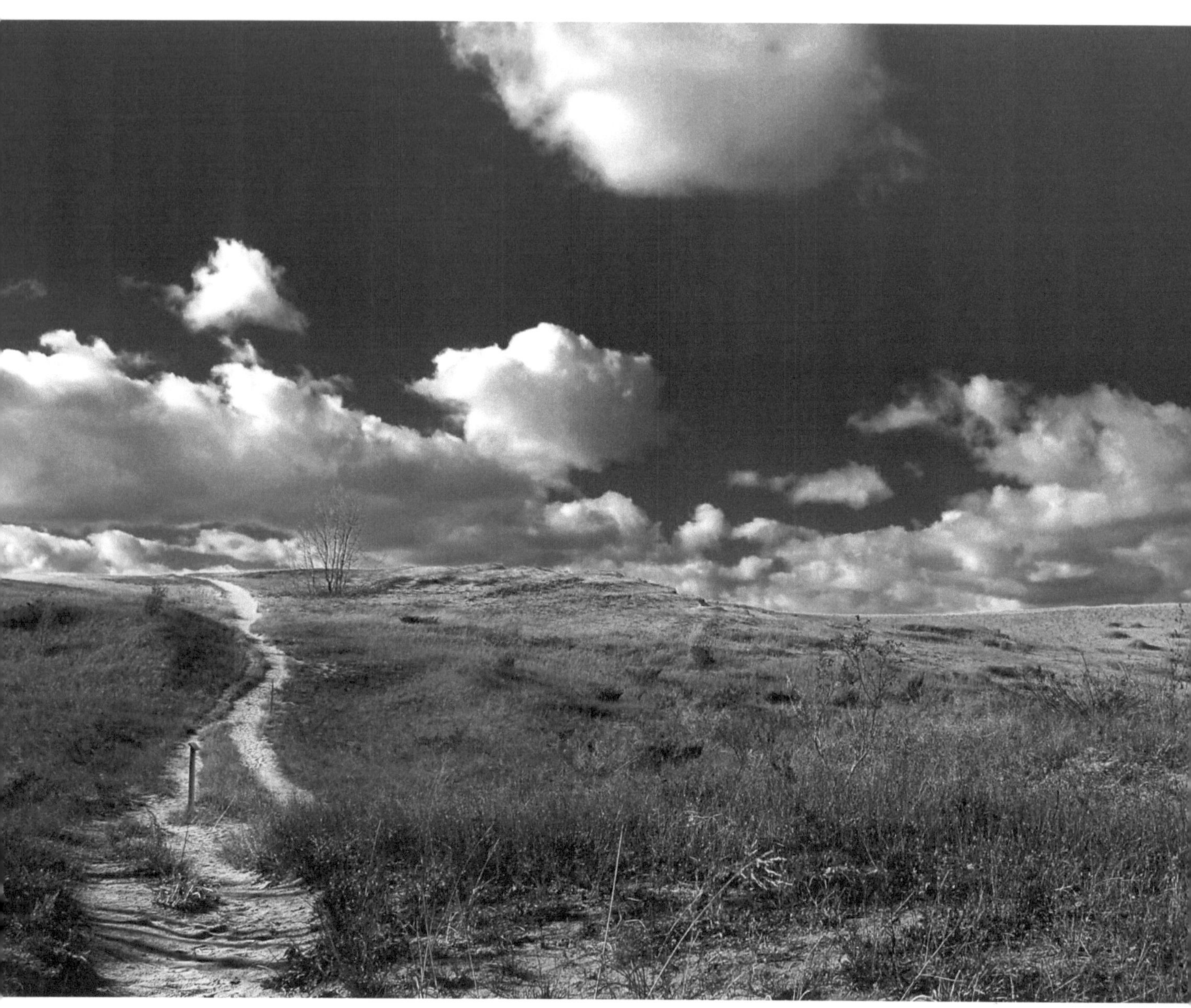

Sleeping Bear Dunes near Glen Haven.

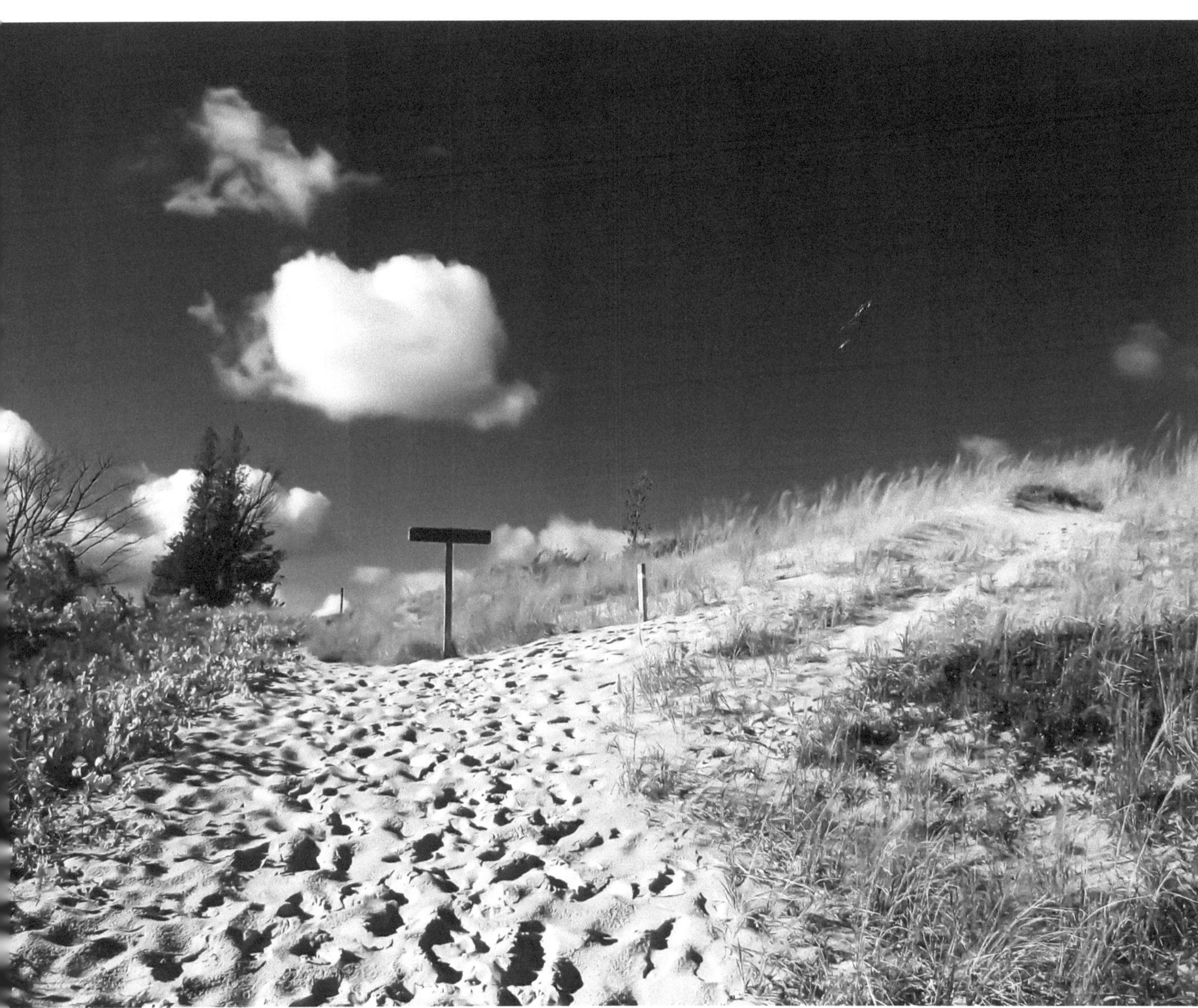

A path through the dunes in black and white.

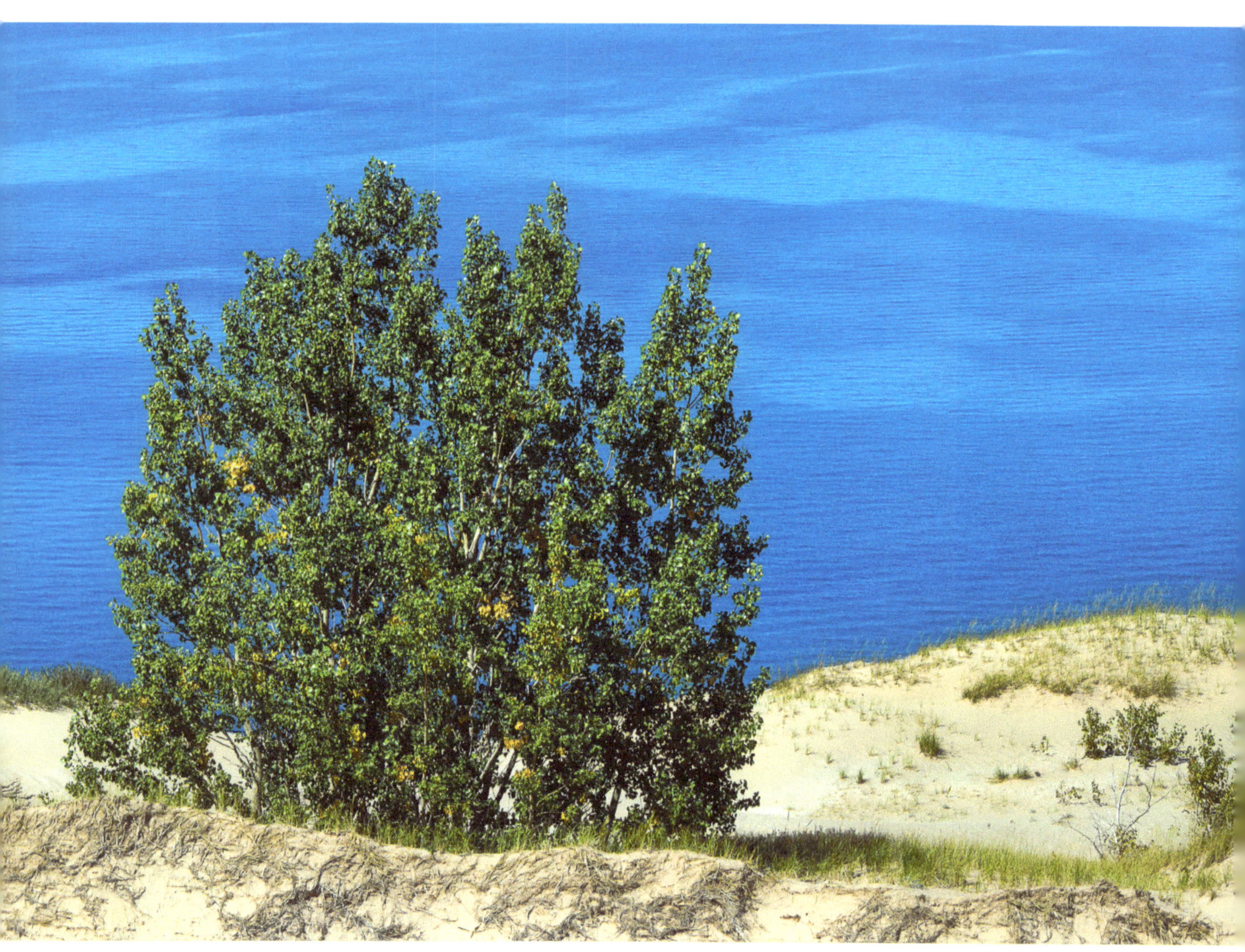

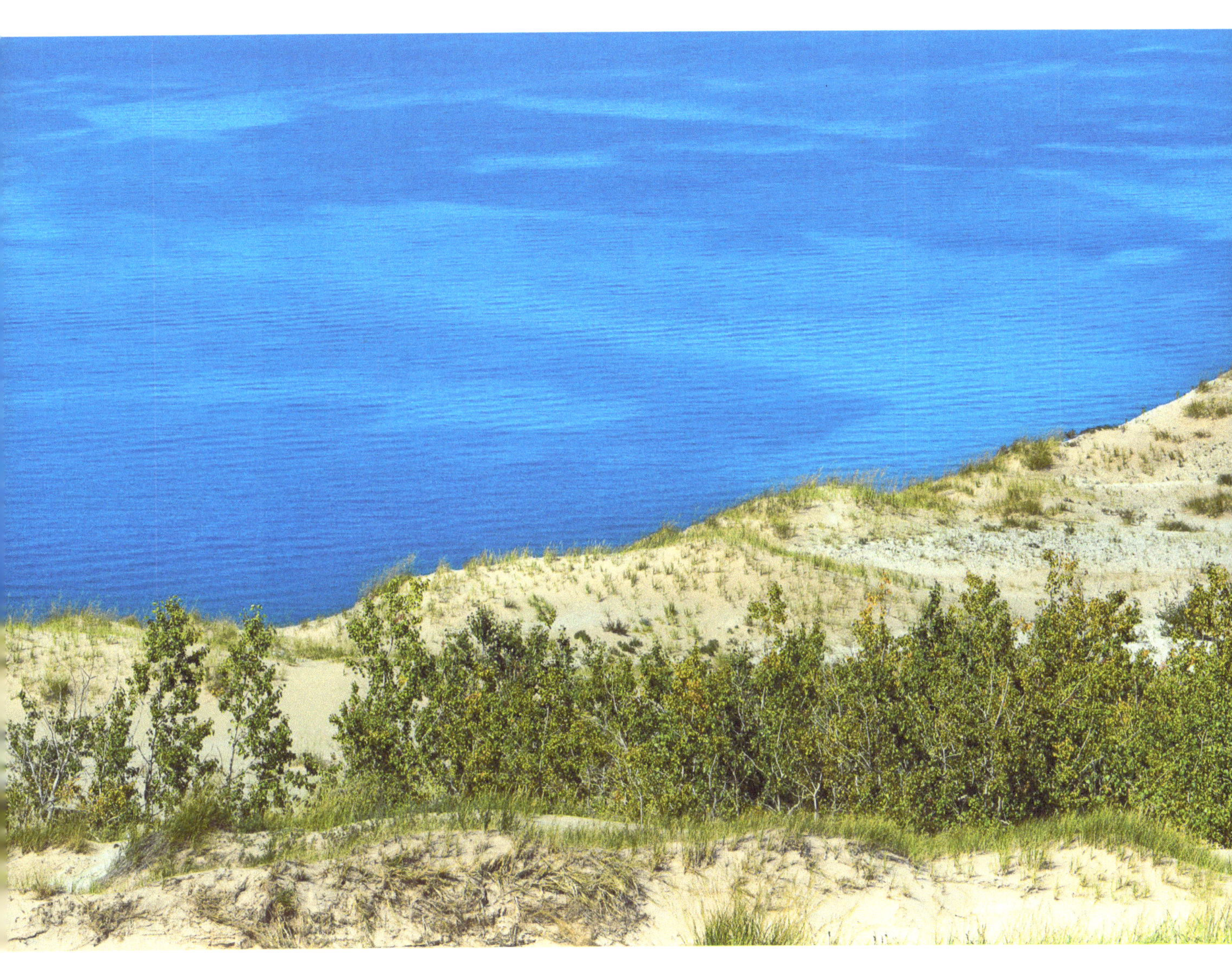

Trees along the dunes descending to Lake Michigan.

Empire

Empire is a small village within the Sleeping Bear Dunes National Lakeshore. It features numerous shops, restaurants, and cafes, with a small lighthouse and beach just a few blocks from downtown. The town sits between the Empire Bluffs to the south and the landmark Sleeping Bear Dunes Bluff to the north, and has a popular hiking trail leading to the top of Empire Bluffs. The Robert H. Manning Memorial Lighthouse, completed in 1990, is the second newest in Michigan.

Empire also has a unique military history. It was home to Empire Air Force Station during the cold war. This radar station was located atop surrounding bluffs and was responsible for protecting the northern United States from threats from the air.

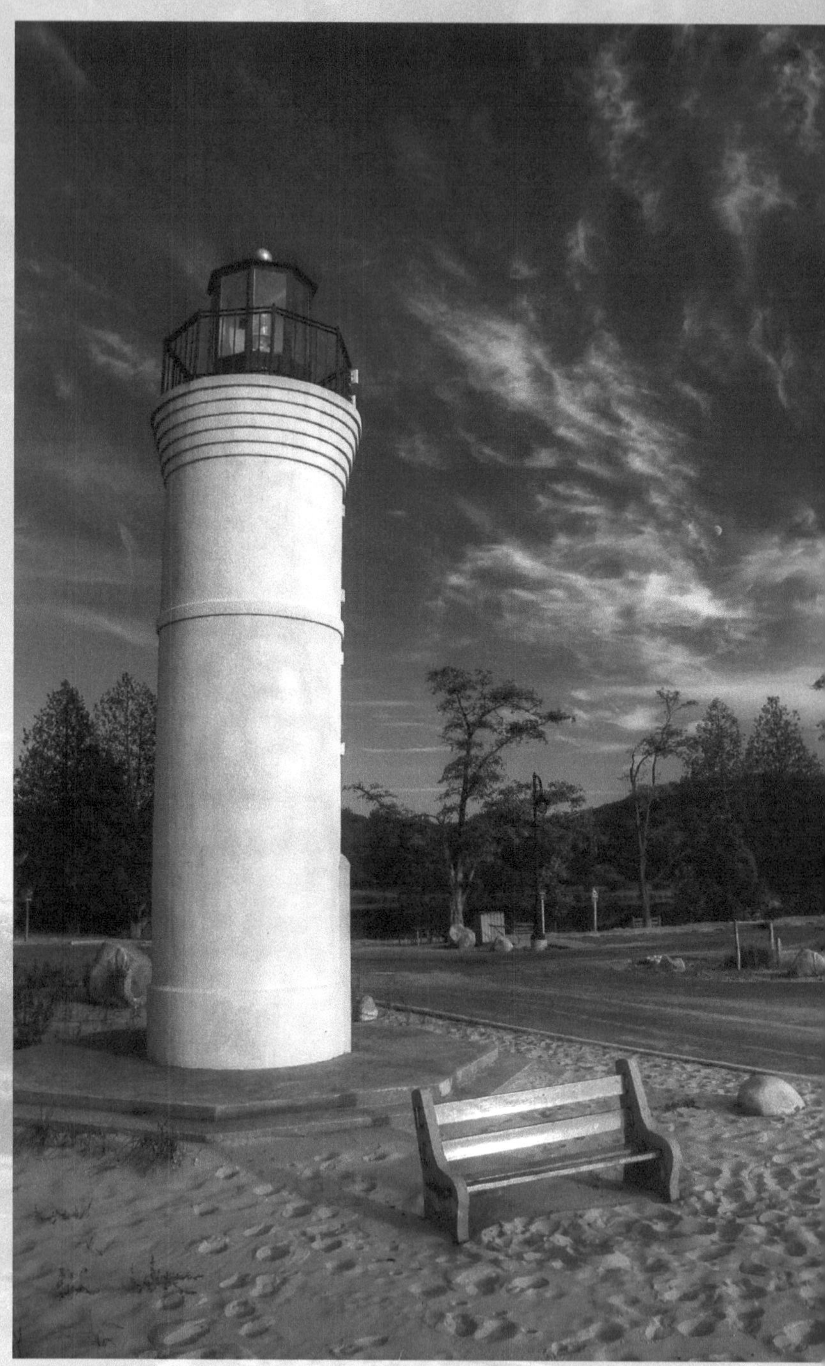

The Robert H. Manning Memorial Lighthouse.

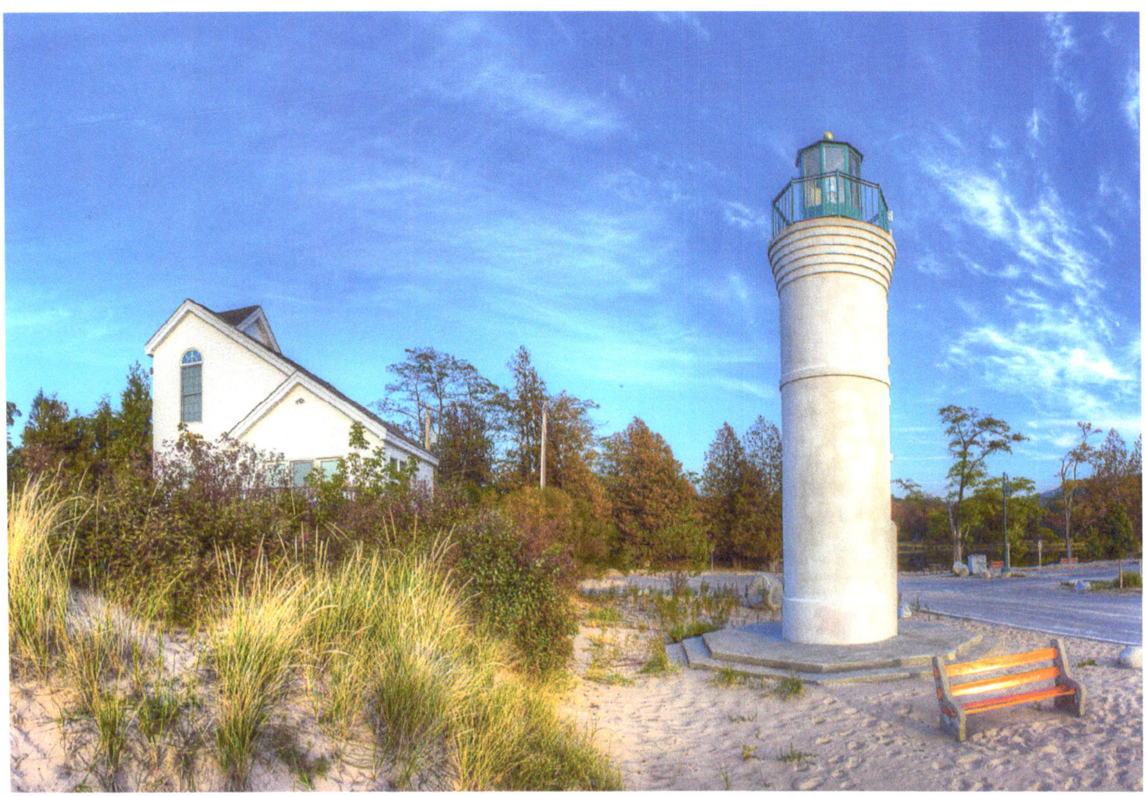

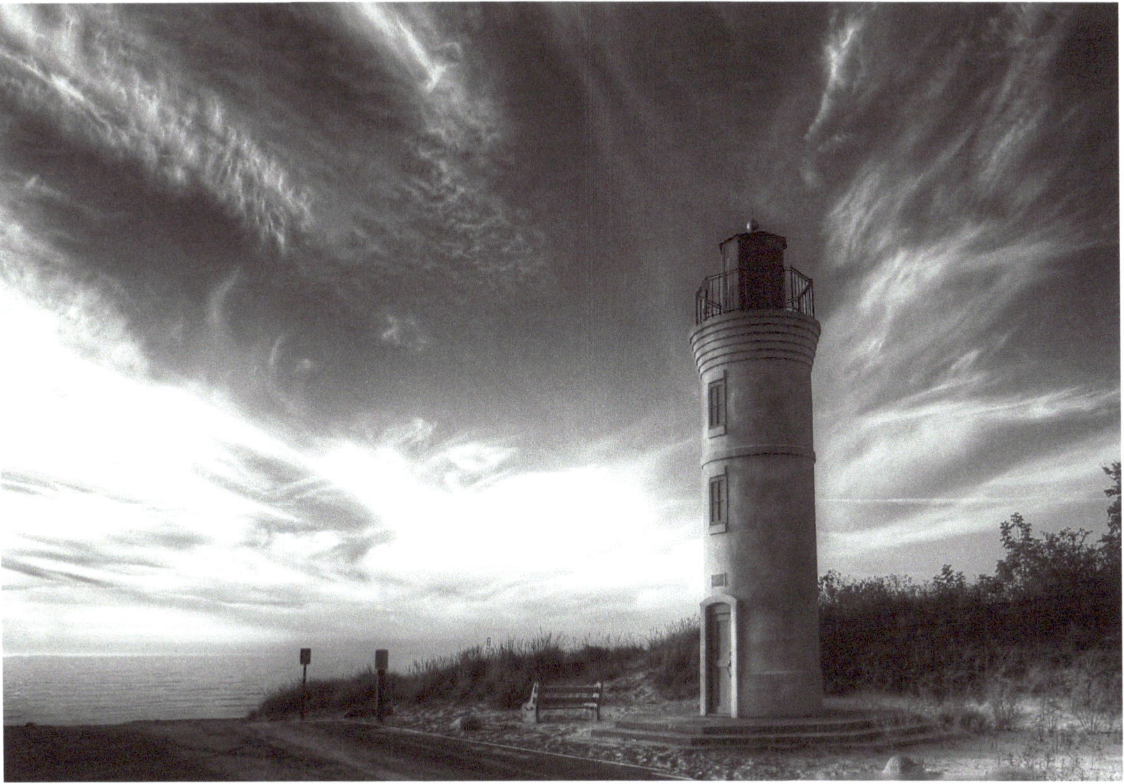

Lighthouse and beach at Empire.

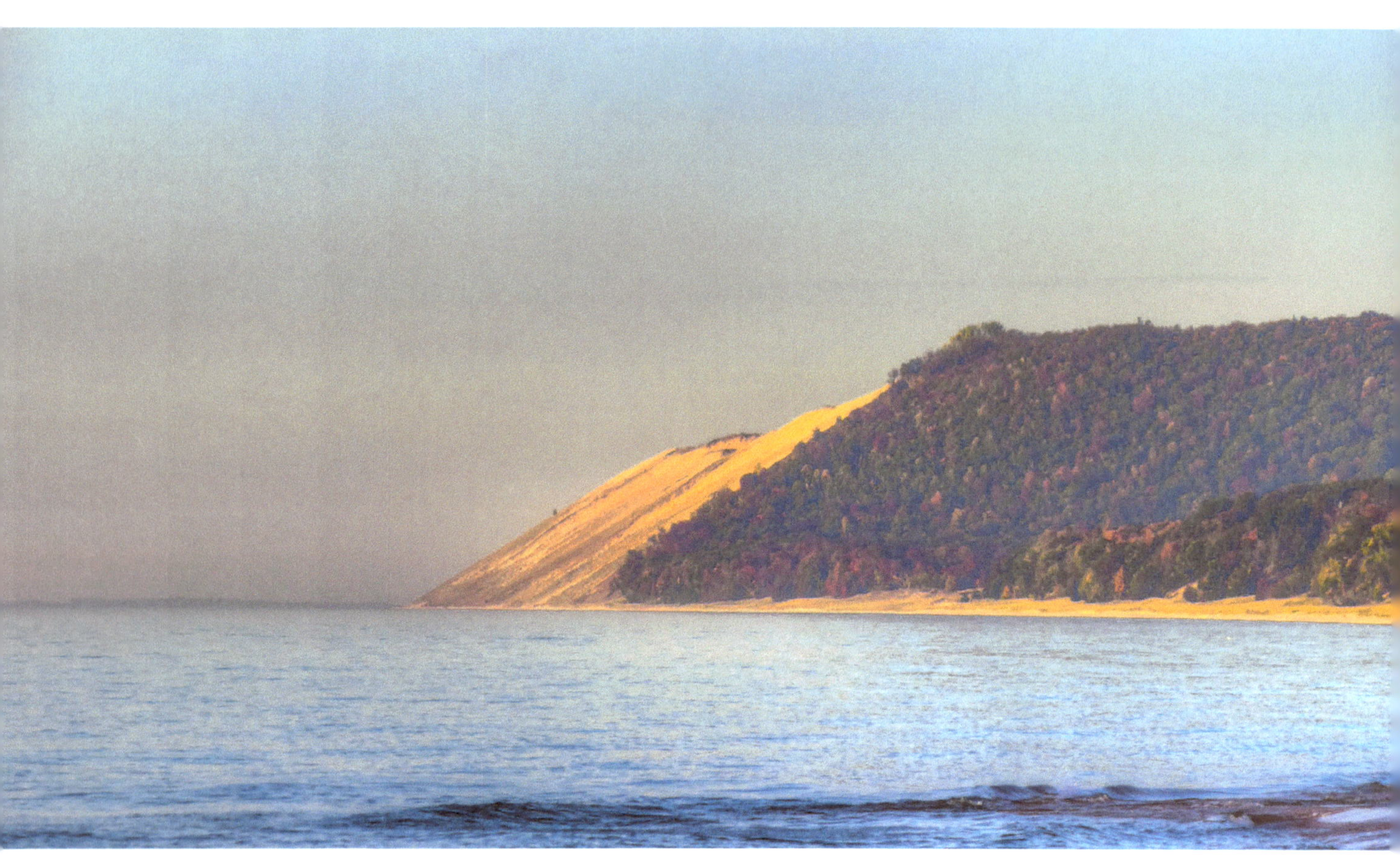

Beach at Empire with Sleeping Bear Dunes Bluff to the north. The beaches around Empire run for miles north and south, and provide great views of Empire Bluff to the south and Sleeping Bear Dunes Bluff to the north.

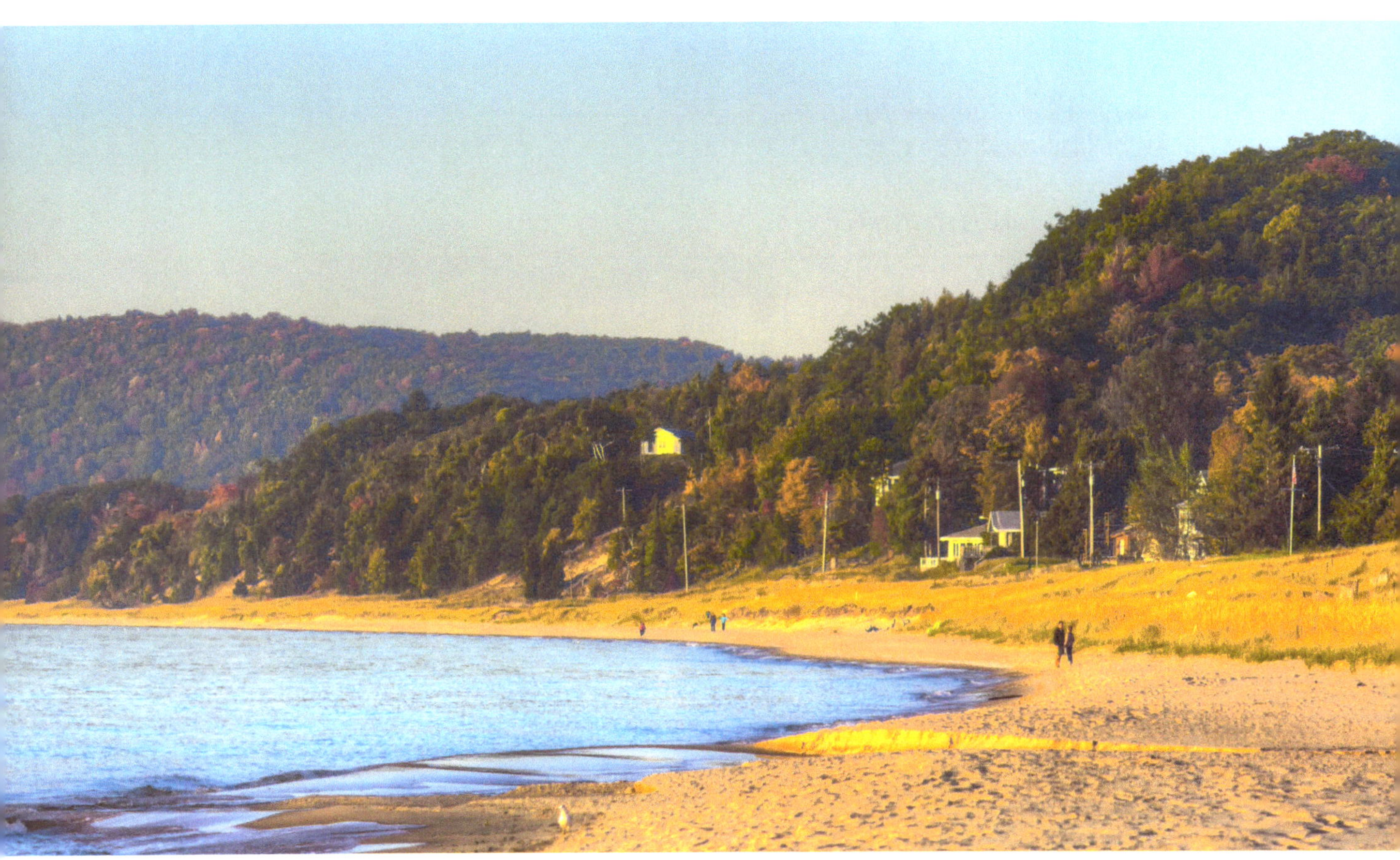

Glen Lake/Glen Arbor

Glen Lake and its surrounding town Glen Arbor sit along M-22 and the Sleeping Bear Dunes National Lakeshore. Glen Lake is surrounded by hills and dunes and can be seen from atop many dunes within the Sleeping Bear Dunes National Lakeshore. Downtown Glen Arbor sits on a small strip of land between Glen Lake and Lake Michigan. The town features numerous shops, restaurants, wine tasting rooms, and other attractions. Glen Arbor is the locus of summer tourist activity in the area, with hundreds of visitors walking the town's streets on summer days. The surrounding hills and dunes are easily accessible. Two of the most popular points from which to get an aerial view of Glen Lake are Inspiration Point just east of Glen Lake and Pierce Stocking Scenic Drive in Sleeping Bear Dunes just west of Glen Lake. Glen Lake is also home to one of the most prestigious resorts in Northern Michigan, The Homestead, just a few miles north of downtown.

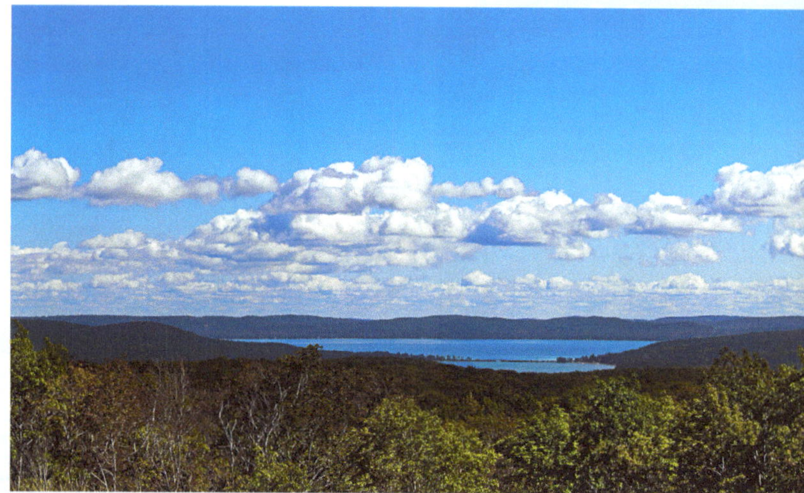

Glen Lake from Sleeping Bear Dunes.

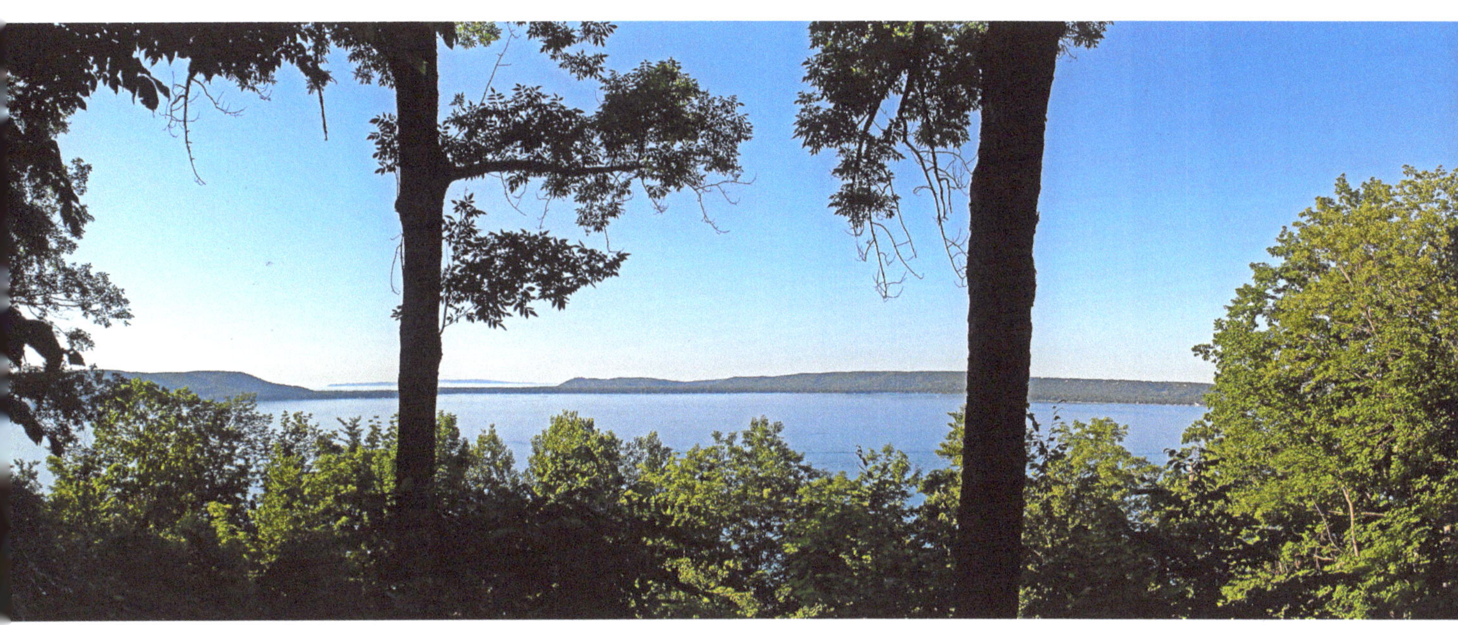

Glen Lake from Inspiration Point with South Manitou Island in the distance. Glen Lake is one of the most popular lakes in Northern Michigan for watersports. Nearby Glen Arbor is one of the most upscale and scenic towns in the area. Inspiration Point sits high above the lake in the surrounding hills off of MacFarlane Road a mile east of M-22.

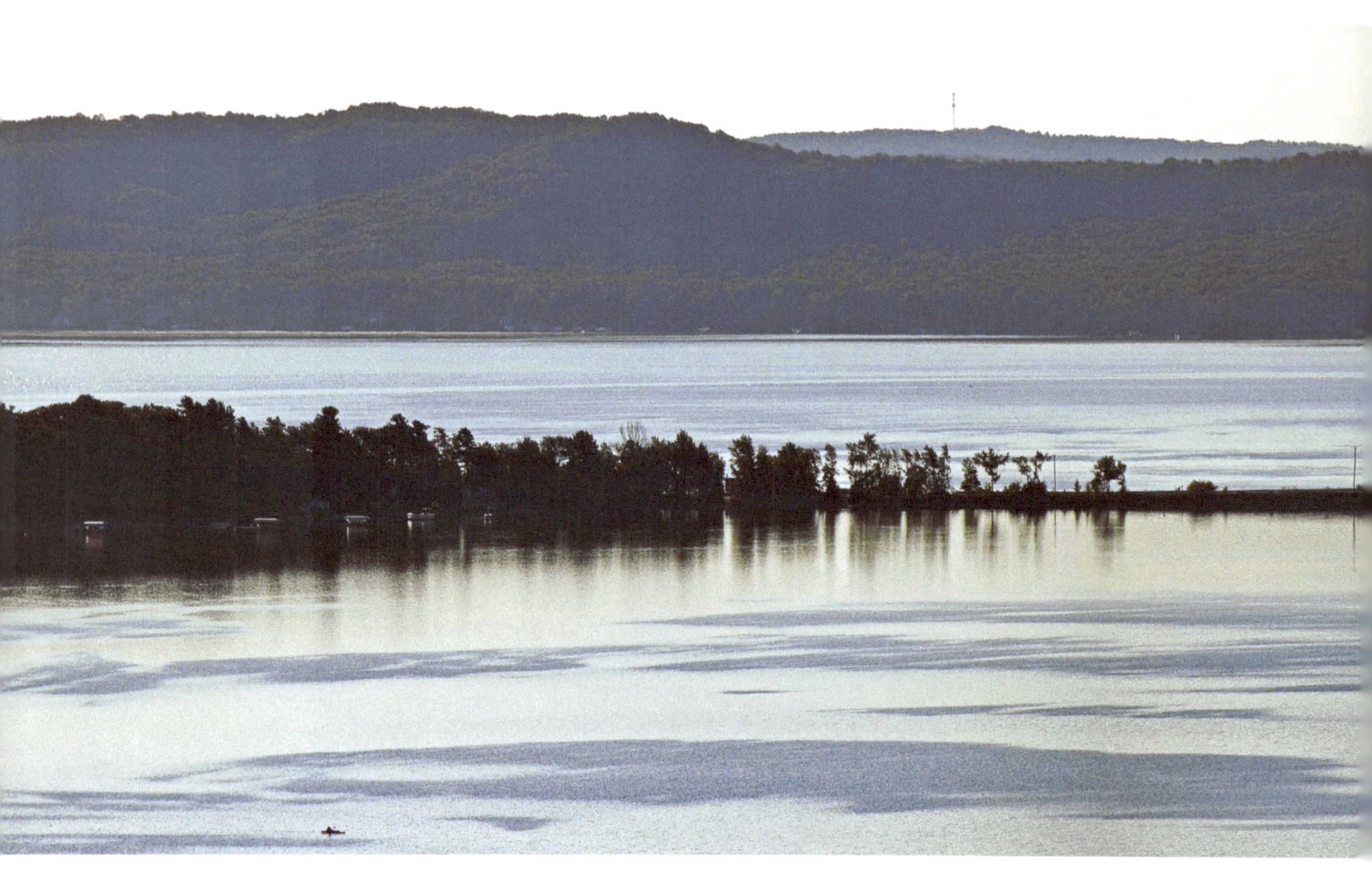

Glen Lake from Pierce Stocking Scenic Drive in early morning. M-22 Scenic Highway splits Glen Lake in two, running north and south through the middle of the lake en route to downtown Glen Arbor.

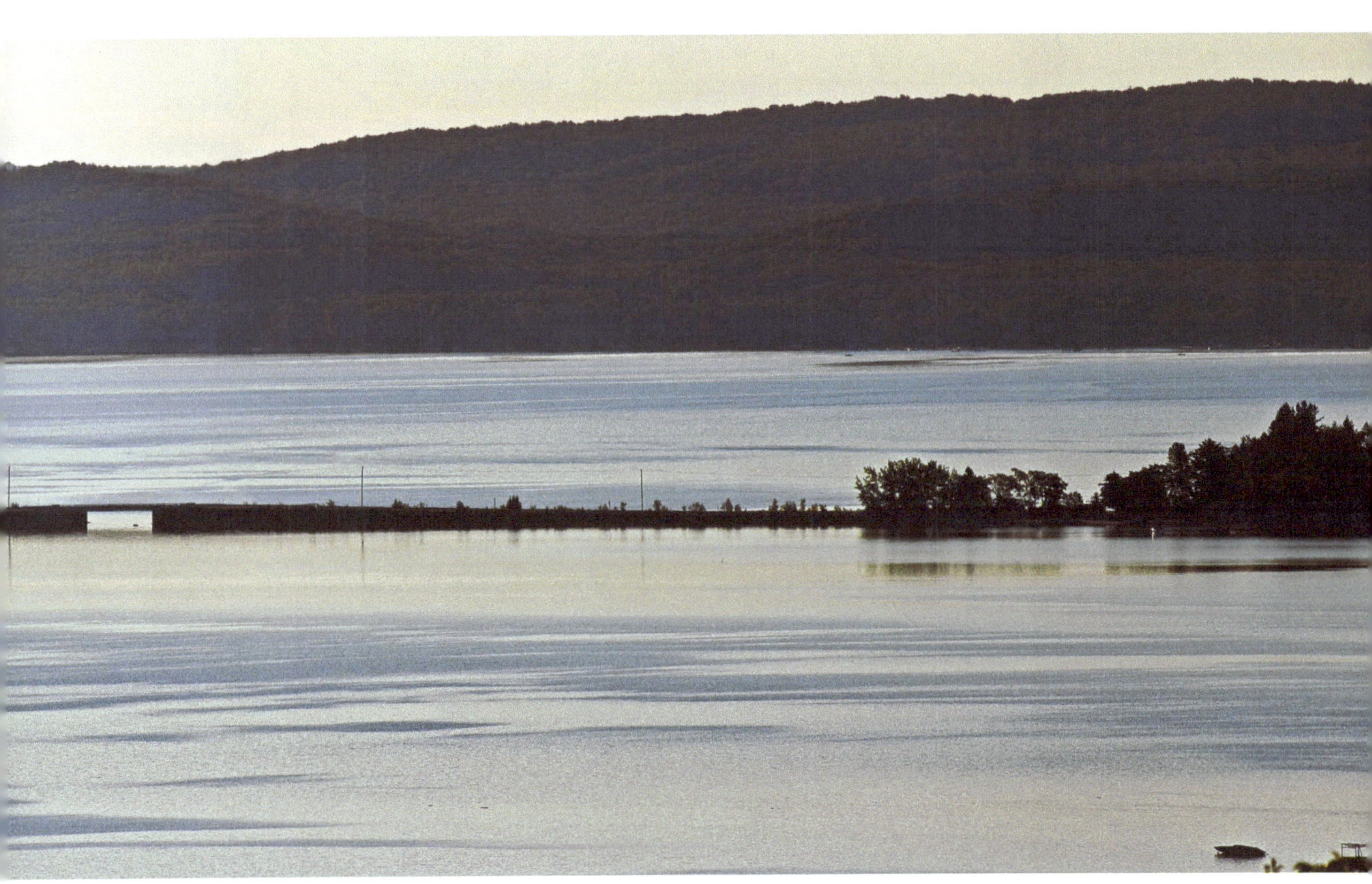

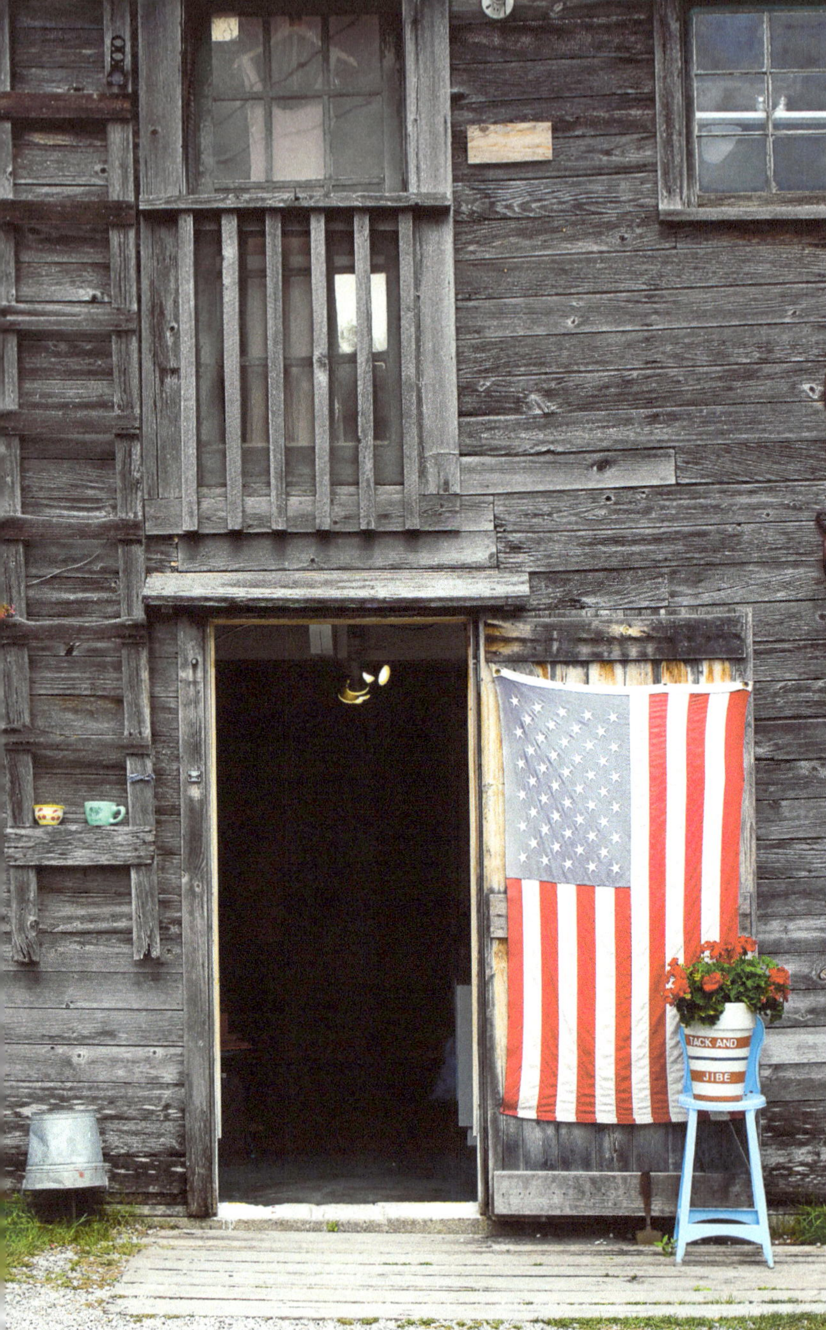

The entrance to a shop in Fishtown.

Leland

Leland sits on Lake Michigan approximately ten miles north of Sleeping Bear Dunes. Its main attraction is Fishtown, a group of weathered shanties along the Leland River between Lake Michigan and Lake Leelanau. Native Americans were drawn to the area because the river had a natural fish ladder where jumping Salmon could be easily caught. Leland maintained its character as a fishing village when white settlers moved in and built many of the shanties that still stand today. Many of the shanties still smoke fresh Great Lakes salmon and whitefish, but many others have given way to gift shops and boutiques. Outside of Fishtown, Leland has numerous galleries, restaurants, bed and breakfasts, and upscale resorts.

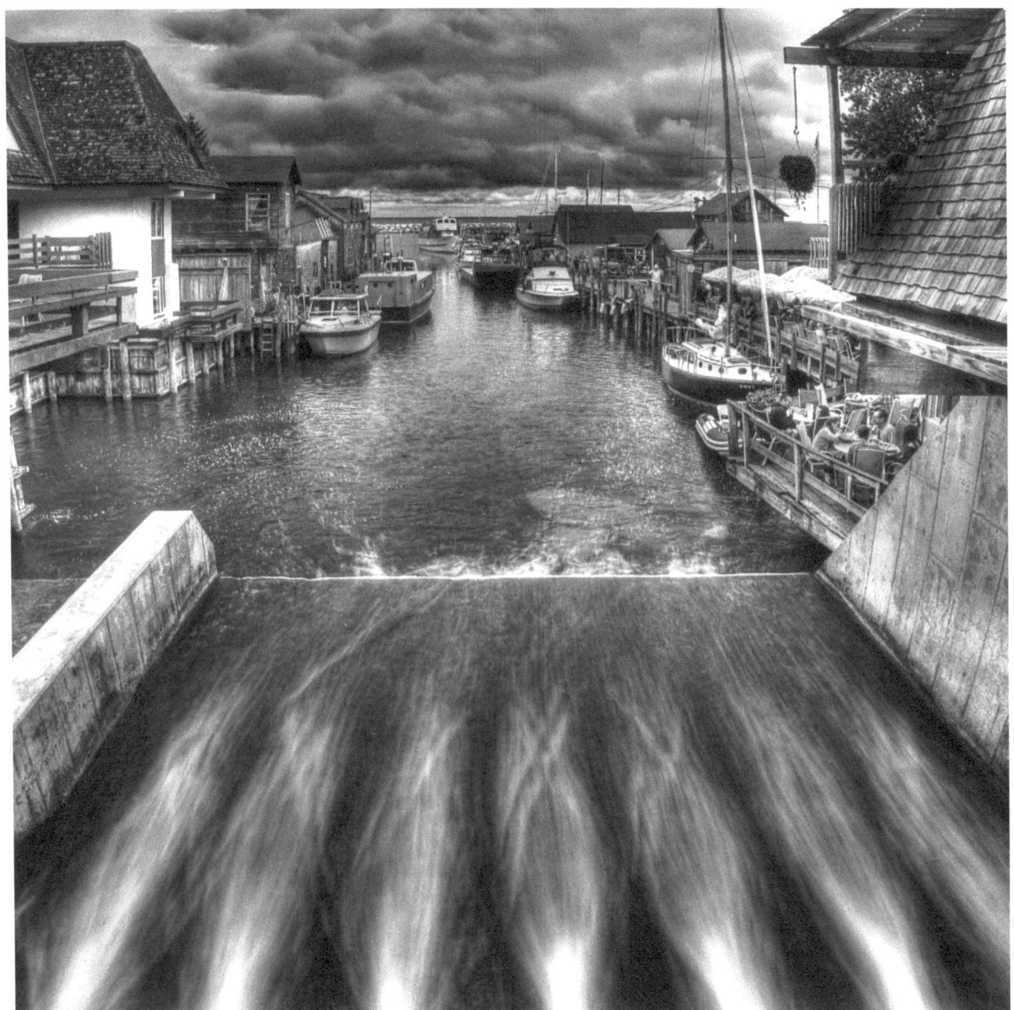

Water flows into the channel in Fishtown. The dam in Leland was built in the 1800s. It raised the surrounding water level twelve feet and transformed three small lakes into what is now Lake Leelanau.

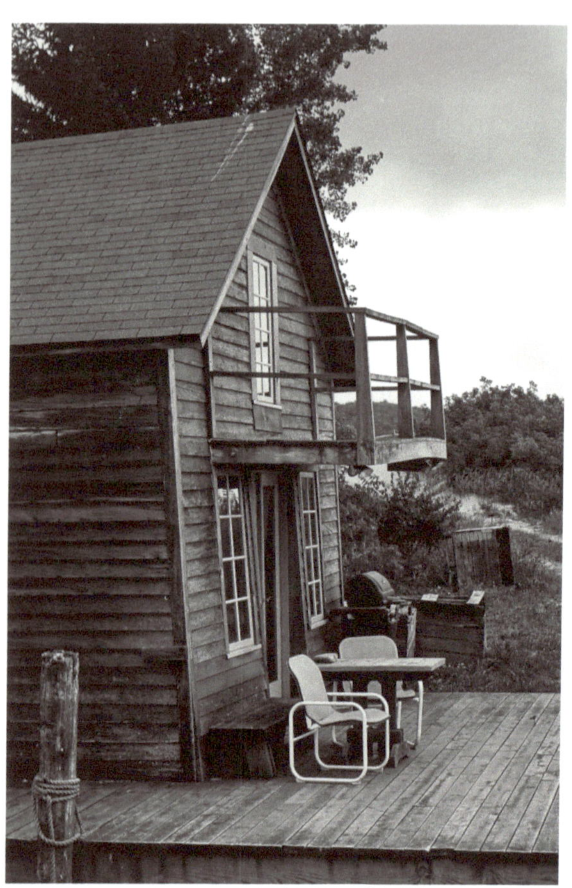

A shanty in Fishtown.

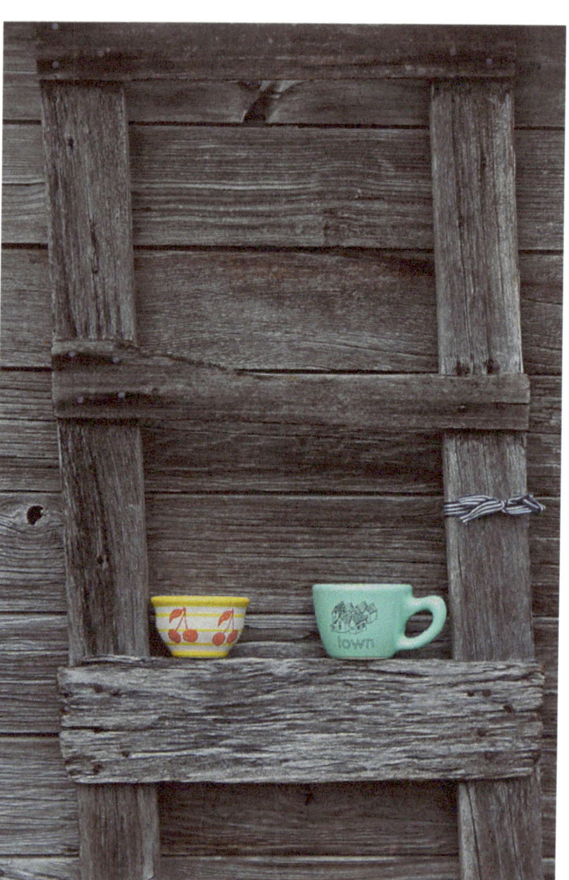

Two cups on the wall of a Fishtown gift shop.

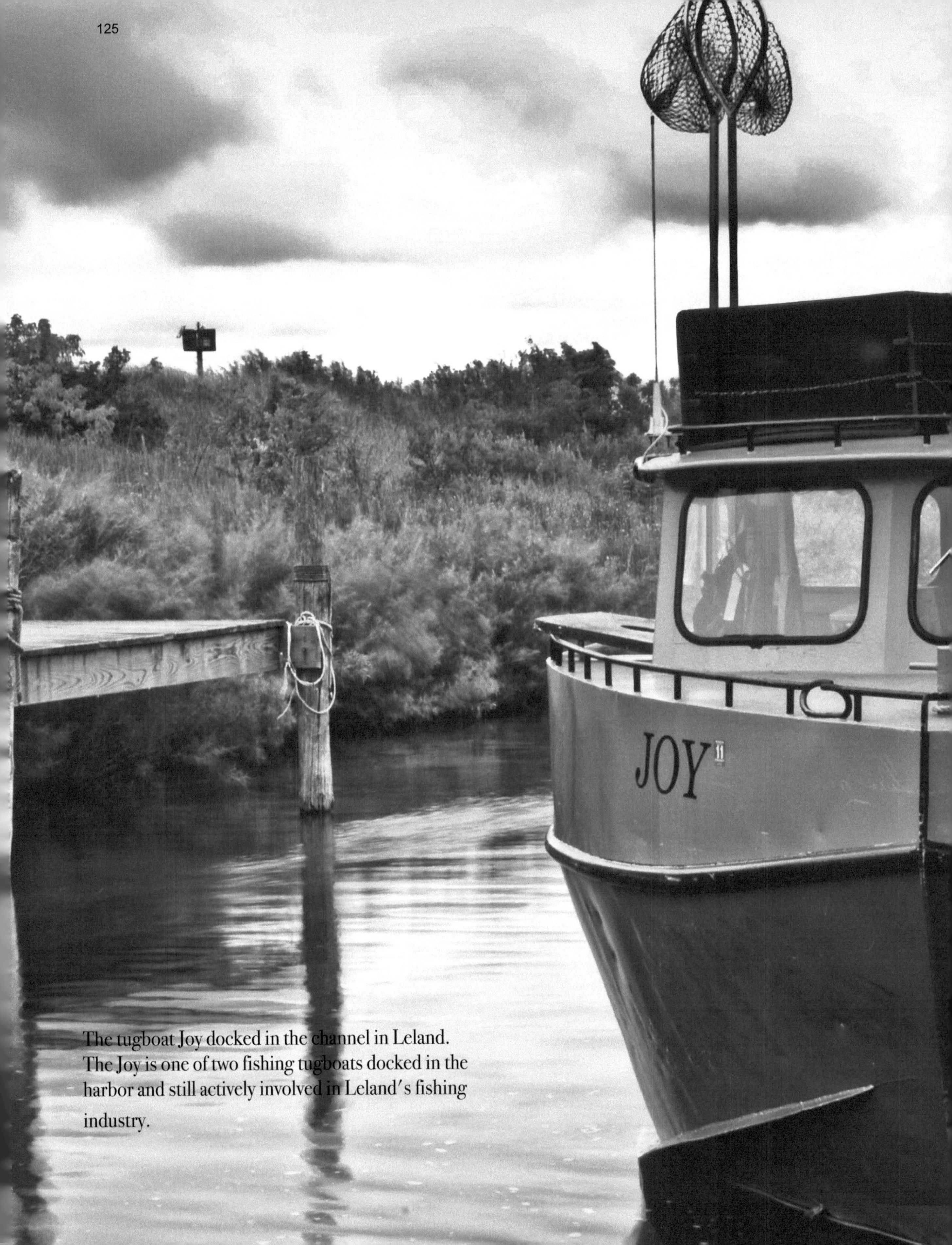

The tugboat Joy docked in the channel in Leland. The Joy is one of two fishing tugboats docked in the harbor and still actively involved in Leland's fishing industry.

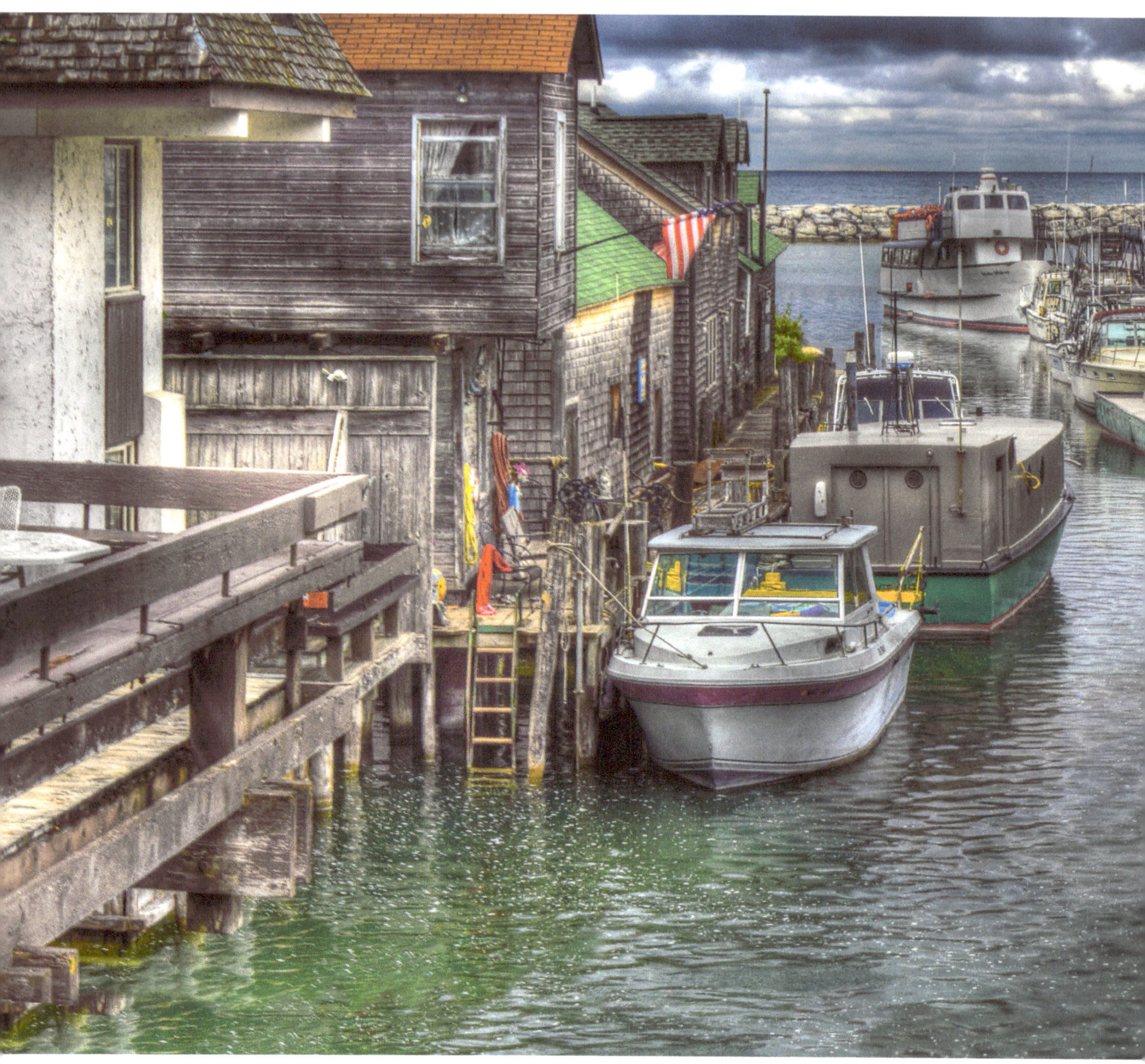

Panorama of Fishtown. Fishing charters and Leland's two fishing tugboats, The Joy and the Janice Sue, are docked in the harbor. The ferry to North Manitou and South Manitou Islands is docked in the distance. Numerous tourists line the north side of the harbor, exploring Leland's shops.

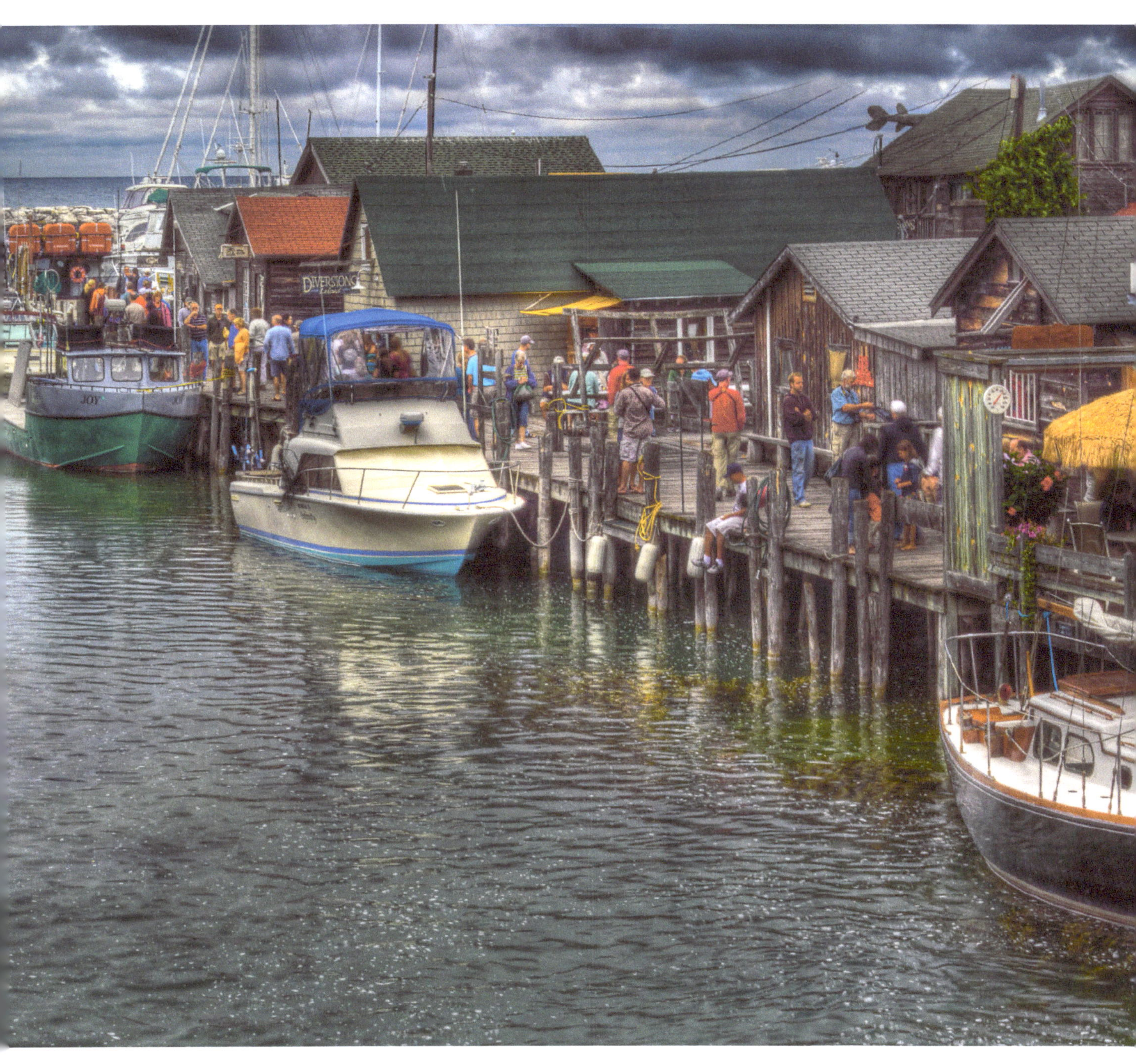

DIVERSIONS
JOY

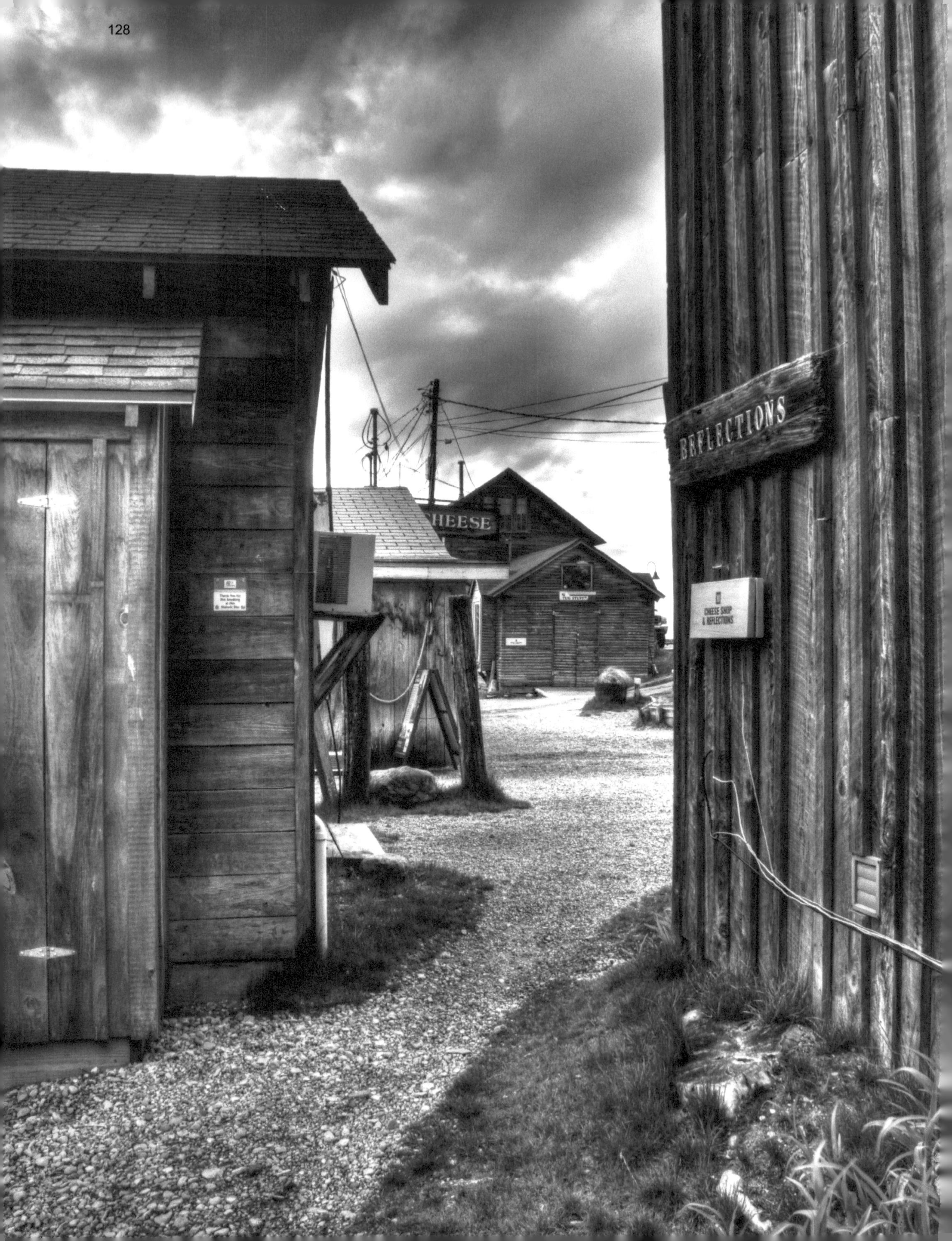
CHEESE
REFLECTIONS
CHEESE SHOP
& REFLECTIONS

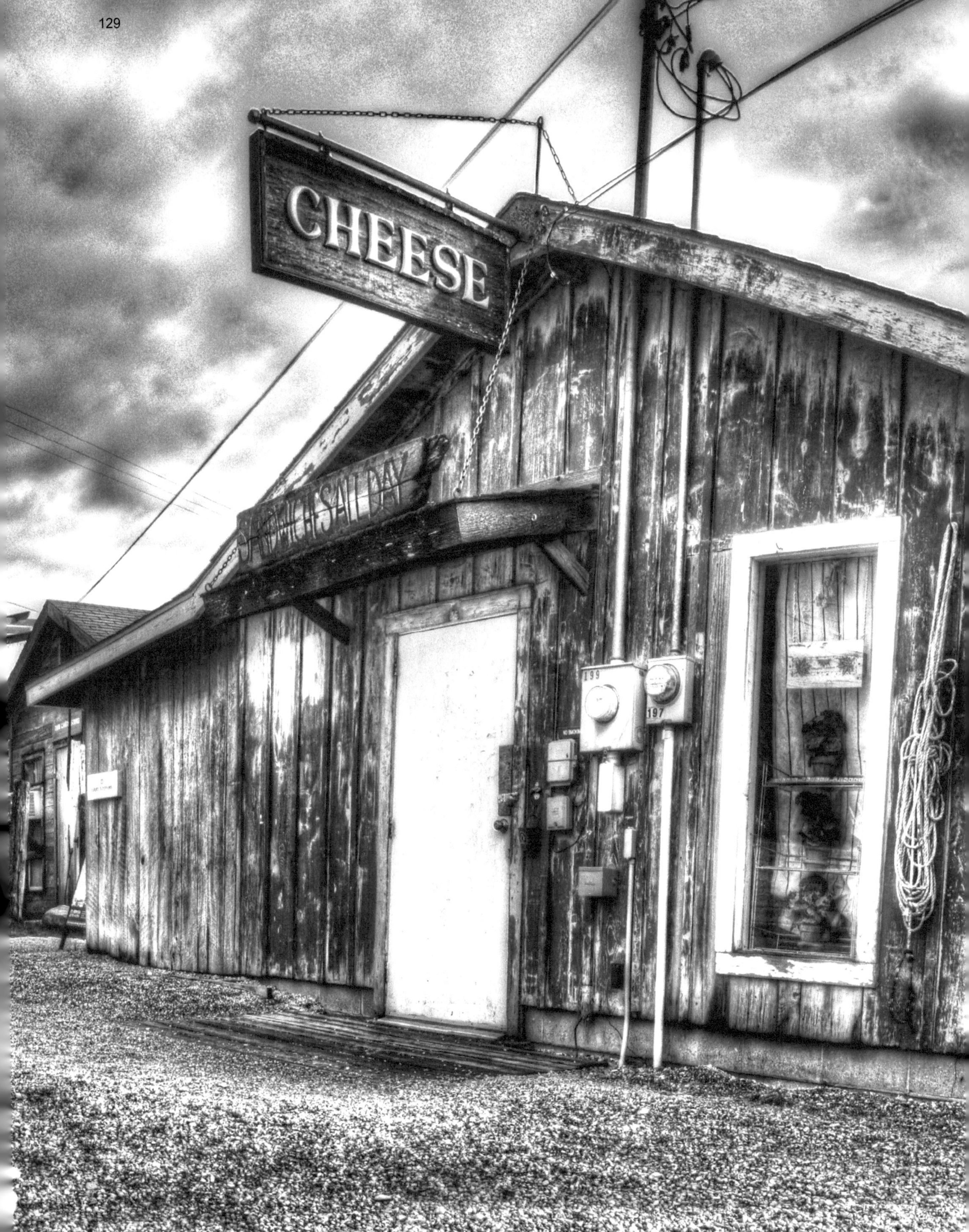
CHEESE
199
197

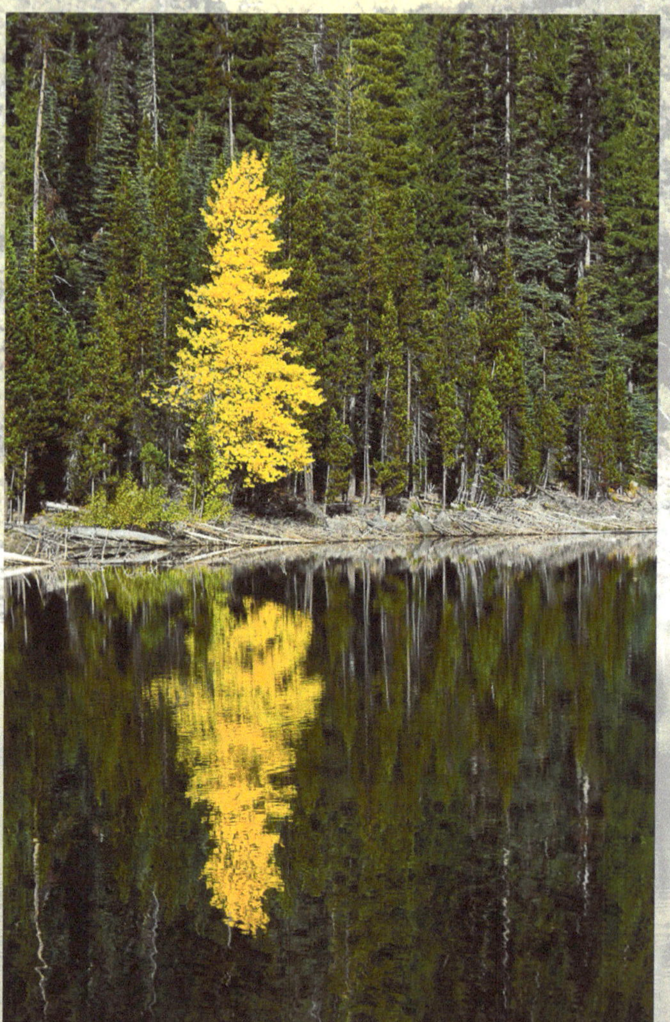

A lone Fall tree among pines.

Fall

In early October the forests of Maple, Birch, Oak, Elm, and Aspen trees turn from their summer green to brilliant shades of yellow, orange, and red. From the Manistee National Forest along the Manistee River, to the rolling hills around Arcadia and Frankfort, to the forests around Sleeping Bear Dunes and Glen Lake, Fall is a stunning time of year along Michigan's Northwest Shore. It is also one of the best times to visit. The Summer heat and humidity give way to crisp Fall days and cool nights. With the throngs of summer tourists gone for the year, the area's attractions are wide open.

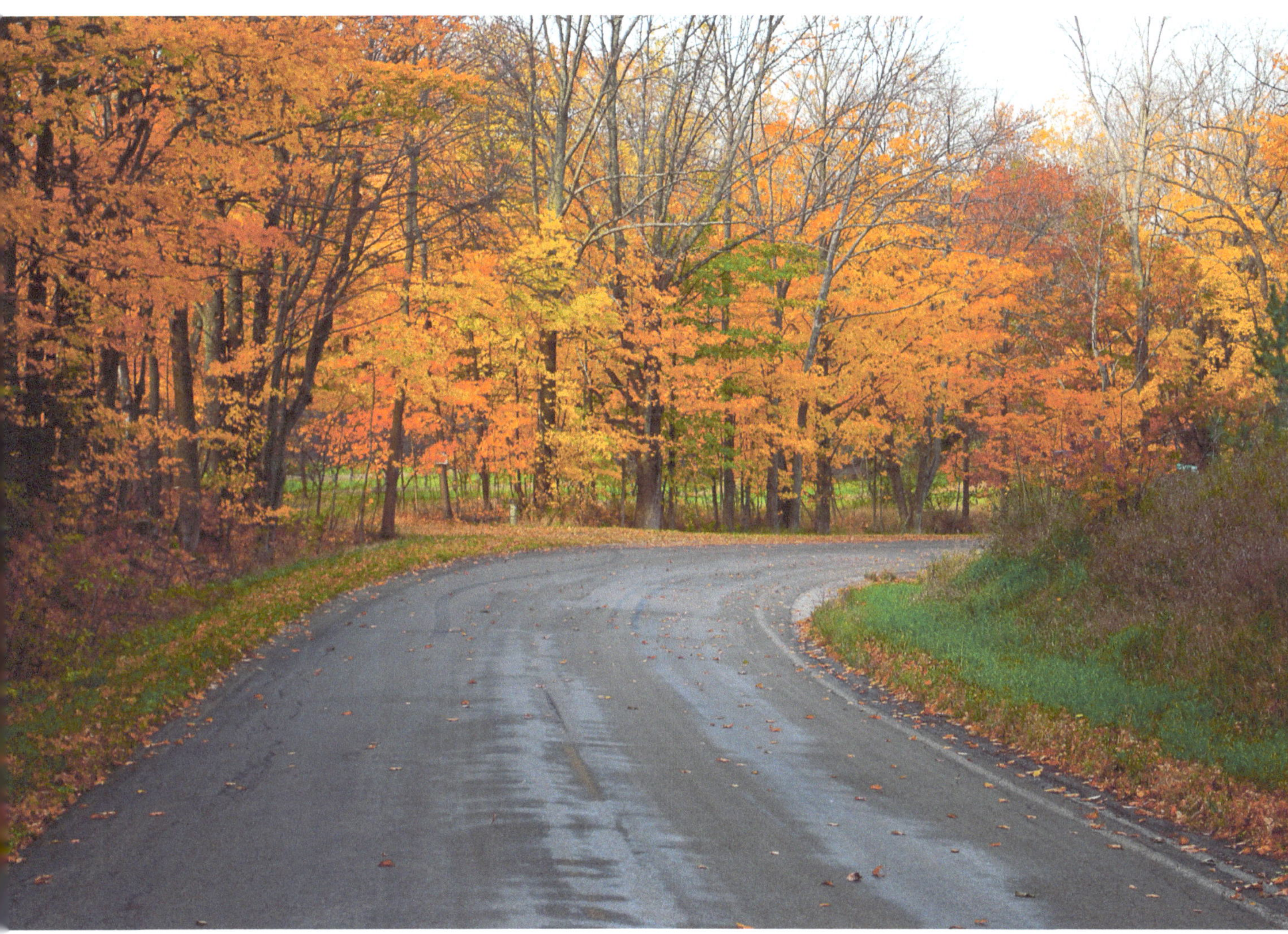

Fall along M-22. While most of Northern Michigan sees prime Fall colors in late September to early October, Lake Michigan moderates temperatures along the shoreline, delaying changes a few weeks.

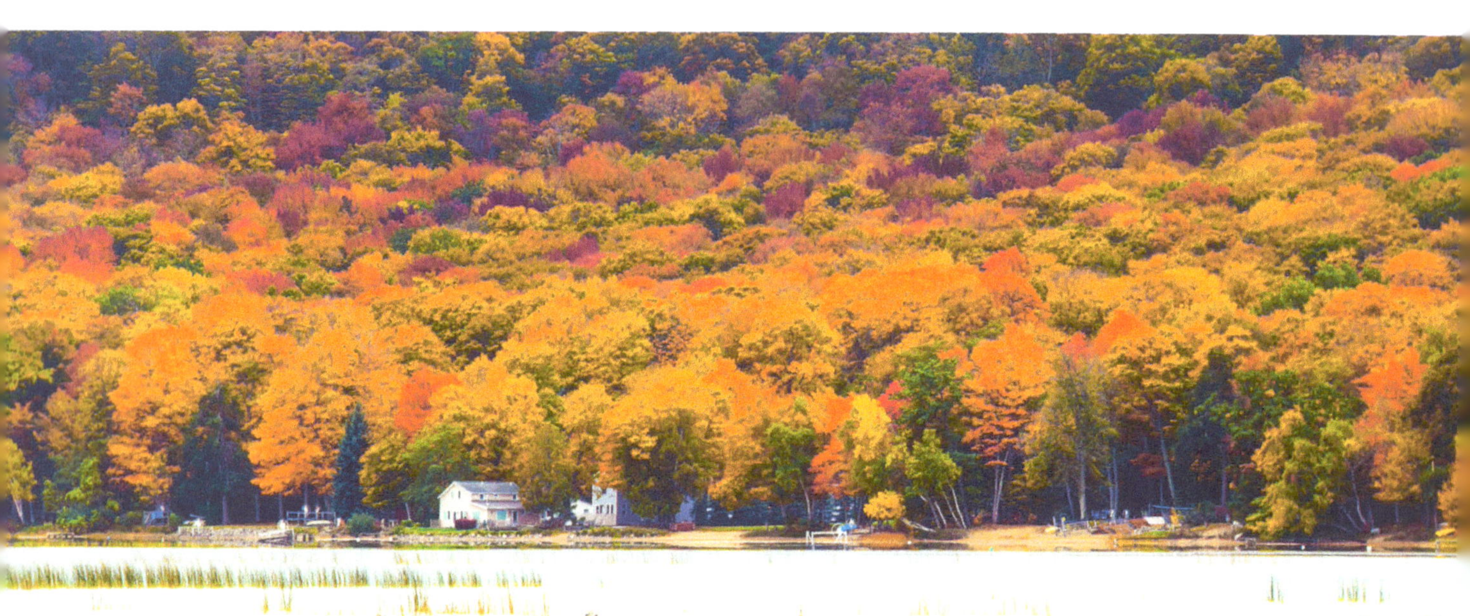

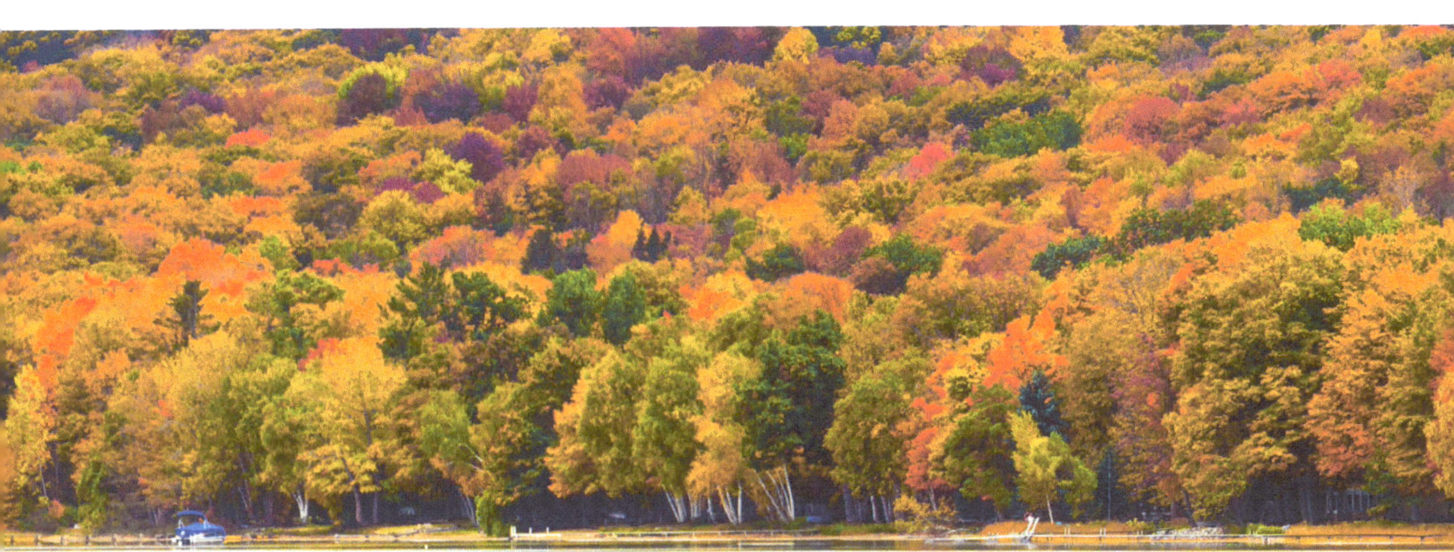

Fall colors over Lake Leelanau. Maple and birch trees are among the first to change color, followed by beech and ash trees, and finally oak late in the season.

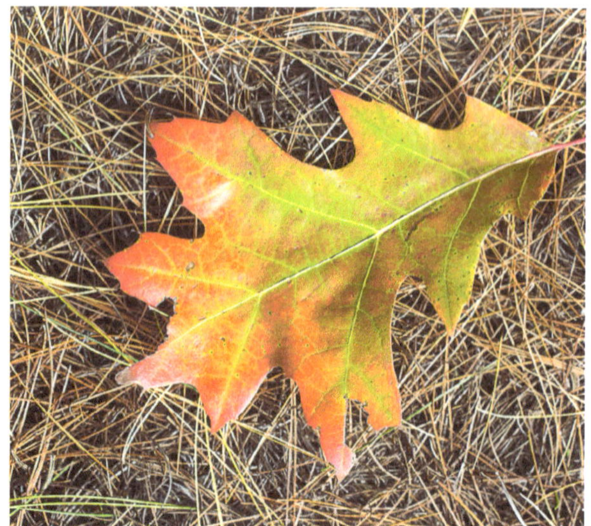

A lone Fall leaf.

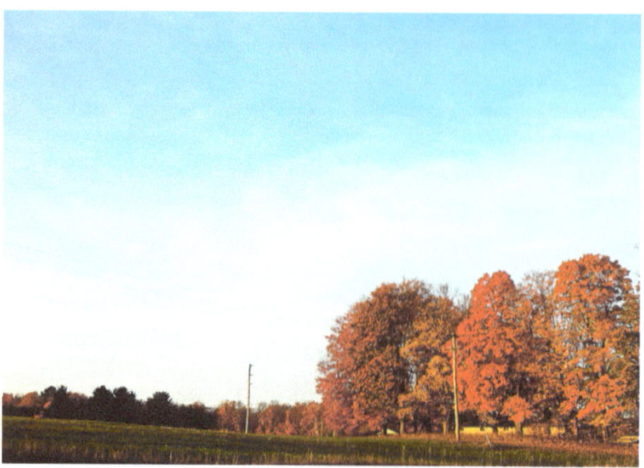

Fall trees on a farm along M-22.

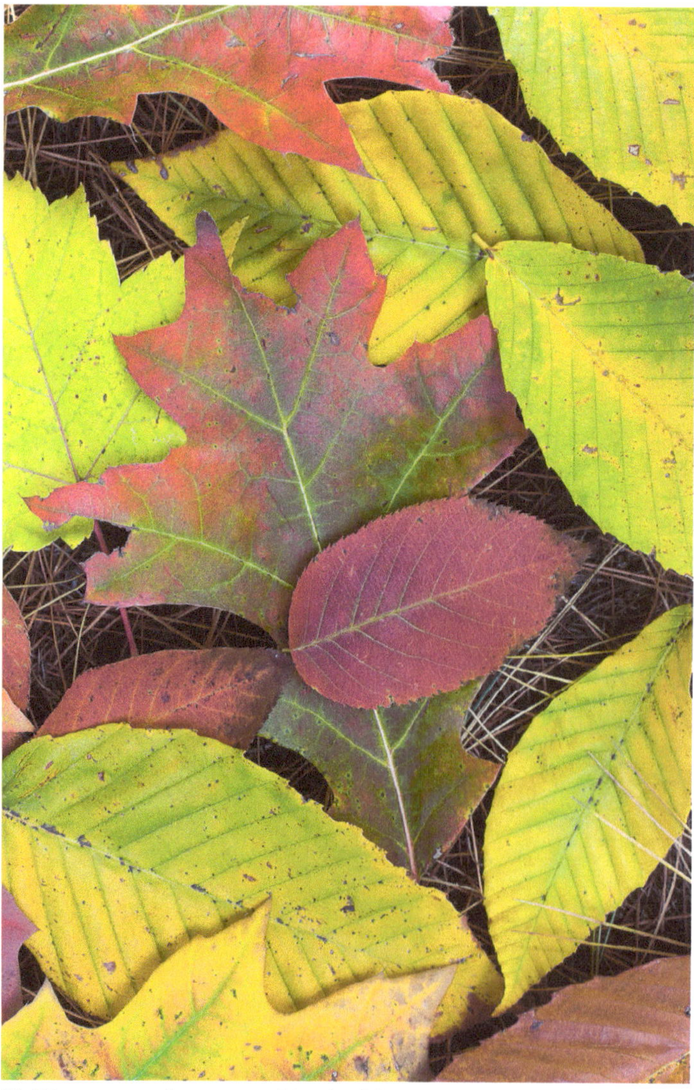

Fall leaves on the ground in the Manistee National Forest.

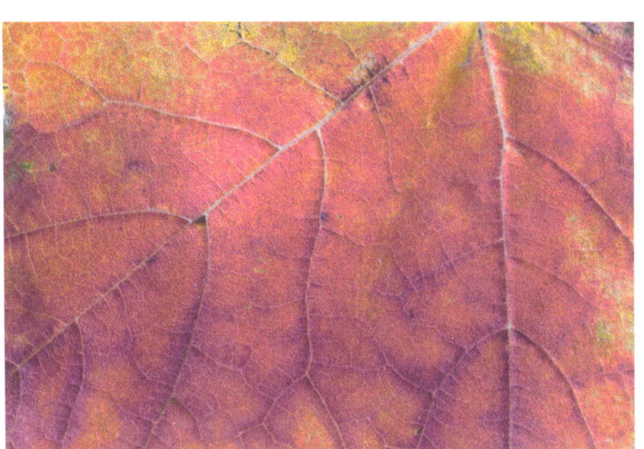

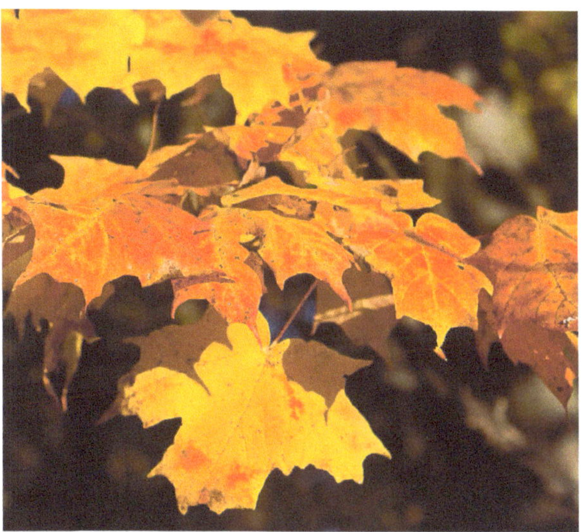

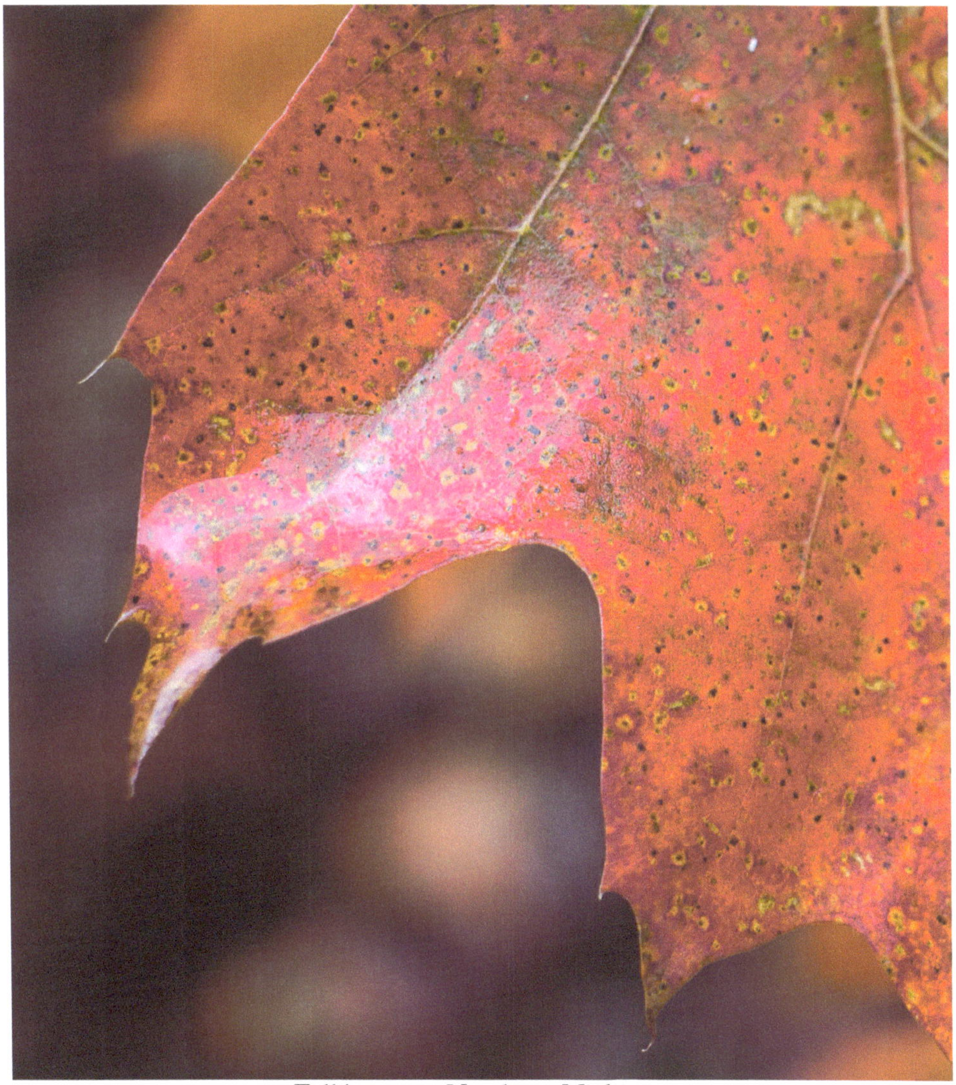

Fall leaves in Northern Michigan.

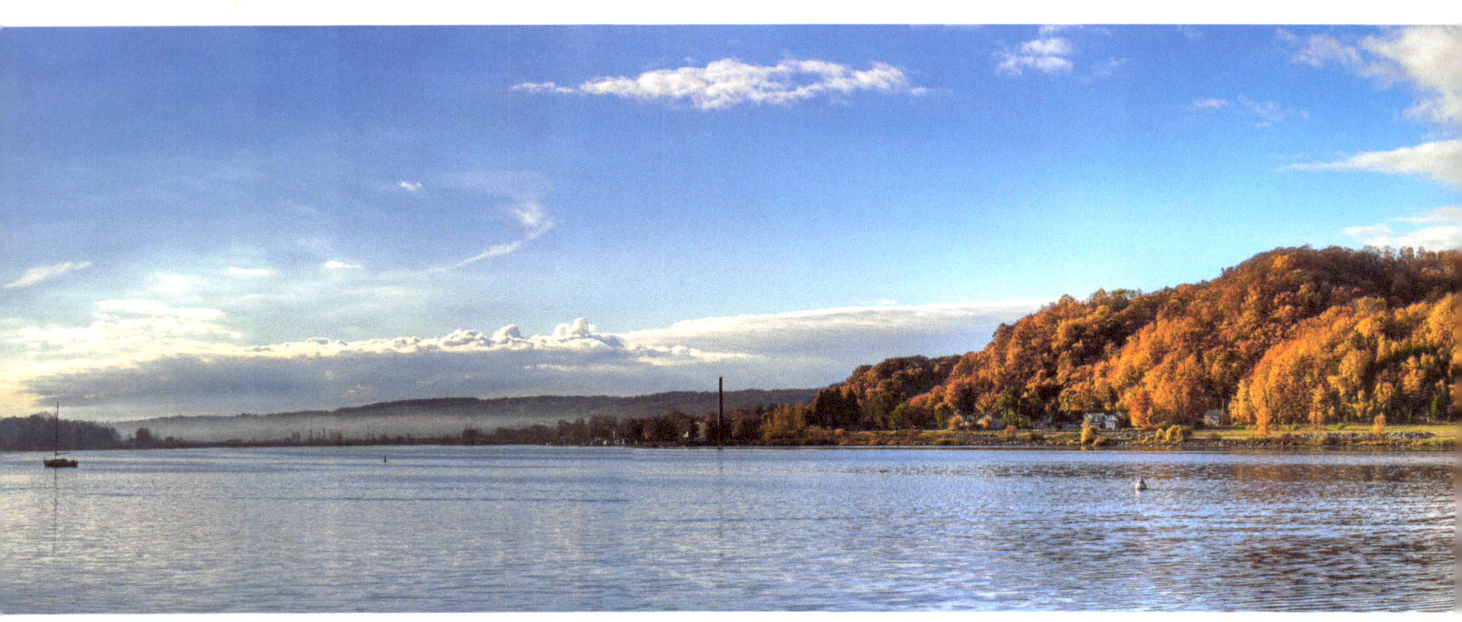

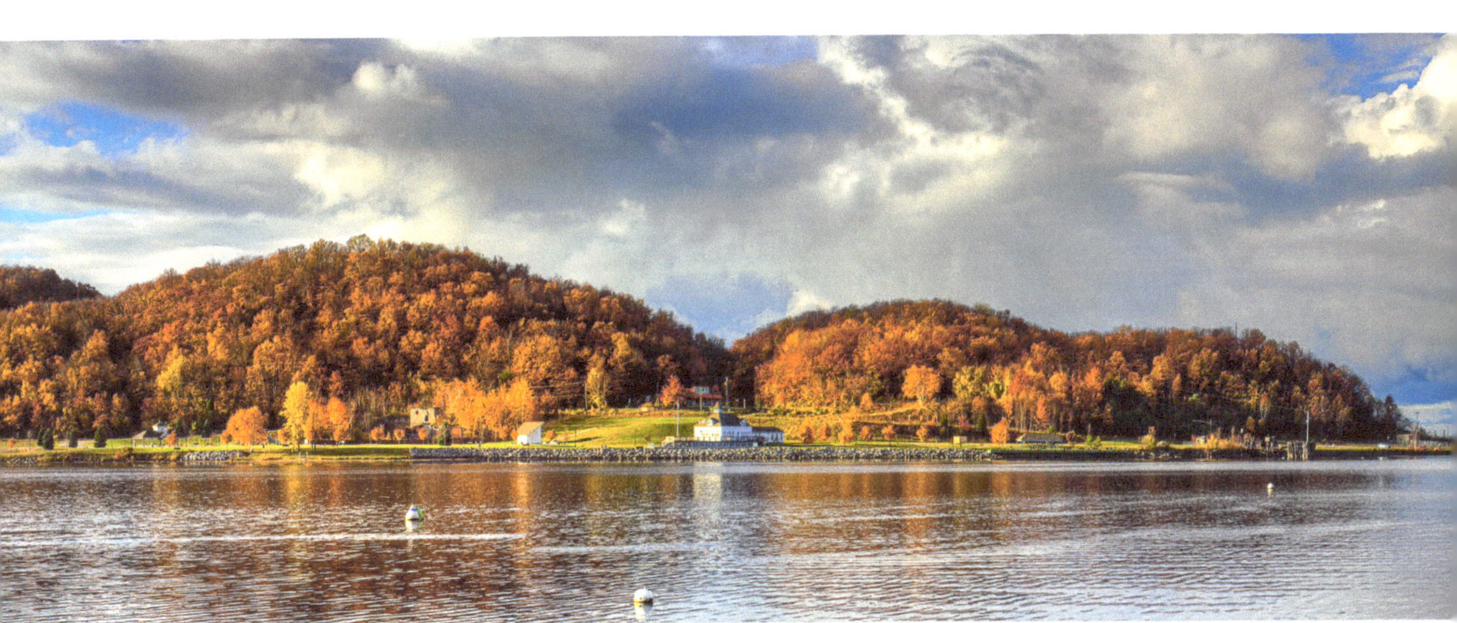

Fall colors in the bluffs around Elberta.

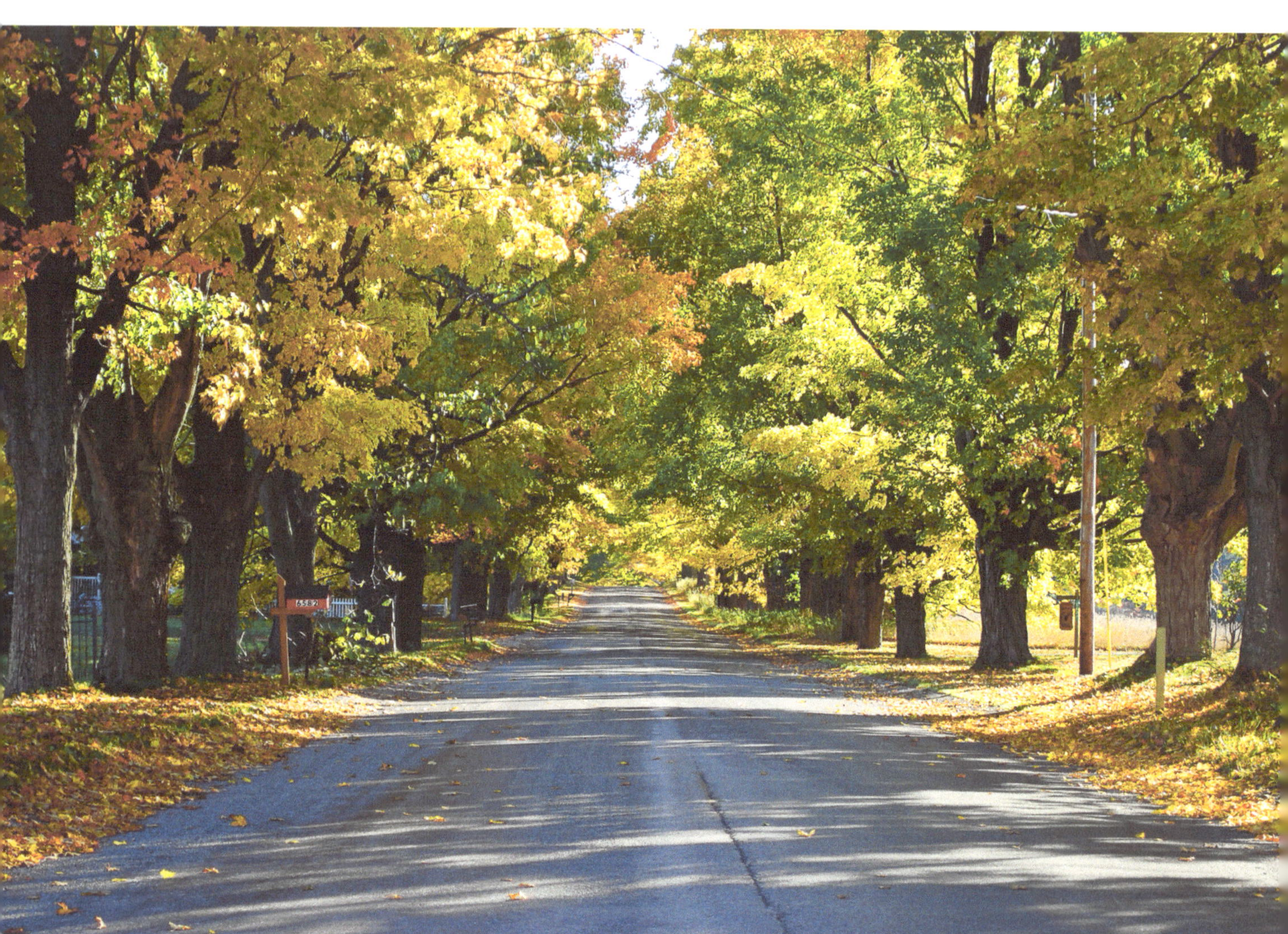

A tunnel of Fall trees along a backroad.

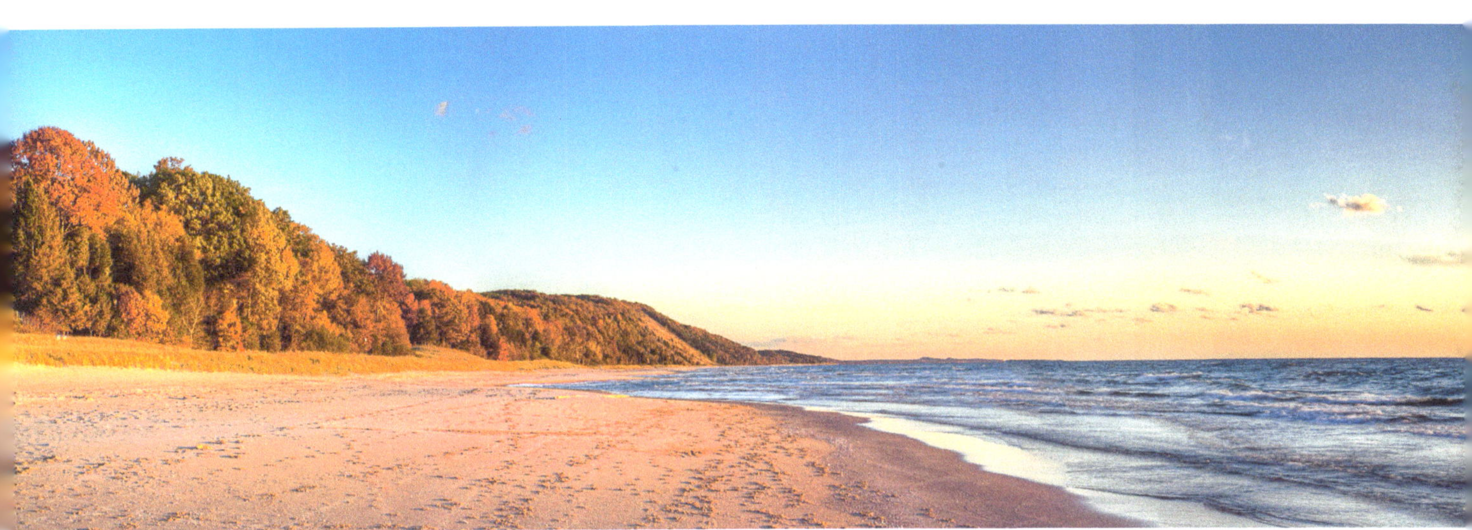

Fall colors along Lake Michigan.

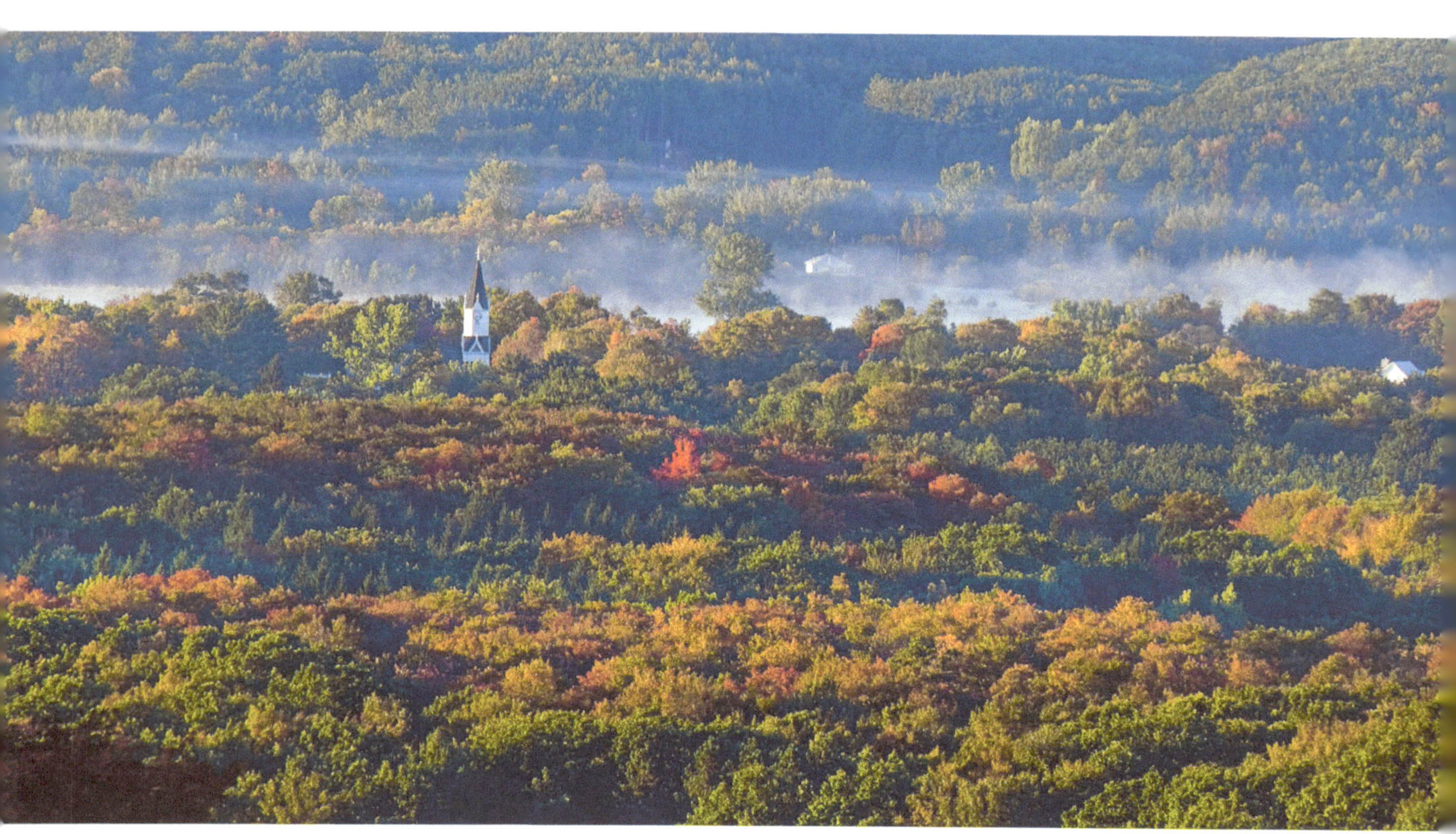

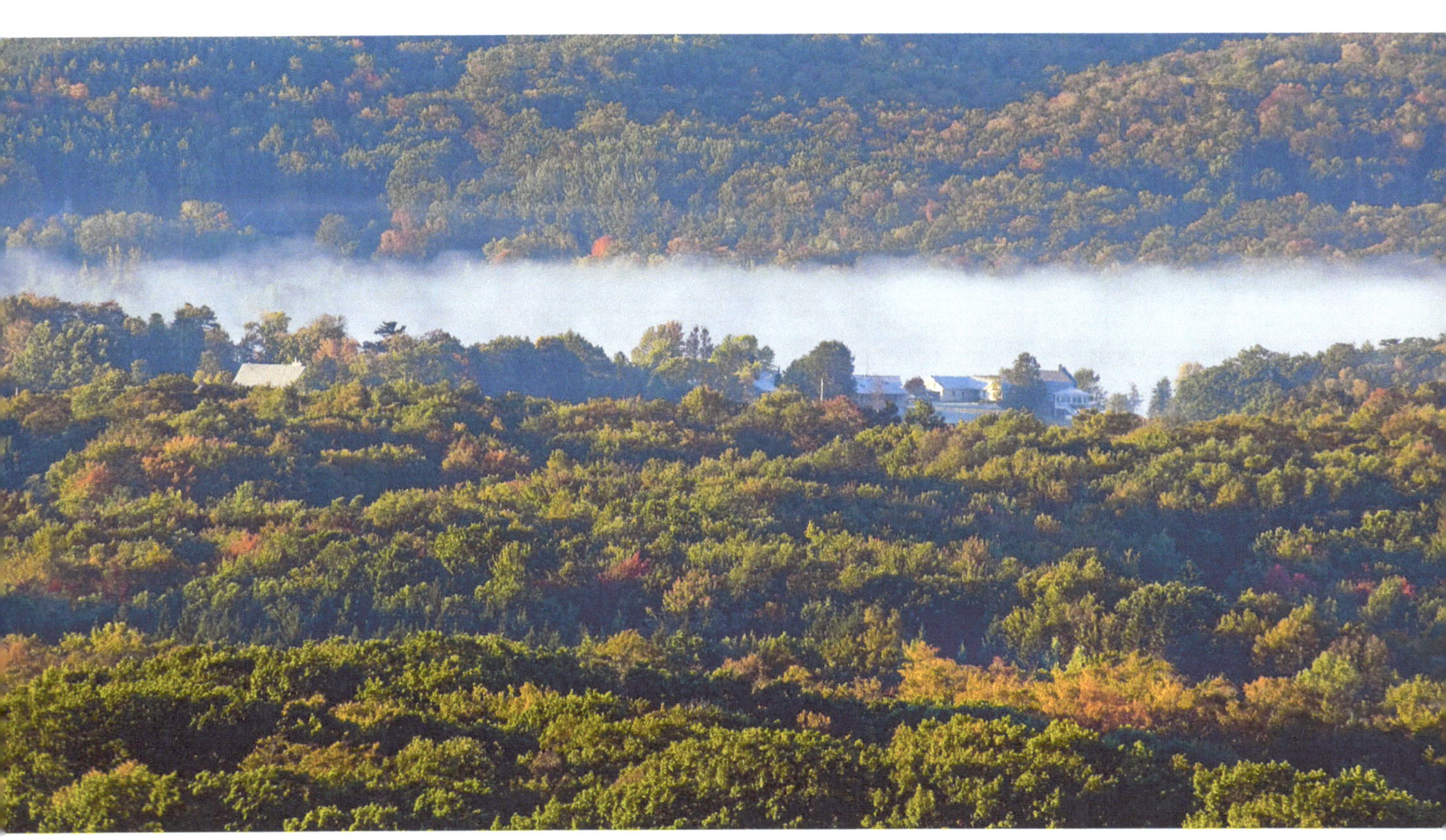

A few trees begin to turn in early Fall in Arcadia. Late September sees a few maple and birch trees start to turn, with peak season coming in mid-October.

Winter

Summer fun on the beaches, lakes, and golf courses gives way to a deep freeze from December to March. All areas along the Northwest Shore see winter snowmobilers and cross country skiers take advantage of the steady snow cover. Three downhill ski resorts sit within a few miles of the shoreline. Ludington and Manistee take advantage of Caberfae Peaks about twenty miles inland along M-55. Further north, Crystal Mountain sits just fifteen miles inland from Frankfort. Leland and Glen Arbor are only a few miles from downhill skiing at The Homestead Resort.

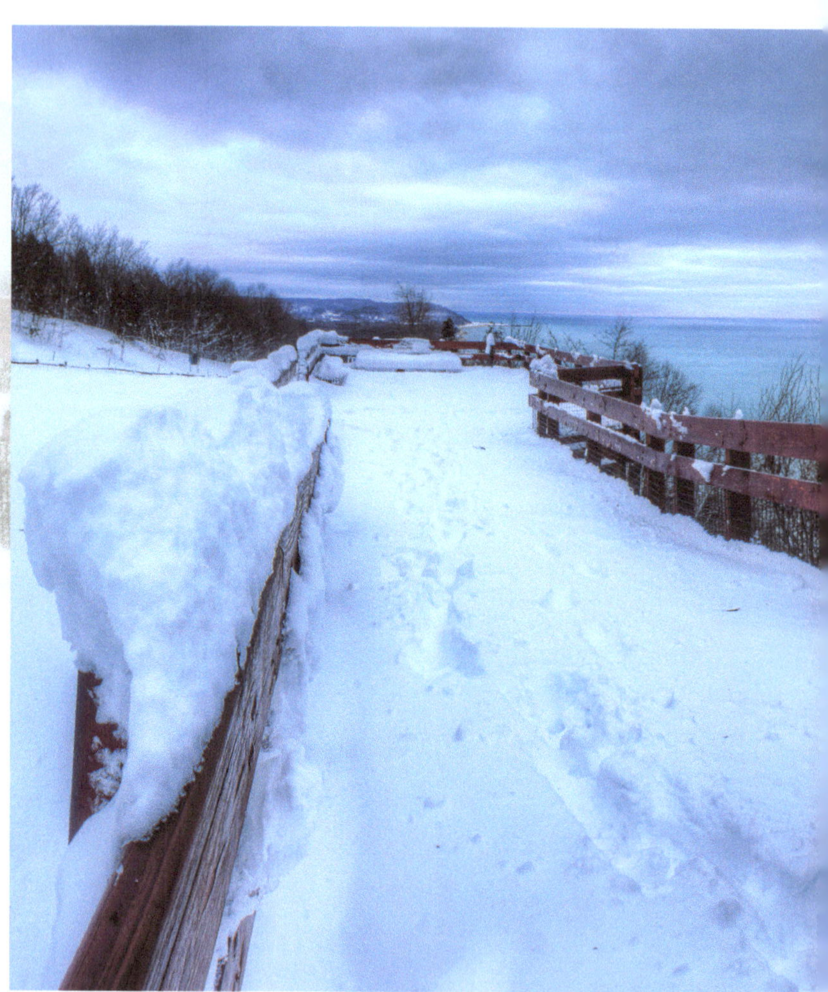

A Christmas Eve blizzard leaves a foot of snow on the Arcadia Overlook.

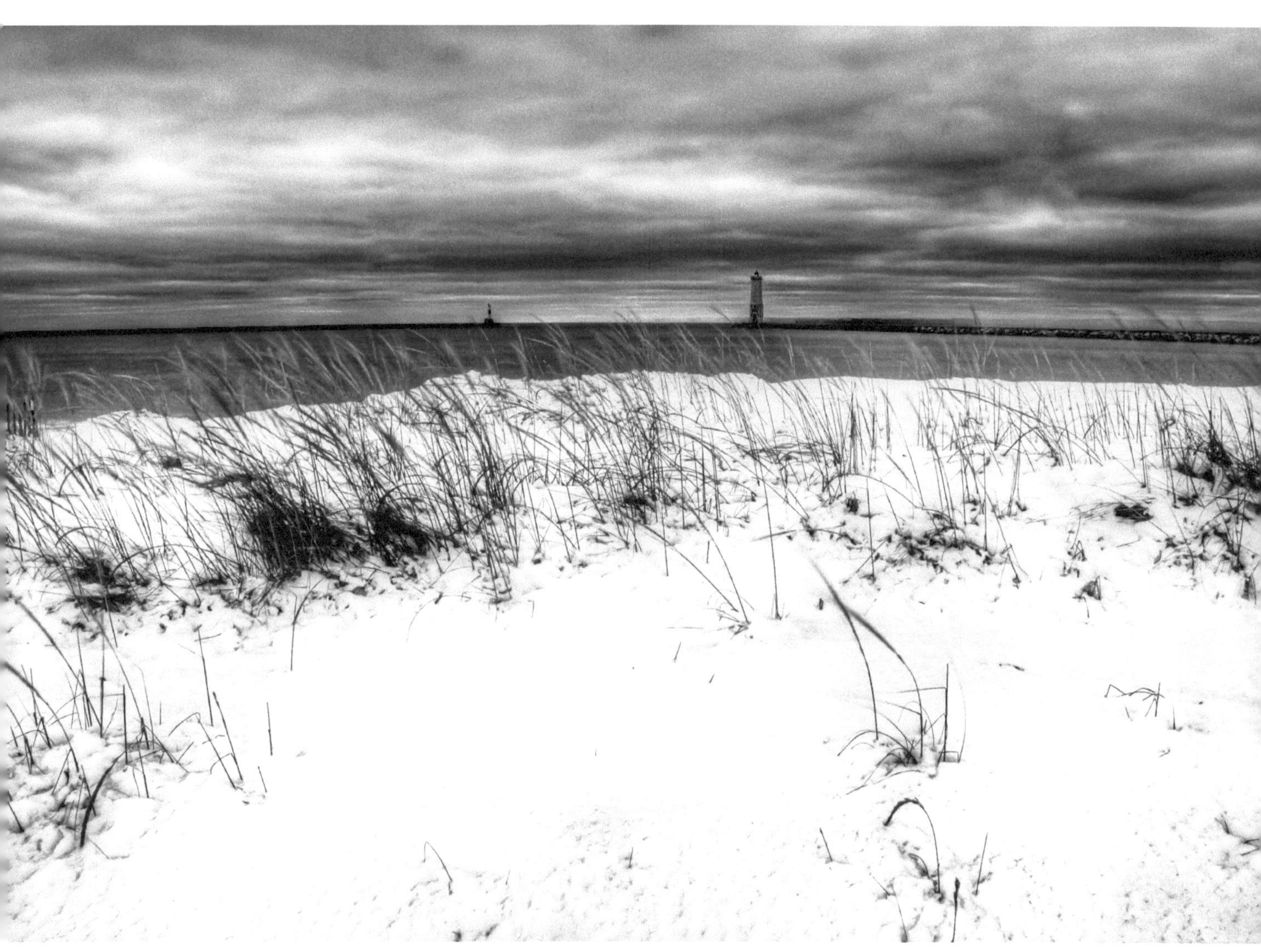

Frankfort in Winter.

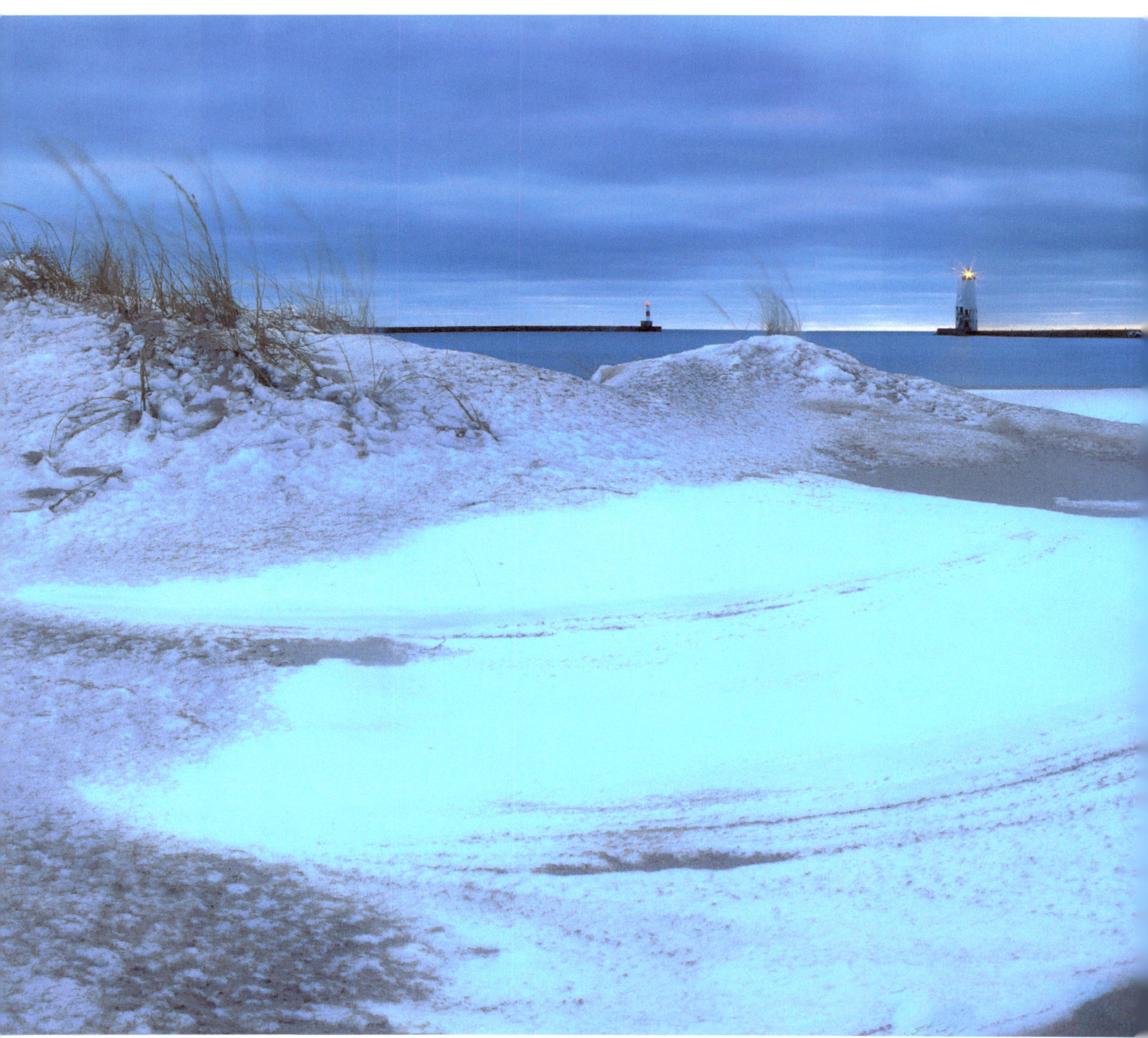

Frankfort beach and lighthouse in Winter.

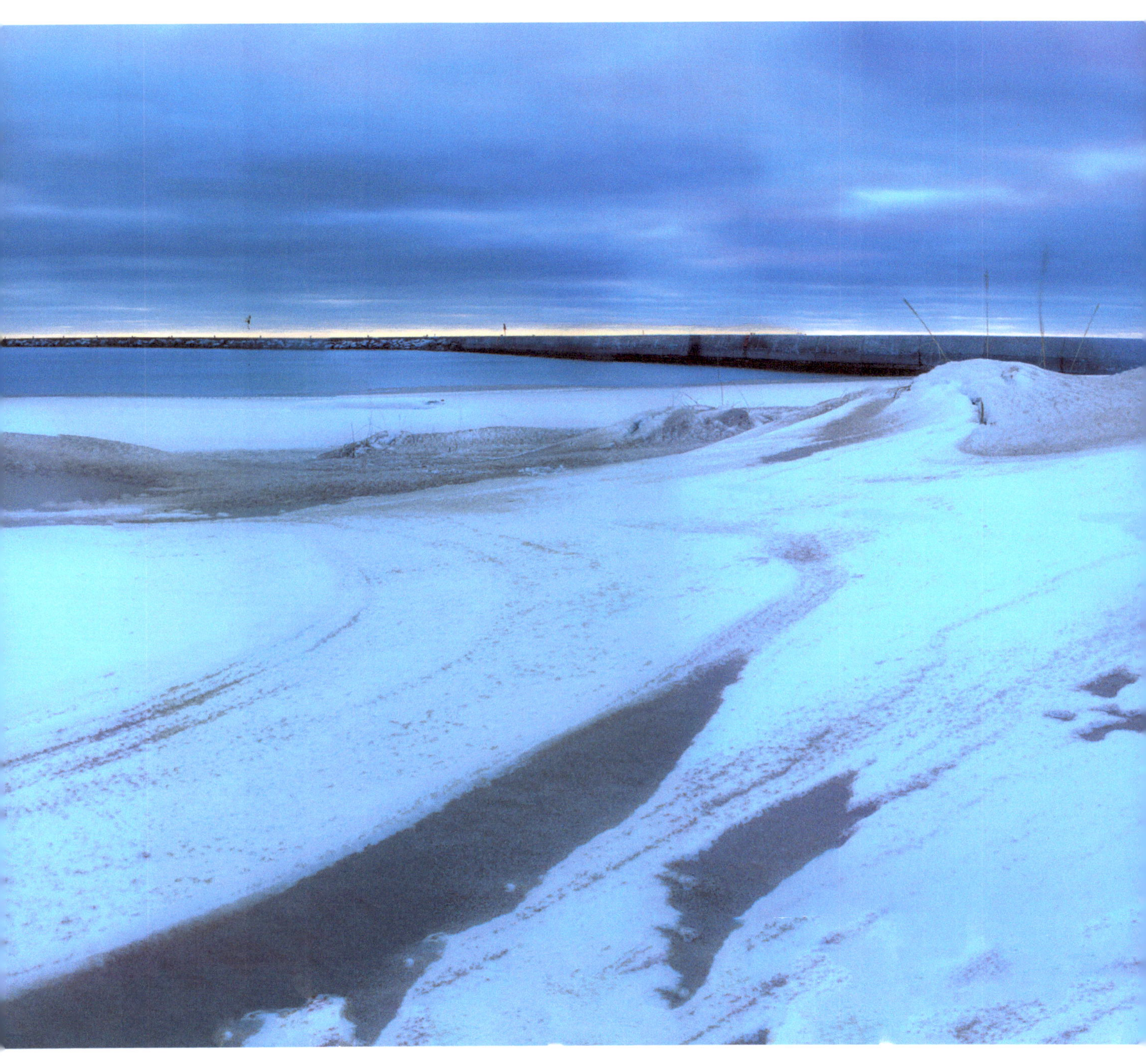

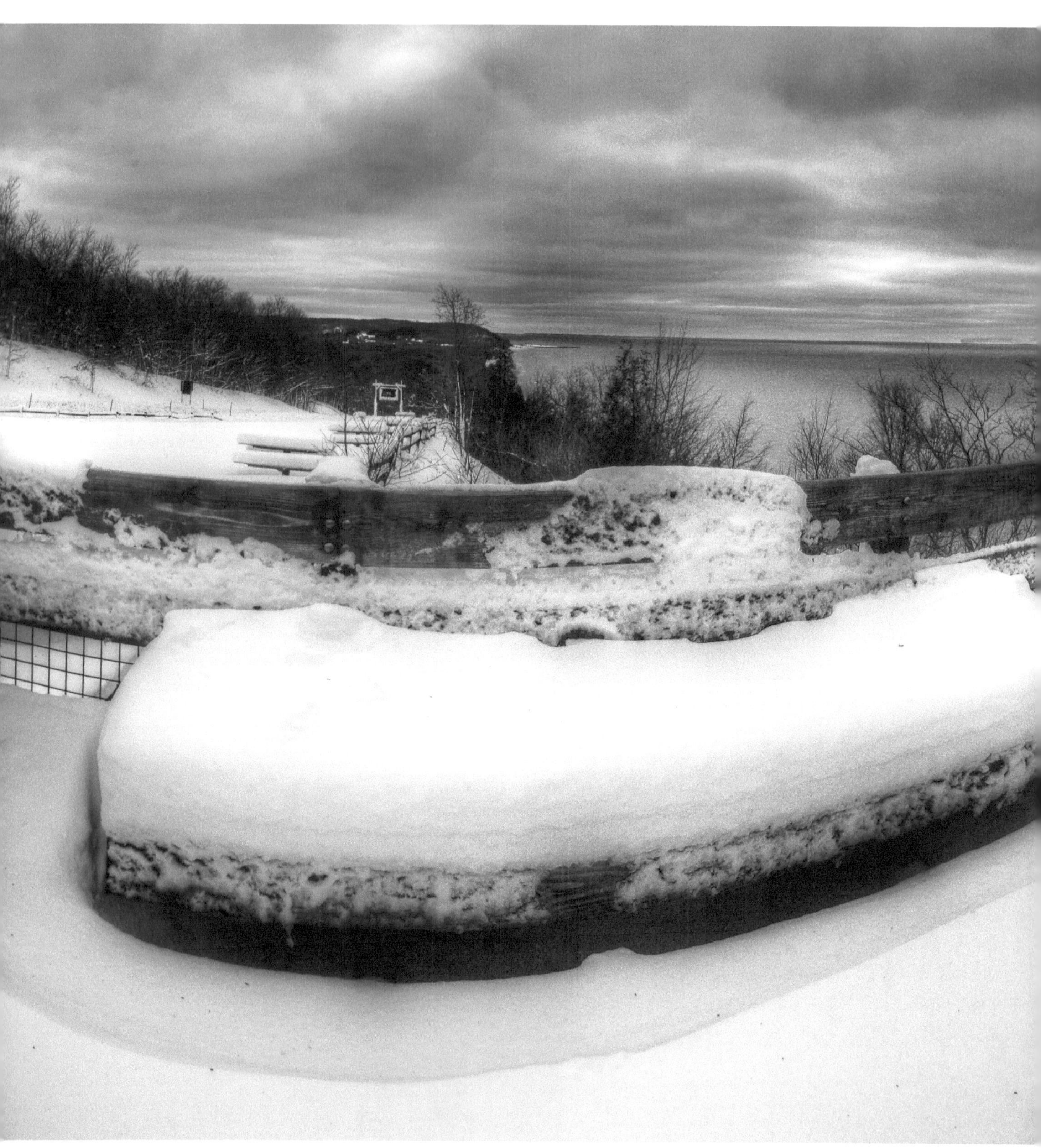

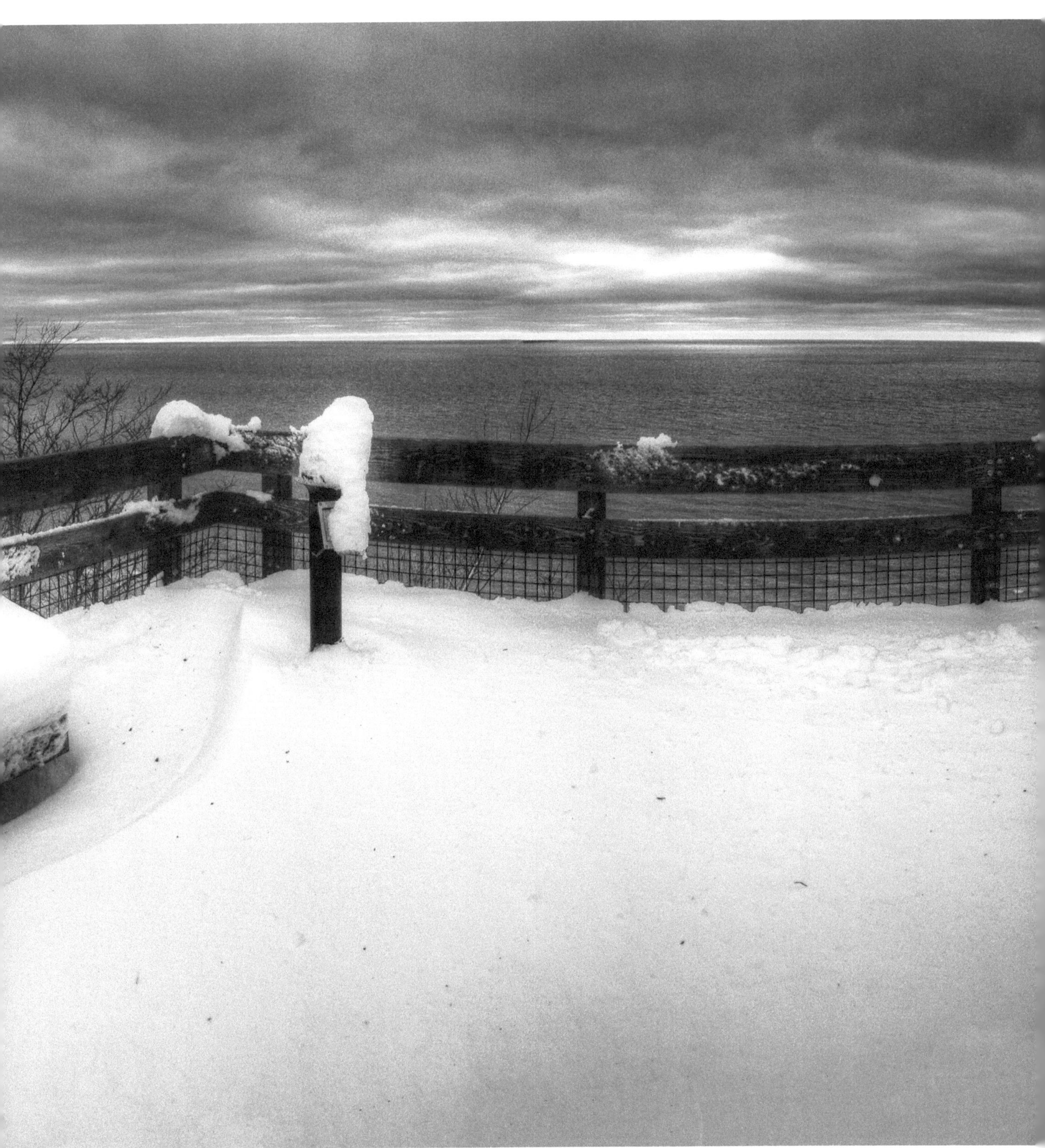

Snow on the Arcadia Overlook.

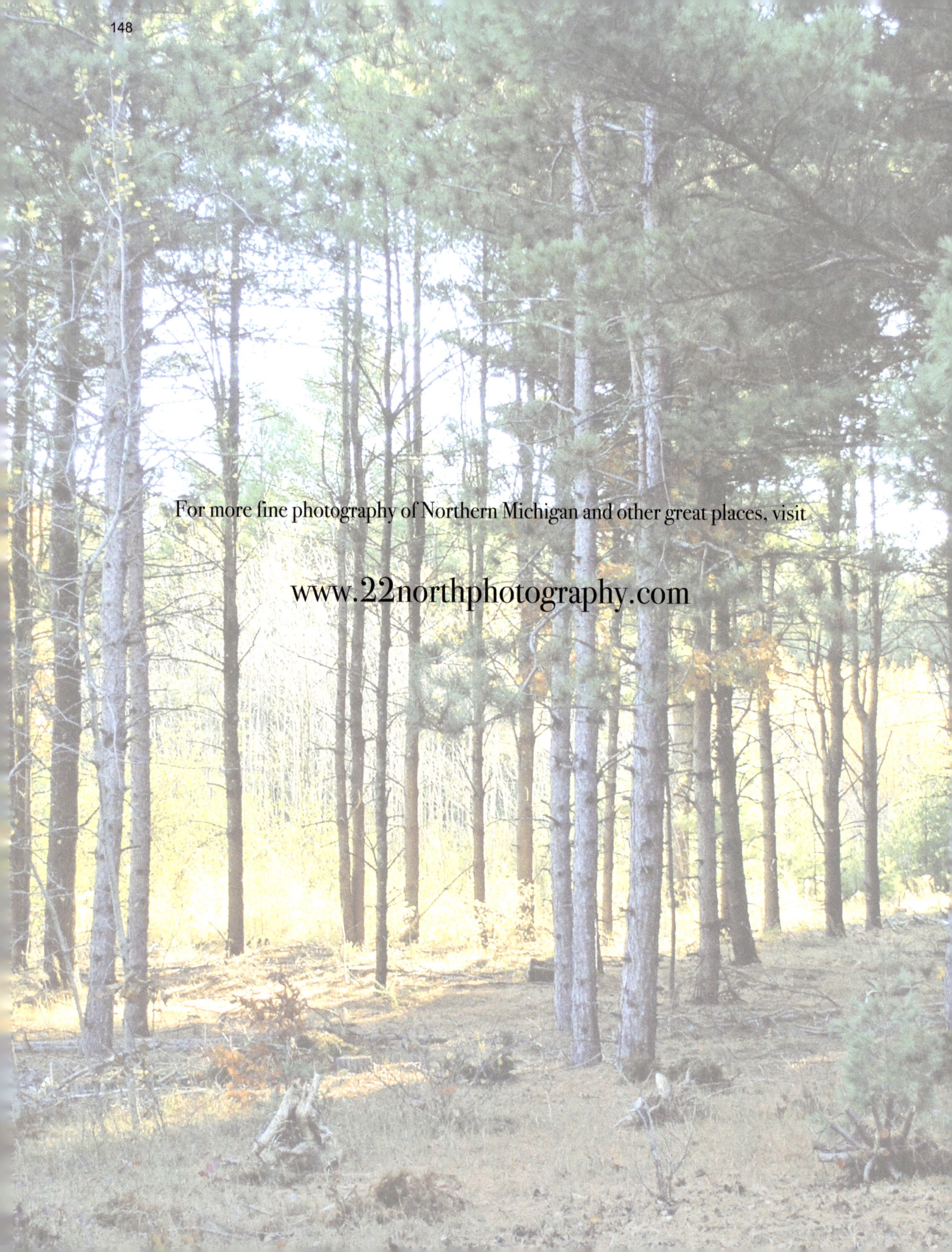
For more fine photography of Northern Michigan and other great places, visit
www.22northphotography.com

About Twenty-Two North Photography

Twenty-Two North Photography is based in Traverse City, Michigan and sells fine photographic prints of Michigan and other landscapes around the United States through www.22northphotography.com. With more than twenty-five years of experience photographing Northern Michigan and other landscapes, 22 North offers some of the most beautiful fine art photography of Northern Michigan available anywhere.